Times.

ONE PENNY

Holidays in sunny ITALY

DAYS fully inclusive from 24 GNS

A DATE WITH THE SUN IN ITALY

and sea or lakes and mountains and in such
cities as Rome, Florence and Venice.
selection of perfect Italian holidays
holiday programme.

● New strain of CJD kills younger victims ● Ministers try to calm fears over children

FOR TO-DAY'S SUMMARY
SEE PAGE 9.
FOR INDEX TO ADVERTISEMENTS
SEE PAGE 8.

SPECIAL ANNOUNCEMENTS (continued).

take cover from battling Mods and Rock

eef linked to brain disease

ow' risk to humans
itted for first time

es, George Jones, Roger Highfield and David Brown

itted for the first time yesterday that m
sed to humans by eating beef
ease, the human form
10 people und

S THE LOT!

es, health, education, F-111
East, roads, school milk,
the Navy, etc. etc.

Report too late, says family of coma girl

By Tom Leonard

THE grandmother of a teenage victim of Creutzfeldt-Ja-
kob disease attacked the
Government yesterday for
not revealing earlier the possible link to beef

BRAND'S
ESSENCE
OF BEEF
AND OF
CHICKEN

ONE HALF-PENNY

Y AT WAR

Take your Holidays at

UTLIN'S
SKEGNESS

OLIDAY CAMP

Y BUILT AT A COST OF £50,000

like it in the world—with all the
omradeship of a camping holiday plus
nities of a first-class Hotel. FREE
Swimming, Bowls, Dancing and
ties, etc. FOUR good meals a day
perienced chefs in hygienic kitchens.
ethan Chalets with electric light,
ors, running water, baths and first-
arrangements. This will be the
your holiday problem—for many
come.

£2. 5. 0. Per Week

for free illus-
descriptive book-

OLIDAY CAMP,
P.O.M.
ESS, Lincs.

ptions—2s 6d

ON charges to be 2s. 6d. in the spring,
s—those over 65, children up to 15,
rs and chronic sick. Maximum charge
ment up from £1 to 30s.

eaving age

ving age deferred to 1973.
in 1968-69 and £48 million
hool-building.

off

ndary

The half-
hearted
cheer

PHILIP MARSHALL

The Prime Minister's 5000
word statement
Government
cuts

LORD
LONGFORD
QUITS

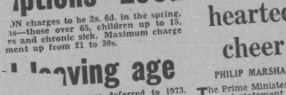

Skytrain undercuts riv
with £78 New York

D IN AND SPACE
S ACID HOUSE '8!

THE WAY WE LIVED

THE WAY WE LIVED

FOREWORD

As the millennium draws to a close, **THE EVENTFUL CENTURY** series presents the vast panorama of the last hundred years – a century which has witnessed the transition from horse-drawn transport to space travel, and from the first telephones to the information superhighway.

THE EVENTFUL CENTURY chronicles epoch-making events like the outbreak of the two world wars, the Russian Revolution and the rise and fall of communism. But major events are only part of this glittering kaleidoscope. It also describes the everyday background – the way people lived, how they worked, what they ate and drank, how much they earned, the way they spent their leisure time, the books they read, and the crimes, scandals and unsolved mysteries that set them talking. Here are fads and crazes like the Hula-Hoop and Rubik's Cube . . . fashions like the New Look and the miniskirt . . . breakthroughs in entertainment such as the birth of the movies . . . medical milestones such as the discovery of penicillin . . . and marvels of modern architecture and engineering.

THE WAY WE LIVED describes the myriad changes that have transformed all aspects of daily life during the 20th century, from coal-fired ovens to microwaves, from the first automated telephone exchange to satellite communications. In the early part of the century, people marvelled at moving stairways, daring stunts by the early aviators, and tinned fruit from faraway countries. By the end of the century, holidays in exotic places, frozen convenience foods, foreign television programmes and computerised banking are taken for granted. Medical advances such as heart transplants and test-tube babies have given people new hope, and developments such as the family car and jet travel have given them new freedoms. At the same time, alongside the scientific and technological innovations, changing attitudes have also helped to reshape everyone's daily life as people have questioned educational methods, social systems, mainstream religions and the very notion of the family itself.

THE EVENTFUL CENTURY

THE WAY WE LIVED

Reader's Digest

PUBLISHED BY
THE READER'S DIGEST ASSOCIATION LIMITED
LONDON NEW YORK SYDNEY MONTREAL

THE WAY WE LIVED
Edited and designed by Toucan Books Limited
Written by Richard Tames
Edited by Helen Douglas-Cooper and
Andrew Kerr-Jarrett
Designed by Bradbury and Williams
Picture research by Julie McMahon

FOR READER'S DIGEST
Series Editor Christine Noble
Editorial Assistant Caroline Boucher
Production Controller Lorine Alexander

READER'S DIGEST GENERAL BOOKS
Editorial Director Cortina Butler
Art Director Nick Clark

First English edition copyright © 1997
The Reader's Digest Association Limited,
11 Westferry Circus, Canary Wharf,
London E14 4HE

Reprinted with amendments 2000

Copyright © 1997
Reader's Digest Association Far East Limited
Philippines copyright © 1997
Reader's Digest Association Far East Limited
All rights reserved

Printing and binding: Printer Industria Gráfica,
Barcelona
Separations: Litho Origination, London
Paper: Perigord-Condat, France

ISBN 0 276 42261 9

FRONT COVER
Background picture: Bathers at Coney Island,
Brooklyn, New York, top; marathon runners,
London, bottom.
From left to right: David Bowie; tins of fruit and
vegetables; boy selling bootlaces, Paris, 1907;
London Underground train, 1930s.

BACK COVER
Clockwise from top left: Cube houses, Rotterdam;
fishwives at Great Yarmouth, 1905; Rudolf Valentino
and Vilma Pankey; children playing 'Squeak, Piggy,
Squeak'.

Page 3 (from left to right): German sidecar
ambulance, 1928; Punk fashions; bathing beauty;
Oklahoma farmer, 1936.

Background pictures:
Page 11: Houses in Bristol
Page 33: Well-stocked shelves at the Piggly Wiggly
supermarket, 1918
Page 79: French students sitting an exam, 1963
Page 123: Bathers at Coney Island, Brooklyn,
New York

CONTENTS

A CENTURY OF CHANGE

IN JUST THREE GENERATIONS SPANNING THE 20TH CENTURY, THE WORLD HAS CHANGED MORE AND FASTER THAN EVER BEFORE

The 20th century has been a century of unimaginable change. A child born near the start of the century entered a world where no one had yet flown in an aeroplane or seen a television programme or used an aerosol spray. The South Pole had not yet been reached. Yellow fever still frustrated all attempts to build a canal across the Isthmus of Panama. Even a child born nearly half a century later, in the aftermath of the Second World War, was coming into a world where

FANTASY AND REALITY The film set for H.G. Wells' *Things to Come* (left) from the 1930s looks strikingly modern, even beside Kansai Airport, Osaka, in the 1990s.

computers were known only to a handful of scientists, the transistor had yet to be invented and the majority of people crossing the Atlantic each year did so by ship, not plane.

Imagine that the child born at the start of the century had an adult grandchild living at its close. The daily detail of their lives would have been radically different – even before either got out of bed in the morning. The child at the start of the century slept under cotton sheets and woollen blankets – not a duvet. His or her bedroom, probably shared with several brothers and sisters, had no central heating. The radio-alarm, shaving-foam, disposable razor, antiperspirant spray, electric kettle, instant coffee, pop-up toaster

and other gadgets that get the modern day under way would all have been complete mysteries to him or her.

What would this child find most bizarre about his or her grandchild's daily life? With lunch approaching, the grandchild might decide, for example, to reheat last night's leftover Indian curry in a microwave oven from the Far East and wash it down with Australian lager – the very notion of these things would have been extraordinary to anyone at the start of the century. Perhaps the child of the 1900s would be reassured by the sight of a 1990s postman bringing the mid-morning mail – but maybe not. Few ordinary working-class people in pre-1914 cities received letters even once a week; even fewer received such things as income tax demands and no one would have known what a credit-card statement was.

Predicting the future

Does changing the viewer change the view? What might a sophisticated, well-informed French or German adult – a businessman or a professor – have predicted about the way

CHANNEL CROSSING Work first began on a Channel tunnel in 1802. The idea was revived in 1909 (left) but the eventual link – by rail (above) – did not open until 1994.

the world would go as he – at that time almost certainly not she – scanned the newspaper headlines in the year 1900?

The supremacy of politics was taken for granted. 'Serious' newspapers gave little coverage to business issues, even less to celebrities, the 'environment' (a word then used only by scientists) or sport. Such newspapers ignored what would become known as 'popular culture'. The first hamburger to be sold, the marketing of the Box Brownie camera and the first international motor-car race, all of which took place in 1900, were not hailed as major portents of the emerging future.

Given the immense self-confidence of Europe at the time, the educated reader in 1900 would probably not be surprised to know that the names making the news that year would still be venerated in the 1990s – in music Puccini, Debussy, Elgar, Sibelius and Mahler; in literature Conrad, Tolstoy and Chekhov; in art Rodin, Renoir and Gauguin. But 1900 was also the year in which the first jazz band was formed and tennis players first competed for the Davis Cup. Readers in 1900 might have been surprised to know that their counterparts at the end of the century found these events significant.

In headline terms, little changed with the dawning of a new century. Politically and internationally, 1900 was the continuation of 1899. France and Italy agreed to recognise each other's 'spheres of influence' along the Red Sea coast and in North Africa. Germany, Britain and the USA negotiated mutually acceptable terms for the administration of Samoa. All three powers, plus France and Japan, cooperated to crush the antiforeign Boxer Rebellion in China. The USA annexed Hawaii, and New Zealand took over the Cook Islands. Russia and Japan quarrelled over naval facilities in Korea. Persia, not to be known as Iran for another three decades, accepted a massive loan that made Russia her main creditor.

Nationalism was the great 'ism' that did not become a 'wasm'. In the first decade of the century it was causing trouble in the Balkans and as the century drew to a close it was doing so again. A liberal free-trader of 1900 might have foreseen all Europe united in a single market. Had he been given the gift of foresight, he would probably have been amused, during the negotiations for the creation of a single European currency, to observe Britain's insistence that it should have its own local version with the sovereign's head on it.

In 1900 the Irish were demonstrating in Dublin for Home Rule. In 1996, as winners of the Eurovision Song Contest for the fourth year out of five, they were facing the expensive prospect of having to host the contest yet again – and consoling themselves with the thought that an Irish poet, Seamus Heaney, was the current winner of the Nobel prize for literature, a prize first awarded in 1901. Cultural power was no longer the prerogative of the traditional big battalions such as the USA. British teenagers were hypnotised by soap operas depicting life in the Australian suburbs, while viewers in the Middle East were transfixed by emotional family sagas produced in Brazil.

The century of the city

'I ... live in a little village ... and help my father and mother, my brother and an aunt, on our little farm ... Everything it is possible to grow, we grow. This is in order to buy as little as possible ... Twice a week the baker comes to the village square and sells bread. A grocer comes twice a month ... We are absolutely cut off from news ... We have few visitors because we are so isolated ... [We are] enclosed by our own habits and daily routines, from which there seems to be no escape. My mother has not even been to the capital of the department, 60 km [40 miles] away.'

When this interview with a French peasant girl of the Isère region bordering the Alps was recorded in the early 1960s, it represented a way of life that had disappeared for most of the population of western Europe and North America half a

FUTURE FASHION Cecil Beaton's prediction, created in 1928, of a fashion style for the year 2000 combined fantasy with nostalgia but would prove impractical in a fast-moving age.

century before. The 20th century was replacing centuries-old isolation with communication, self-sufficiency with interdependence. The suburb, town or city, not the village, was where most people in the Western world now lived, and cities, unlike villages, are anything but self-sufficient.

In 1900, London was the biggest city in the world, with a population of just over 6 million. By mid century it had been pushed into second place by New York, which by then had a population twice that of London

PLEASE SPEAK AFTER THE TONE The first answerphone, or 'mechanical secretary', marketed in 1932, used a gramophone record for the outgoing and incoming messages.

in 1900. By the mid 1990s New York would be overtaken by Tokyo, with a population more than twice as big again. London by the 1990s was no longer even in the top 20 of the world's biggest cities.

Even so, covering some 400 000 acres (160 000 ha) and embracing 12 per cent of the population of the United Kingdom, the British capital was a ferocious consumer. Each week it burned enough oil to fill two supertankers. Each year it consumed 1.2 million tons of timber and an equivalent weight of metals, 2 million tons of foodstuffs and equal quantities of paper and of plastics. Each year it spewed out 7.5 million tons of sewage, twice that much waste and eight times as much carbon dioxide. Each year it was visited by almost four times as many people as actually lived there.

London was by no means untypical of the world's great cities. Among them they covered just 2 per cent of the world's surface but consumed 75 per cent of its resources. They were also drawing in more and more people. In 1975 some 1.5 billion people lived in cities. This figure was forecast to pass 3 billion by the turn of the millennium – more than the entire population of the planet in 1960.

Science and technology

For people pondering the future in 1900 it was not hard to imagine that science and technology would transform their daily lives. The World Exhibition staged in Paris in 1900 – visited by 50 million people over the course of six months – was dominated by a Palace of Electricity, which featured a continuous cinema show and the first public demonstration of the escalator. Would the same observers, however, have grasped the long-term implications of less publicised technological achievements? These included the first exploration for oil using offshore rigs, the opening of the first automated telephone exchange, controlling 10 000 lines, and the first successful transmission of speech by wireless telegraphy.

Readers brought up on the futuristic fantasies of Jules Verne or H.G. Wells knew all about the possibilities of space travel. The pioneer French film-maker Georges Méliès

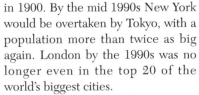

TWO UP, TWO DOWN The family house of the future, 1950s style, was made from steel and welded together on site. The ladder leads to the guest bedrooms.

even faked up a jokey Moon voyage in a backstreet Paris film studio in the early 1900s. So the visionary of 1900 would probably not have thought it too fantastic that men should be standing on the Moon in 1969. But he or she would quite possibly have been amazed to learn that large fleets of 'jumbo' jets, which made their inaugural flight in the same year, 1969, would later be used to transport tens of millions of ordinary European and North American working people to holiday destinations in a sunshine belt stretching from Florida and Jamaica in the west, through Majorca and Corfu in the Mediterranean to Goa and Thailand in the east. As for space travel, it has happened, and its chief impact on the way we live has been in the application of the technologies that made it possible to other areas of life. Concorde, laptop computers, carbon-fibre optics and nonstick frying pans – all these are spin-offs of space technology.

Jules Verne and H.G. Wells enjoyed great popular success with their writings, but they were generally regarded as harmless fantasists. The most influential 'futurological' writers of the turn of the century were concerned with institutional change. *Looking Backward: 2000–1887*, written in 1888 by the American Edward Bellamy, told the story of a Bostonian, Julian West, awaking at the end of the 20th century to find that squalor and injustice have disappeared, thanks to the replacement of capitalism by a benevolent state that is the sole employer. This hugely influential utopian romance actually provoked the formation of a political party in the USA to advocate its vision as

a programme for reform. It also inspired turn-of-the-century political groups in Europe, notably in the Netherlands. Ironically, Bellamy died, of tuberculosis, in 1898, before his new century of transformation had even begun. The concern for social justice and change that he articulated would, however, be a constant – waxing and waning in influence, but always there – throughout the century.

Coca-colonisation?

Have television and tourism and global marketing created a universal consumer culture of soccer and sweatshirts and soft drinks? Certainly there are now events and experiences that are shared worldwide in a way that was never possible in any previous century. The 1902 coronation of the British monarch Edward VII was seen by fewer than 7000 aristocrats and ambassadors crammed into London's Westminster Abbey. The 1981 wedding of Prince Charles and Lady Diana Spencer was witnessed by 700 million people around the world. The 1984 Live Aid concert, raising money for famine-ravaged Ethiopia, was broadcast on 95 per cent of the television receivers then in operation. In 1900 even some of the participants in the second Olympic Games in Paris were unaware what exactly it was that they were participating in. Few within reach of a television set could have remained oblivious to the progress of the centenary Olympiad staged in Atlanta, USA, in 1996.

Cultures and societies overlap and interpenetrate each other more than ever before, yet they retain their distinctiveness. Peter Rabbit, Tintin, Asterix and Popeye have transcended their national origins to become

MOBILE SITTING ROOM One view of the future envisaged cars being guided along superhighways by electronic devices embedded in the road.

children's favourites in dozens of countries. But cultural exports do not receive an automatic welcome everywhere. There can be few people in North America who do not know what soccer is, but it has yet to make much headway there against the dominance of basketball, ice hockey and other, very different forms of football. Kentucky Fried Chicken nearly sank without trace in Japan – until salty soy sauce was added to the batter recipe and mother-and-child-sized portions became available at railway-station kiosks.

The forces of change

This has been the century of More! and New! and Faster! Daily life in the world's great democracies has been transformed by technology and by terror, by the trivial and by the tremendous – by zips and Biros, tampons and condoms, sticking plasters and contact lenses and the two most destructive wars in human history.

In 1900 the average life expectancy of the American male was just over 48 years. While some optimists might have believed that, as the century closed, it would be 50 per cent longer, most would have been astounded that a man would have a better chance of living to 65 in Bangladesh, the 12th poorest country in the world, than in the Harlem section of New York.

AN EDUCATION REVOLUTION   In France at the turn of the century, it was thought that by the year 2000 technology would turn schools into models of efficient learning.

COMMUNICATIONS The 1990s videophone, while more compact than one envisaged by an artist in 1905, does not enable the speakers to shake hands.

The first five years of the new era blessed the world with tea-bags, teddy bears, free mail-order catalogues and powered flight. But a hunger for novelties was seldom matched by an understanding of their implications. The first newspaper reports of the Wright brothers' achievement were low-key: 'Balloonless Airship' read an inside-page space-filler in the *Daily Mail* – one of the few to report it at all. It was another five years before the US Army Signal Corps was

persuaded to invest in an aeroplane, thus creating the world's first airborne military unit. In the 1930s, after a decade of dedicated effort and the expenditure of tens of millions of dollars, the Du Pont corporation finally succeeded in producing a new wonder material – nylon.

Technologies have proved slippery in their implications. Women pilots were commonplace in the 1930s, when new airlines were trying to take the fear out of flying. In America's Midwest some women's colleges sought to steal a march on more staid rivals by putting aviation on the curriculum. News-reels of the day suggested that within a decade or two homes would have a family plane in their driveway, rather than a saloon. But aviation has remained the prerogative of professionals – and mainly male ones at that.

The way we live has been changed as much by institutions as by innovations. Self-service has arrived; domestic service has all but departed. We celebrate Mother's Day in an age where the extended family headed by a matriarchal figure has been replaced by single parent families, DINKYs (career couples with Dual Income but No Kids Yet), and fragmented families spread not just around a village but now often around the globe. The century of space travel and heart transplants has not found solutions for ethnic cleansing, poverty and road rage, and however significant the triumphs of Western science, for many people they cannot replace the wisdom of ancient religions such as Hinduism or Buddhism. As the century – and the millennium – draws to its close, we are far less optimistic than our forebears that more and new and faster will necessarily mean better or wiser or happier.

EN L'AN 2000

THE WORLD AROUND US

SINCE THE 1900S, THE HOME ENVIRONMENT HAS BEEN CONTINUOUSLY RESHAPED BY TECHNOLOGY, ALTHOUGH SOCIAL PATTERNS HAVE ALSO PLAYED THEIR PART. HOUSEWORK AND TRANSPORTATION WERE ONCE SERVICES THE RICH PAID THE POOR TO PROVIDE; INCREASINGLY THEY HAVE BECOME UNPAID TASKS WE PERFORM FOR OURSELVES. AND OUR HOMES AND CARS NOT ONLY MEET OUR NEEDS FOR SHELTER AND MOBILITY – THEY ALSO EXPRESS OUR TASTES AND DREAMS.

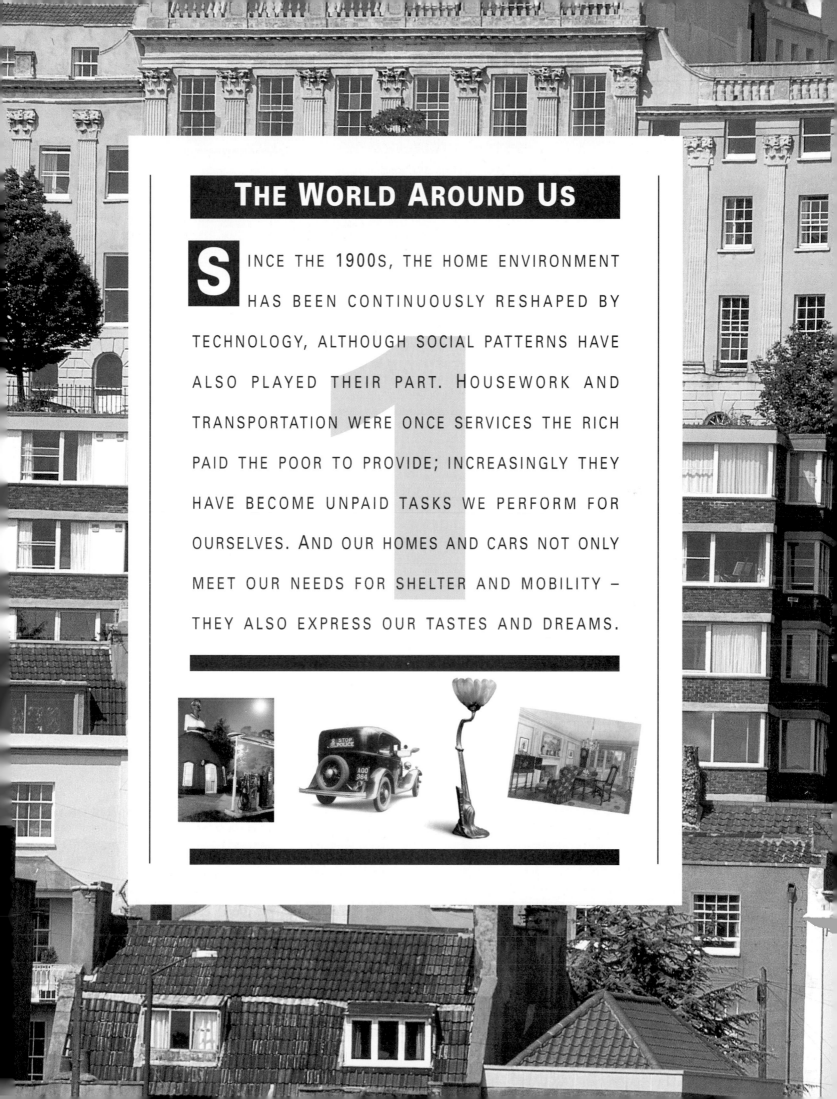

THE HOMES WE LIVED IN

SWISS ARCHITECT LE CORBUSIER CALLED THE HOME 'A MACHINE FOR LIVING IN'. THIS CENTURY HAS SEEN THAT MACHINE INVADED BY MANY OTHERS

ACCLIMATISATION In a spacious turn-of-the-century home in Brisbane, Australia, features such as gables and a verandah were used to accommodate the hot climate.

In the character of Mike Dobrejcak, the American novelist Thomas Bell re-created the experiences of his father, a Slovak immigrant, arriving in the United States in the first decade of the 20th century. Mike begins to court a young nursemaid who works in the home of a factory owner, and his first visit there comes as a revelation:

'The Dexters' [home] was the first private house Mike had ever set foot in which was wired for electricity. For that matter it was the first private house he'd ever been in that had a bathroom, a telephone, steam heat, and in the kitchen a magnificent icebox . . . Mike's interest in houses, in house furnishings, was no greater than most young men's . . . but in the Dexters' dining room, in their parlour and bedrooms, he saw furniture, dishes and silverware which were desirable and beautiful in themselves and not merely as articles of use. For the first time he perceived how graceful the business of eating and sleeping and entertaining one's friends could be, and how one could be proud of one's possessions, the way one lived. . . .'

Home comforts

Home for the 'comfortably off' at the start of the 20th century was not usually as grand as the Dexters' house. But in the Western world the benefits of industry and technology meant that even those with comparatively modest means could aspire to higher levels of comfort than their forebears had ever known.

In Continental European cities the typical middle-class home was a flat or apartment. The largest had up to a dozen rooms, including separate

CHEEK BY JOWL The terraced housing that has accommodated British working-class families for a century or more is plain in style and densely packed.

quarters for servants, and most had the benefit of some form of central heating. This was still a rarity in the English-speaking world, where even the rich deployed an army of screens, shawls and door curtains to fight an unending war against draughts. It was said on the Continent that designers of heating appliances in Britain observed five main principles. They were, in descending order of priority: safety, economy, ventilation, looks – and heat.

In North American cities, the typical home for middle-class people was a brownstone row house; in most British cities it was a red brick terraced or semidetached house. For the British – and the English in particular – a garden, however minute, was still regarded as an essential feature for those aspiring to a respectable status. Only the poor lived in houses whose front doors opened directly onto the street.

In Australia, New Zealand and small-town North America even quite well-off people lived in houses made of wood, an almost inconceivable notion to most Europeans. In the warmer parts of those countries most houses had a wide verandah, which was often the focus of social life, especially in the evenings during the summer months, when warm or humid weather encouraged families to savour every breath of breeze.

Gas was available in most big Western cities but many women still cooked and boiled their water on a cast-iron solid-fuel 'range'. In the rural areas of Canada, South Africa and Australia pioneer conditions prevailed. In these parts of the world, many homes of families that were otherwise moderately affluent still used kerosene lamps for lighting and had no indoor lavatory. Galvanised iron had begun to replace wooden shingles on the roofs of such homes and was sometimes used even for walls. Only time and rust would soften its patent ugliness.

Middle-class Americans definitely led the way in home conveniences in the early years of the century. Between 1912 and 1914 John B. Leeds of Columbia University in New York surveyed the living conditions of 60 American families 'earning enough for decency', a figure which ranged from the $700 a year of a farming family to the $3750 of a professional man – the average was around $1300. No fewer than 53 of these families lived in homes with electricity and 42 in homes with mains gas. Fifty-one homes had some form of central heating and Leeds did not even enquire whether they had a bathroom; he took it for granted that everybody had.

How people used their homes varied, then as now, from country to country and region to region. Flat-dwelling Continental Europeans tended to socialise outside the home, in cafés or beer gardens, in parks or on esplanades. Americans and Australians sat on their front steps or verandahs and chatted, read, played board games or hailed passersby. The English preferred to relax in privacy behind neatly clipped hedges.

The wealthy

The truly wealthy were rich enough to build new houses that looked old – assuming they had not inherited or purchased a genuinely old house. They built in pseudo-medieval, Renaissance or Neoclassical styles – or whatever combination of periods, motifs and details appealed to them.

Others could adapt existing dwellings. What the Victorian British architect William Burges had contemptuously dismissed as getting 'the picturesque by any and every means'

DOMESTIC PALACES Large detached houses in a Vermont town (below) contrast with a Berlin apartment block (right). Even wealthy Continentals favoured apartment living.

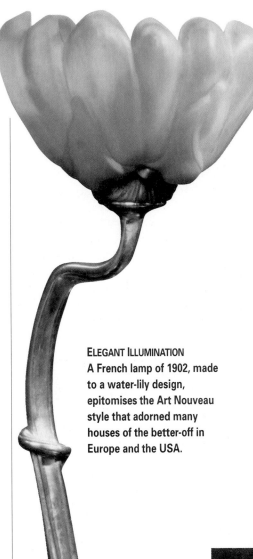

ELEGANT ILLUMINATION
A French lamp of 1902, made to a water-lily design, epitomises the Art Nouveau style that adorned many houses of the better-off in Europe and the USA.

usually involved obscuring the outlines of a conventional house by festooning it with gables, dormers, scrolls, oriel windows, bow windows and panels of hung tiling or half-timbering and then punctuating its outer walls with asymmetrical arrangements of unusual windows – round or oval, long and narrow, lozenge-shaped or semicircular.

The largest houses were virtually palaces, the most extravagant examples including the string of ornate country mansions built in the late 19th century by the different branches of the Rothschild banking dynasty in Austria, France and England, and the vast 'cottages' built at the fashionable American resort of Newport, Rhode Island, by such families as the Vanderbilts. Mansions like these had dozens of rooms, the principal ones set aside for particular forms of leisure and entertainment: a ballroom with chandeliers and a floor specially sprung for dancing on, a grand dining room with a table that could seat 20 people

RICH LIVING   An English lady's light and airy boudoir (top), an American parlour (centre) and the heavy opulence of a New York millionaire's drawing room (bottom) reveal contrasting styles, all fashionable in the early years of the century. Nor were individual styles confined to one country.

In Europe, 'old money' brought with it a ready-made inheritance of antique furniture which was seldom discarded, though particular pieces might be relegated in large houses to corridors or less public parts of the house when they were reckoned to have become ugly and out of date.

There was also a choice of avant-garde styles, particularly popular with the newly rich European middle classes. These styles were dominated by the heirs of the arts and crafts movement that had started in Britain in the mid 19th century,

in comfort, a salon for receptions, a music room with grand piano (at which one's daughters could show off), a billiard room (to which the gentlemen could retreat after dinner) and finally a book-lined library and a conservatory crammed with tropical greenery – either of the last two providing an appropriate setting for genteel flirtation, depending on the weather and time of day.

More intimate rooms for family use, apart from the individual bedrooms, might include a boudoir for the mistress of the house, a

---

SLOW-TECH

The earliest electric kettles, first marketed in the 1890s, took 18 minutes to boil a pint (600 ml) of water. Washing machines on sale at the same time stood about 6 1/2 ft (2 m) high, weighed half a ton – and were operated by turning a handle.

---

dressing room or a study (or both) for the master, a breakfast room for informal meals and a smoking room where the younger gentlemen could read raffish magazines and indulge themselves in smoking cigars without offending the ladies.

The basement was invariably the servants' realm. Here, behind the green baize door that led down to their subterranean kingdoms, the butler presided over the pantry and wine cellar and the cook reigned over the kitchen, where meals were prepared, and the scullery,

where dirty cleaning jobs were done. The attics would be subdivided into small bedrooms, where the female servants slept, while the younger male servants were relegated either to corners of the basement or perhaps to a room above the stables outside.

Home decor

For the wealthy, opulence was the hallmark of the period, particularly in the United States. Rich Americans were, after all, even richer than rich Europeans and had no qualms about displaying their wealth. The merely comfortably off paid more attention to more homely details, however, especially when it came to furniture.

Almost all well-to-do Americans represented, in Old World terms, 'new money', but new money enjoyed old furniture. Rich and well-off Americans were eagerly collecting antiques, and not just European ones. The 1876 Centennial celebrations had renewed interest in the colonial period of American history. As early as 1883 the author of *The Hearthstone, or Life at Home* had been urging her readers to acquire homely Shaker sewing chairs for their drawing rooms, and another author suggested that it was a good idea to hang on to 'one's own or someone else's great grandmother's candlesticks'.

HOME WITH THE RANGE Heat for cooking and hot water is supplied by a coal-fired iron range in a modern kitchen in New England (top), just like its older English counterpart.

spawning imitators all across Europe. Later, in the 1890s, the Belgian architect Henry van de Velde had developed the sinuous Art Nouveau style. By the turn of the century, this had spread to most other European countries under a variety of names – Jugendstil in Germany, Sezessionstil in Austria and *modernista* in Barcelona where wealthy merchants, shipping families and factory-owners were enthusiastic patrons of the new style.

The writhing curves of Art Nouveau lent themselves particularly well to metal, glass, plaster, wallpaper and textiles but were difficult to render in wood. This limited it as an overall decorative style; it tended rather to be a way of treating individual items, such as lamps or door handles. More exotic motifs and decorative items were also drawn from

'Celtic' sources or 'the Orient', especially from Japan, a prolific supplier of richly decorated Imari export-ware vases, lacquer chests inlaid with mother-of-pearl and delicate

SLUM LIFE Inhabitants of New York's Mulberry Bend district, one of the city's worst slums at the turn of the century, stare into the camera of reporter Jacob Riis.

paper screens, painted with spiky, floral designs.

At its worst, this eclecticism could fall into mere confusion. A catalogue of Shoolbred and Company of Tottenham Court Road, London, carried an illustration of a 'Drawing Room furnished and decorated in the Old

LIFE IN THE RAW Ragged clothes hang across the room where a Berlin mother lives with her children. On the left is a sewing machine which she uses to earn a precarious living.

English taste', which combined medieval, Renaissance, Japanese and contemporary elements. A very similar scheme was labelled 'Jacobean'. A better term for both would have been '"Artistic" furnishings (Commercial)'.

The struggling

The poor, who in every advanced country still made up two-thirds or more of the population, lived with very different preoccupations. Their homes were grubby tenement blocks, grimy terraces, damp cottages, leaky shanties and cabins.

In Berlin in 1901 more than 45 per cent of all dwellings consisted of one or two rooms only. In London the percentage was lower at under 35; in Paris it stood at over 55 and in Glasgow at over 70. In most of the cities of Continental Europe, Scotland and North America, the labouring poor were crammed into barrack-like blocks in inner-city areas or around port facilities. In England and Belgium, the poor clung doggedly to terraced cottage-style houses, even though these could be quite as bleak as tenements. In 1908, a British Board of Trade enquiry into working-class housing noted the difference in this respect between England and Scotland: 'In an ordinary English industrial town, street after street of two-storey cottages built on an almost uniform plan are met with. In Scotland the cottage disappears . . . in Edinburgh, for example, the most usual type of tenement house is that of four storeys, each with four flats, or 16 in the block. As regards the flats themselves the rooms are generally much larger than those in an English cottage, and

moreover, in nearly all tenements additional accommodation is afforded in one or two of the rooms . . . by a "bed recess". . .'

Whatever architectural shell encompassed their living space the poor lived in the closest proximity within it. Smoke, smells and noise were their constant companions. Most families consisted of an adult couple plus several children and often an aged relative and a

---

STRUGGLING FOR SURVIVAL IN THE SHANTYTOWNS

By the second half of the 20th century, the most squalid urban living conditions were in the shantytowns of Third World cities. In the 1950s, Carolina Maria de Jesus, with only a primary school education, kept a diary recording her life in the *favelas* (shantytowns) of São Paulo in Brazil. She was a single mother with three children:

Christmas Day, 1958: 'João came in saying he had a stomachache. I knew what it was for he had eaten a rotten melon. Today they threw a truckload of melons near the river.

'I don't know why it is that these senseless businessmen come to throw their rotted products here near the *favela*, for the children to see and eat.'

December 28: 'I lit a fire, put water on to boil, and started to wash the dishes and examine the walls. I found a dead rat. I'd been after him for days, and set a rat trap. But what killed him was a black cat. She belongs to Senhor Antonio Sapateiro.

'The cat is a wise one. She doesn't have any deep loves and doesn't let anyone make a slave of her. . . .'

January 4, 1959: 'In the old days I sang. Now I've stopped singing, because the happiness has given way to a sadness that ages the heart. Every day another poor creature shows up here in the *favela*. Ireno is a poor creature with anaemia. He is looking for his wife. His wife doesn't want him. He told me that his mother-in-law provoked his wife against him. Now he is in his brother's house. He spent a few days in his sister's house, but came back. He said they were throwing hints at him because of the food.

'Ireno says that he is unhappy with life. Because even with health life is bitter.'

January 7: 'Today I fixed rice and beans and fried eggs. What happiness. Reading this you are going to think Brazil doesn't have anything to eat. We have. It's just that the prices are so impossible that we can't buy it. We have dried fish in the shops that wait for years and years for purchasers. The flies make the fish filthy. Then the fish rots and the clerks throw it in the garbage, and throw acid on it so the poor won't pick it up and eat it. My children have never eaten dried fish. They beg me.

' "Buy it, Mother!"

'But buy it – how? At 180 cruzeiros a kilo? I hope, if God helps me, that before I die I'll be able to buy some dried fish for them.'

---

lodger as well. This meant that overcrowding was the norm and rooms could rarely be used for one purpose only. Baths, when taken at all, were taken in the room where you ate, because that was where water could be heated. Children usually slept two or three or more to a bed, sometimes top-to-tail, divided by gender or age for the sake of 'decency'. Parents, and often lodgers, slept in the same room, which made passion a furtive business.

The poorest of the poor slept on rags and straw and sat on tea chests and orange boxes. Even those in work could rarely afford cabinets or closets and kept their few possessions in chests stowed under beds, hanging on wall-pegs or ranged on open shelves if they were objects in daily use. A solid-fuel stove supplied the only heat for cooking and hot water and so often had to be kept going all day, even in sweltering summers.

In multistorey tenements it was often necessary to haul both fuel and water up from ground-floor level or to use a shared wash-house built in the back yard. Washing and drying clothes was therefore a major chore and much less frequently done than in better-off households. Cooking was liable to be limited to one pot dishes, such as soups and stews, or else to whatever could be fried up in a pan. Tut tutting home economists declared that the poor could not possibly afford canned goods, 'shop' bread, sausages, salted fish, cheese and other prepared or takeaway foods. In fact, these often made up their basic diet because the more elaborate preparation involved in roasting and baking brought such households to chaos.

The table the family ate at was the same one at which the mother earned a few pennies by assembling matchboxes or stitching cheap garments. The same greasy towel might be used for wiping hands, windows, pans and the baby's behind. Vermin abounded – one doctor working in the Gorbals district of Glasgow at the turn of the century had to tie string round the bottoms of his trousers when he visited the tenements to prevent rats from climbing up them. Cleanliness might indeed be next to godliness, but both were usually remote for the slum-dweller.

With servants and without them
In 1900 the great social dividing line was between those who employed a servant of some sort and those who did not. For the middle and upper classes servants were a

CONDEMNED This photograph of a tenement block in Glasgow's notorious Gorbals district was taken in the 1950s shortly before the clearance of Glasgow's slums began.

necessity, not a luxury. Advertisements for domestic appliances invariably showed them being used by a maid in cap and apron, rather than by a housewife herself. Anyone who could afford a carpet-sweeper could almost certainly also afford to have someone to push it around for them.

In the 'middling classes' there was a clear distance between those at the upper end, who had several domestics living in, and those at the bottom, who paid for a sturdy girl to come in once a week to do the laundry, scrub the floors, clean the toilets and scour the pans. But this gap was less significant socially than the one between families who could afford even a little help and the families who sent their womenfolk out to provide it.

The First World War and its aftermath brought noticeable changes to this and other aspects of middle-class life. In Germany many middle-class people saw their way of life disappear altogether as catastrophic hyperinflation in the early 1920s wiped out the value of their property and savings. Elsewhere, the change was less dramatic, though it still made itself felt – in the so-called 'servant shortage', for example. Not only were fewer women willing to tie themselves to the long hours habitually demanded of them 'in service'; but, having experienced wartime employment in factories and with growing opportunities opening up for them

MIDDLETOWN As railway networks increased around the major cities of Europe and North America, former fields were developed into suburban comfort zones.

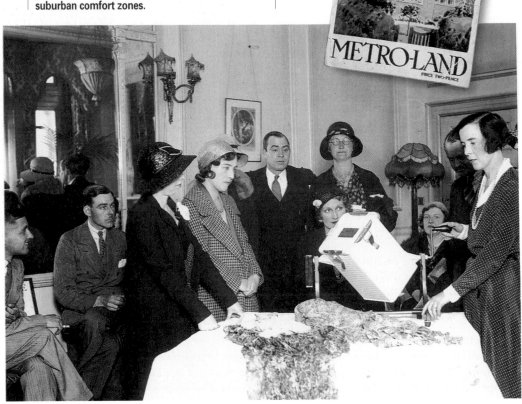

METRO-LAND
PRICE TWO-PENCE

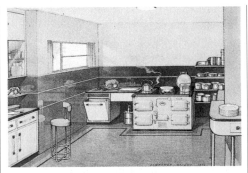

MOD CONS Appliances such as a miniature washing machine and the fuel-efficient Aga cooker (left) that appeared in the 1930s made housework quicker and cleaner.

in offices, they also expected to be paid much more. In the England of 1914, £100 a year would have paid the wages of a cook and four maids; ten years later it paid for only a cook and a housemaid.

For the very rich this made little difference, though some English people began to experiment with American-style 'service apartments' where central heating did away with the need for someone to light and stoke half a dozen fires each day and even meals could be ordered from a central kitchen.

For the middle classes, however, it meant that the housewife now did more of her routine housework with her own hands and spent less time making sure that it had been done

properly by someone else. Advertisers no longer presented labour-saving devices as something one bought for the staff but as miracle-working innovations which would give back to the housewife some of the leisure hours she remembered her mother having. Sales of vacuum cleaners, electric irons, kettles and toasters boomed in response to this new demand. For the same reason new houses for the relatively affluent began to be built rather smaller; less space meant less to clean. Even having stainless-steel knives, instead of silver ones, helped, getting rid of one more messy, time-consuming job.

Many middle-class wives tried to substitute a 'daily' for the traditional live-in maid. This had released the former servant's room for use as a dressing or utility room or a nursery or child's bedroom. But, to readers of the British magazine *Good Housekeeping*, it also conjured up 'a vista of inconvenience' such as bells going unanswered outside 'kitchen

hours' – which were still expected to stretch from 7.30 am to 9 pm. Beyond inconvenience there lurked even worse nightmares: 'to the mind's eye the daily maid appears as slovenly, unpunctual, perhaps actually dishonest, introducing burglars, and herself vanishing from sight or, it might be, not appearing at all on some critical occasion'.

Prospective employers were advised to recruit only through a reputable staff agency and to look, preferably, for the wife of a disabled ex-serviceman who, as her family's main breadwinner, would be anxious not to lose her position. In large country houses it was recommended that, rather than engage

ALL IN A WEEK'S WORK

In 1918 the *American Journal of Home Economics* published an account of the household routine of Marion Woodbury, the wife of a university professor and mother of three small children. Describing herself as a woman who 'did her own work', she did not feel that the assistance of a weekly laundress and a student part-timer contradicted this.

Mrs Woodbury estimated that she put in ten hours' work a day, five days a week, plus five hours on Wednesdays and Sundays. Monday was her day for stripping dirty linen from beds and gathering dirty towels from the bathroom and then assembling the week's washing, which she put in to soak overnight. On Tuesday the laundress came in to do the actual washing and give the kitchen and bathroom their weekly once-over. Mrs Woodbury meanwhile focused on darning, letting out clothes and other sewing tasks. On Wednesday the laundress came in again for half a day to iron. Thursday meant replenishing the linen cupboard and wardrobes.

Having a telephone, Mrs Woodbury was able to order most of her groceries, which were brought to her home by an errand boy – in effect, another part-time helper. Actually going to market only took up a Friday afternoon every other week.

Mrs Woodbury did all the cooking and ate meals with her children, but the clearing away and washing up were done by a student helper, who also baby-sat when needed. The student also did most of the dusting, sweeping and floor polishing, leaving Mrs Woodbury to do only superficial 'straightening-up'.

Mrs Woodbury's housework therefore consisted more of supervising than carrying out manual tasks. It allowed her to pursue the more 'creative' aspects of housework, such as cooking and needlework, and gave her time for social and charitable activities.

an additional maid, one should employ a handyman who would combine the roles of chauffeur, gardener and repairman, as well as cleaning brass and windows, hauling coal and laying fires.

Life in 'Middletown'

American lifestyles between the wars illustrated the way patterns were changing. In 1925 the sociologists Helen and Robert Lynd produced a study of the lives of 40 'business class' housewives in 'Middletown' (Muncie, Indiana). They showed that on average these women bought in only about half the number of servant-hours per week that their mothers had done – and paid five times as much for it. As a result almost all of them possessed a range of labour-saving electric appliances.

Efficient washing machines, for example, enabled them to dispense with the services of a laundress. In 1932 the Secretary of the American Washing Machine Manufacturers Association announced triumphantly that for the first time ever this severely practical appliance was being offered for sale on New York's fashionable Fifth Avenue and shrewdly noted that 'an entirely new class, never before

BARE MINIMUM Although standards of living had improved for many by the 1960s, there were still areas of great poverty, as seen in this sharecroppers' shack in South Carolina.

directly interested in the washing process or in the details of household economics has come into the buying market . . . These housewives have the money to buy anything.'

A follow-up study of 'Middletown' in 1935 showed that 40 per cent of such homes had also acquired a refrigerator. Whereas in 1910 the affluent American housewife had been a manager of people, a quarter of a century later she was a manager of technology.

Even in the booming USA the affluent were still a minority, but the urban hard up did also benefit to some extent from modern conveniences. A 1926 study of the working-class population of Zanesville, Ohio,

STATE OF THE ART A porcelain sink of 1900 (top, left) contrasts with the sparkling stainless-steel surfaces of a 1990s Australian sink (bottom, left). The kitchen of tomorrow (above) – a 1955 vision from Frigidaire.

revealed that nine homes out of every ten had running water and gas; three-quarters had electricity; seven out of ten had a telephone and six out of ten had an indoor toilet and a bath. The larger electric appliances, however, which would have taken much of the drudgery out of raising a big family, were still beyond their means. A washing machine would cost a factory worker the equivalent of an entire month's wages.

Living conditions were much worse among America's rural poor, especially in the South, and among the black community. A 1934 survey of 200 Tennessee tenant farmers showed that only 4 per cent could afford electricity and none had running water. Other investigations made in the same year established that four-fifths of Missouri farmhouses lacked a kitchen sink with a drain, 93 per cent in Kentucky had no bathroom, and 75 per cent in supposedly prosperous Washington state had no flush toilet. As late as 1940 only a third of American homes had central heating, only half had a bath and only two-thirds had running water.

Ideal homes

In Europe, too, changing lifestyles from the interwar years through to the end of the century brought changing homes. The 1920s and 30s saw some notable experiments, all in

their different ways attempts to rethink what made a home attractive and convenient. In the mid 1920s, in the German city of Dessau, the architect Walter Gropius – a leader of the Bauhaus movement, a later offshoot of the arts and crafts and Art Nouveau styles – built startlingly avant-garde houses, all straight lines and large glass windows, to accommodate teachers at his school of arts and design. Around the same time, the Swiss-born Le Corbusier, near the start of his career, built a model 'workers' city' of 40 houses at Pessac near Bordeaux. In Vienna in the 1930s, the socialist city authorities constructed huge blocks of flats for working-class families, the most famous of which was the Karl Marx Hof built around three sides of a common garden, with a railway station next door so that people living there were just 15 minutes from the city centre.

Less revolutionary in intent were the mass-produced 'dream houses' put up by speculative builders, catering for people's desire for privacy and life in a 'respectable' neighbourhood. These remained a feature of both European and American cities, towns and suburbs through the rest of the century, though the precise dimensions of the dream changed over the decades, tending to become smaller as the paraphernalia of home life became more compact. In 1919, the author of the British manual *Ideal Workers' Homes* envisaged working-class occupants having some 900-1000 sq ft (80-90 m²) to move around in, not much short of the 1100 sq ft (100 m²) typical of a 1990s four-bedroom 'executive' estate house. The basic format was that of a cottage, with a front parlour and a back living room, with a scullery off it. The ground floor also had a larder and storage space for a bicycle and a baby's pram. Some sample designs boasted extra fittings, such as wall-mounted drop-flap tables and built-in dressers.

The 1922 *Daily Mail Book of Bungalows*, aimed at mid-market British purchasers, assumed a 1500 sq ft (140 m²) overall floor plan and still allowed space for a maid's bedroom and sitting room. The principal rooms in its homes were not labelled parlour and living room but more grandly as drawing room and dining room. There were often double doors between them so that they could be used en suite. Larger models had a

SMART SIMPLICITY Advanced taste in 1962 favoured 'open plan' layouts for an airy atmosphere. Even the houses are portable in a 1950s Long Island suburb (below) being shifted to make way for a new road. The giant house mover will reinstall them elsewhere.

vestibule, to take coats and umbrellas, as well as a spacious hall, where handsome items of furniture could be displayed.

In the 1950s, a generation and another world war later, 'open plan' was all the rage, with dividing walls taboo. Houses were no longer thought of as arranged sets of rigid boxes but fluid volumes of space. Many owners of existing properties knocked through the wall between front parlour and back living room to create a 'through lounge' – a trend that carried on until the end of the century.

For a while, in the 1950s and 60s, period features went out of fashion in favour of streamlined modernism. Moulded plaster ceilings and parquet floors were removed or covered with plastic tiling. Panelled wooden doors were disguised with hardboard and their brass handles and fingerplates were replaced with shiny new ones in plastic, chrome or aluminium – later, in the 70s and 80s, fashion changed course again and many of these features were laboriously reinstated.

Central heating became a virtual necessity in the post-Second World War decades, as did wall-to-wall fitted carpets. Open-tread staircases were briefly popular but proved

HOMES FOR HEROES

With thousands of homes destroyed by bombing, Britain's wartime government predicted a postwar housing crisis, so they got the munitions industry – which would face a run-down after fighting stopped – to design prefabricated homes, which would be replaced after ten years by 'proper' houses. The 'prefabs' were hailed as a great success. Because erecting them was essentially an assembly process, they could be completed in three weeks.

READY MADE Prefabs were supposed to be demolished after ten years, but many were still standing 30 years later.

For men who had spent years in barracks, and women who had been obliged to share a home with in-laws or evacuees, they represented privacy and a home of one's own. The future Labour Party leader Neil Kinnock remembered the prefab his family moved into: 'It had a fitted fridge, a kitchen table that folded into the wall and a bathroom. Family and friends came visiting to view the wonders. It seemed like living in a spaceship.'

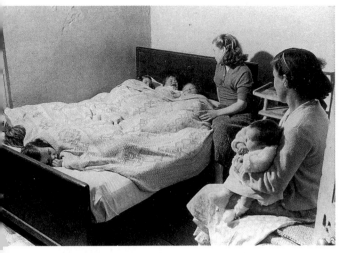

ROOM TO BREATHE? In Liverpool in the 1950s, large areas of housing were condemned as damp and overcrowded. In this household the children sleep six to a bed.

hazardous to families with small children. Later, as these children grew into teenagers with a fondness for loud music, the concept of shared living space began to pall, though sliding doors helped, providing partitions when needed.

North American fashions such as split-level rooms and 'conversation pits' were known about in Europe from films and were often aspired to, but European homes were mostly too small for them to be practicable. Only the rich could indulge in such trans-atlantic eccentricities as L-shaped rooms and, even more daring, freestanding fire-places in the centre of the room. Large picture windows could, however, be taken over from the American 'ranch house' style and featured widely in European homes built in the 1960s. Later, novel devices such

SUBURBAN RANCHES Ranch-style homes are firm favourites in Johannesburg's middle-class suburbs. There is room for garden barbecues and even a swimming pool.

as solar panels for heating were tried out – though these were more suitable for sunny climates than for overcast northern ones.

Late developers

Germany, Britain and the United States all saw feverish building activity through most of the inter-war and postwar decades. France lagged behind, adding little to her housing stock between 1914 and 1954. A quarter of what was built in France in the interwar period was simply replacing what had been destroyed during the First World War. Rent controls, hastily introduced in 1914 to protect sol-diers' families from profiteering landlords, had never been lifted, making building for letting too unprofitable to be worthwhile and encouraging landlords of existing properties to allow them to fall into premature decay. Defeat and occupation after 1940 brought

EUROPE IN A SPIN

In 1988 Spain was the western European country with the highest proportion of households – 94 per cent – that owned a washing machine. Neighbouring Portugal had the lowest – 31 per cent. But, thanks no doubt to their country's sunny climate, only 2 per cent of Spanish homes felt the need of a tumble drier. Damp Britain headed the ownership league at 31 per cent.

such building activity as there was to a halt, and in the immediate postwar period indus-trial recovery, rather than home building, was the number one national priority.

The 1954 census revealed that 73 per cent of French homes did not have a flushing lavatory, while 42 per cent had no running water. Only 7 per cent of homes had a refrig-erator and 8 per cent a washing machine. About 100 000 new homes a year were being built by then, but this was only about a third of what the British were doing and a fifth of the annual output being achieved in Germany. By the 1960s, however, French home-building had expanded rapidly and was running at 400 000 homes a year.

The 1968 census showed marked improve-ments. Almost half of all French homes now had a bath or shower and a flushing lavatory and less than 10 per cent still lacked running water. Even so almost a third of all homes

were officially acknowledged to be over-crowded (defined as having more than four people in three living rooms); and no less than 52 per cent of all French homes dated from before 1914, many being in an appalling state of repair. Some 100 000 houses a year were estimated to be collapsing because they were so far decayed that they could no longer be repaired.

Although the French government did promote subsidised public housing for workers, the building industry was much keener to cash in on the demand of the wealthy for

MODERN AFFLUENCE Densely packed apartment blocks are still the favoured style in Barcelona (left), while expensive austerity is the keynote of a Thames-side penthouse in 1990s London (right). Solar panels stud the roofs of 'cube houses' in Rotterdam (below).

smart apartments in the capital and villas on the Riviera. The industry also remained highly inefficient compared with Germany or the USA, where there was much greater use of prefabricated components and standardised parts. Around 1970 an artisan working for one of France's 243 500 building firms could choose from no fewer than 300 types of door and 1000 different taps. Rigid regulations, local government corruption and speculator profiteering further marred continuing efforts to rehouse the nation.

By 1990, 58 per cent of French homes were owner-occupied but this was still well below the proportion attained in Italy, Belgium, Britain and Spain over a decade

SUNSHINE CITY A futuristic house in Arizona has all the latest gadgets. In such regions solar technology may come to supply all the energy needed for domestic efficiency.

previously. Home-ownership was, however, as much a matter of cultural preference as of economics. In affluent Sweden, Germany and the Netherlands almost 60 per cent of the population still chose to rent their homes rather than buy them.

Death of the hearth

The way people lived at home was still changing as the 20th century drew to its close. In 1900 a typical home, almost anywhere in the Western world, was occupied by five, six or more people, was subject to draughts and heated by coal. Warmth in the form of an open fireplace or a stove provided the focus for family life. By the interwar period this focus had a rival in the form of the wireless. A generation later the wireless had, in most homes, lost the battle to the television set and solid-fuel heating had given way to gas, electricity, radiators or even ducted air circulating through grilles.

With the arrival of the gramophone and radio in the interwar years the home became a centre for entertainment – a trend that was reinforced in the postwar decades by the advent of hi-fi, television, video recorders,

CD players, computers, cable TV and satellite receivers. But whereas whole families had once gathered together to 'listen in' after supper, increasingly the entertainment came to be provided for an audience of two, or even one, as individual members of the family started to entertain themselves separately, and as single-person households became more common, especially in big cities. Even people living together wanted to be apart. By 1960 rent allowances to the poor in New York were calculated on the assumption that a four-person family needed a five-room apartment – a degree of luxury almost inconceivable to a family half a century earlier.

This shift was reflected in falling demand across the Western world for larger family homes and the construction of more compact residences, apartment buildings and 'sheltered' complexes for the retired and the elderly. Most large terraced houses in inner-city areas, originally built for wealthy families with servants, were subdivided into

TOGETHERNESS In the interwar period, and through the dark years of the Second World War, the family radio was the focus of home life

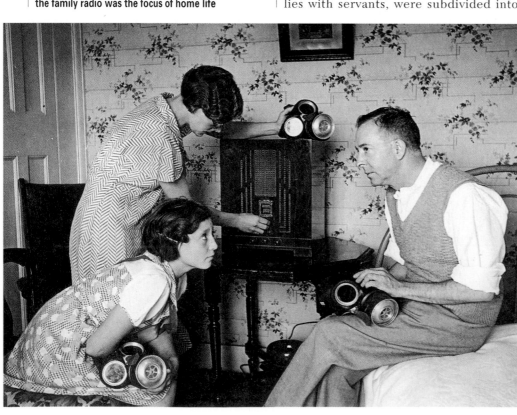

CONTRASTING STYLES A French family in the 1950s enjoy a celebratory drink in a rather formal home setting (left) . An 'arty' New York interior towards the end of the century presents a more relaxed scene. Homes changed over the course of the century as families changed, often with more easy-going attitudes between the generations.

small self-contained flats or bedsits. Living alone, many individuals became increasingly concerned for their personal security, so new homes were routinely fitted with window locks and alarms.

At the same time, greater environmental awareness and rising energy costs prompted many householders and homebuilders to invest in better insulation and double glazing. Experimental energy-efficient houses were being built and 'smart' houses with computers that automatically controlled heating and lighting to optimum efficiency no longer appeared the stuff of science fiction. Homes looked set to change even faster in the 21st century than they had in the 20th.

THE WORLD ON OUR DOORSTEP

WE ARE MORE MOBILE NOW THAN EVER. DURING THE 20TH CENTURY THE WORLD ON OUR DOORSTEP HAS STEADILY EXPANDED ITS LIMITS

The family motor car, more probably than anything else, has transformed our relationship with the world on our doorstep, and well beyond it, during the 20th century. Apart from air travel, the transport revolution of the 19th century had already introduced most of the key forms of public transport, from tram

AT HOME ON WHEELS An American mother and daughter enjoy the panelled luxury of a 1905 Pullman railway carriage.

to train, that are with us to this day. But none of these offered the degree of freedom to go where one liked, when one liked, at the pace one liked, that the family car would give growing numbers of people during the course of the 20th century. At the start of the century, when the motor car was still predominantly a toy of the rich, the bicycle offered many people a chance to roam more freely than ever before. The mass-produced motor car, invented by the American Henry Ford, would

extend that freedom to much wider horizons. It would also bring its own problems, as traffic congestion in the late 20th century made many people take a fresh look at the virtues of public transport.

For its part, public transport has seen refinements, improvements – and drastic changes. In 1900 there was no challenger to the railway and ocean liner for travelling long distances. This remained true for most of the first half of the century. But air travel, once properly established after the Second World War, changed all that, transforming both intercontinental travel – previously the

EARLY AUTOMATION A customer buys a ticket from a machine on London's Underground in 1928.

domain of the liner – and long-distance travel within continents – previously the domain of the railway. The great liners of the past have long since gone, their successors devoted to holiday cruises. The railways, however, have fought back more successfully. Japan's highly efficient Bullet Train and France's TGV (Train à Grand Vitesse), which travels at speeds of up to 320 mph (515 km/h), are working proof of the value of modern high-speed rail links.

Local transport, meanwhile, has had its ups and downs. At the start of the century, London had an expanding underground

CAPITAL SYSTEMS
The Paris Métro's first stations were built in the Art Nouveau style. New trains transformed London's Underground in the 1930s.

most long-haul journeys in the Western world for the next half century. But already electrification was promising new standards of speed, smoothness and reliability for shorter-haul journeys – the Italians inaugurated their first mainline electric service as early as 1902. Then came the diesel engine. The Germans began operating a two-car diesel service between Berlin and Hamburg in 1932. Later in the same decade, long-haul diesel engines, capable of cruising at 90 mph (145 km/h), were introduced on the American railways. The journey from Chicago to Los Angeles was cut from a pre-First World War average of almost 60 hours to just under 40. Other countries followed suit, though more gradually – Britain, for example, did not phase out its last steam locomotives until 1968.

Some long-distance rail journeys in the first half of the century could be undertaken in what were virtually hotels on wheels. Europe had its legendary Orient Express, linking Paris with Istanbul. The United States had several such services. The New York Central's Twentieth Century Limited service to Chicago, inaugurated in 1902, had two buffet cars, a library and a smoking car, two observation cars and a dozen drawing-room and stateroom cars. The Santa Fe Railway's Chicago-Los Angeles service, inaugurated in 1911, had business travellers in mind, offering them the services of a stenographer, daily market reports and access to telephones at stations en route, as well as the comforts of a library, club room, barber, bathing facilities and Pullman sleeping cars with brass beds. Further refinements on the American rail network came in the 1930s with streamlined stainless-steel carriages, complete with air conditioning.

By the interwar years, the European railways were facing

CITY TRANSPORT
Tramways crisscrossed most cities, including London until the 1950s and Berlin (below).

railway system, and other cities were following suit – Paris opened its Métro in 1900, Berlin its U-Bahn in 1902 and New York its Subway in 1904. In 1933 the British capital again set a worldwide trend when it created the London Passenger Transport Board, integrating the operations and timetables of all its underground, bus, tram and trolley lines. Employing 71 000 workers, the LPTB carried some 4 billion passengers a year. As late as the 1960s, traffic experts were coming from the Netherlands to study the system. A generation later, it was the Netherlands whose transport system was a model for the industrial world, integrating road and rail services and providing for the hire and storage of bicycles at stations to encourage cycling.

Change on the rails
Although the railways have held their own through the 20th century, just about everything about them has changed. In 1900 steam reigned supreme, and would do for

OPEN ALL HOURS The driver of this 1929 London double-decker bus still has to sit in an open cab, while the passengers are glassed in against the elements.

a serious challenge from the roads. Motor trucks, offering door-to-door delivery, were creaming off much of their freight business. Charabancs or coaches began to challenge them for passenger traffic, particularly for excursions and touring holidays. The railways responded with electrification and more comfortable rolling stock.

In 1936 a London-Paris overnight service was introduced which took sleeping cars right onto the Dover-Dunkirk ferry, enabling passengers to sleep on undisturbed. Another response was for governments to take over and run the increasingly unprofitable railways as public services. France completed the nationalisation of its network in 1938, before the Second World War; Britain carried out its own nationalisation ten years later in 1948.

The 1950s brought airline competition on intercity routes, beginning in North America. They first vied for passengers and soon afterwards for high-value or perishable freights. The American and Canadian railways, still privately owned, were severely pruned. Across the Atlantic in Britain, a radical review of rail services in 1963 resulted in the closure of 2128 stations and a quarter of the nation's network – the so-called 'Beeching axe', named after the chairman of British Railways who introduced

the reorganisation. In 1995 the Canadian Pacific Railway finally closed down its transcontinental rail service – which had originally been created in the 1880s as a way of uniting the nation.

High-speed trains held the key to the railways' survival in the late 20th century. This was symbolised by the inauguration in 1964 of Japan's 130 mph (209 km/h) Bullet Train between Tokyo and Kyoto, the two major venues for the Olympic Games that year. In 1981 Paris and Lyons were linked by the first TGV. By 1992 a 160 mph (260 km/h) version of the Bullet Train was in service in Japan. The opening of the Channel Tunnel, bringing London and Paris within three hours of each other by 1995, was another milestone. Allowing passengers to travel rapidly from the centre of one city to the centre of the other, without having to battle out to or in from airports, the Eurostar service showed that the railway had plenty of life in it for the 21st century. Long-haul journeys by rail were no longer luxurious affairs with drawing rooms and observation cars, but in the age of executive travel they could match the airlines within a continent or country for speed and convenience. Intercity routes, in particular, were so profitable that some governments, in Sweden, Germany and Britain, for example, set about reprivatising them.

OBSERVATION CAR The design of the General Motors Scenicruiser imitated railway observation cars to give its 43 passengers a clear view on long cross-country journeys.

For travel within cities nothing was more advanced at the start of the century than London's Underground. A sub-surface, steam-powered system dating back to the 1860s had been supplemented from the 1890s by a true Underground, set hundreds

of feet deep and electrically powered. In 1900 the new Central Line came into operation, providing the first direct east-west link across the capital. In a city whose streets were already clogged with motorised and horse-drawn traffic, a clerk working in the financial districts of the City could get on a train and be whisked underground to the shopping and residential areas of the West End, all for a flat-rate fare of twopence.

But only very large and wealthy cities could contemplate the expense of an underground railway. Most cities, in both Europe and North America and well beyond, relied

on the vehicle running on tracks and driven from overhead powerlines that the British called a tram and the Americans a trolley car or streetcar. The tram was then entering its heyday. By 1917 the USA alone had 80 000 trolley cars carrying 11 billion passengers a year. It would have been possible, if somewhat laborious, to travel from eastern Wisconsin all the way to New York, a distance of more than 1000 miles (1600 km),

just by changing from one trolley system to the next at each terminus. Later, the trolley bus – electrically driven from overhead powerlines but without tracks – was introduced in many cities, notably in Italy.

The tram made possible a new feature of urban living: the working-class suburb. Now manual workers, as well as the middle classes, could afford to commute to and from their places of work each day. The tram also opened up the countryside to them. In

STEAM OR GAS? Gas-turbine locomotives (above) were an experiment of the 1950s. In the end, diesel and electricity won the day to replace traditional steam power.

Europe, tram routes often defined the boundaries of a city. Where the tramlines ended, the countryside, by definition, began. At weekends the young and the poor could refresh their lungs simply by riding to the end of the line and then wandering off into fields and forests.

In many parts of northern Europe – Scandinavia, Germany and the Low Countries – the clatter and clang of trams as they rattled along their tracks would remain one of the characteristic and endearing sounds of urban life. Elsewhere, however, they were ousted by the motorbus. At the start of the century, this was a rudimentary, extremely noisy vehicle, often with an open upper deck. But in 1920 Frank and William Fageol of Oakland, California, produced a bus specifically designed for carrying passengers in comfort. It had a low floor for easier boarding, an inside seat for the driver, upholstered seats for passengers and a smooth braking system. With no overhead powerlines, the bus had the great advantage of flexibility and by the 1960s many cities had abandoned their tram and trolley-bus

HARD TRAVELLING Early cars, like this Peugeot 'wagonette' taking part in the 1900 Paris-Rouen race, offered few comforts despite being the prerogative of the rich.

services. The bus is, however, much more of a polluter than its rivals, and as people became more aware of the dangers of pollution some cities turned back to older forms of transport. In England, for example, Manchester reintroduced trams in the 1990s.

Long-distance bus services, meanwhile, flourished. By 1933, the Greyhound company in the United States was operating a network covering 40 000 miles (64 400 km). Sixty years later, in 1993, American intercity bus services were still carrying 350 million passengers a year, and for 15 000 American communities bus services were the only form of public transport available to them.

The not so open road

Motoring was an adventure at the start of the century. In Britain it had recently been released from the restrictions of the 'Red Flag' Act according to which drivers of 'horseless carriages' were restricted to a speed of 4 mph (6 km/h) – 2 mph (3 km/h) in towns – and had to be preceded by a man carrying a red flag as a warning to other road users. The repeal of the Act on November 14, 1896, was celebrated by car users with an 'Emancipation Run' from the Hotel Metropole in London to its namesake in Brighton over 50 miles (80 km) away on England's south coast. This became an annual event, which is still held for veteran cars on the first Sunday in November.

There was nothing streamlined about early motoring. Some manual braking systems relied on the strength of the motorist's arm to halt the vehicle. Crank-starting a car could dislocate a thumb or even bring on a heart attack. Speedometers and fuel gauges were sold as extras. Drivers and passengers, exposed to the elements, went swathed in fur-lined garments, gauntlets and goggles which could cost almost as much as a car itself. Without a network of filling stations (hotels and chemists were among the earliest petrol distributors), touring motorists were advised to strap jerry cans of fuel around their vehicles to avoid running out. Breakdowns were expected to happen daily. Many hotels provided pits where chauffeurs could make running repairs overnight.

In Europe, France and Germany were the biggest producers of motor cars, with the names Daimler, Benz, Peugeot and Renault

Motor transport had come to stay. In 1910 an advertisement threw American businessmen and farmers the challenging query: 'Can your horses deliver your goods fast enough?' It then promised that 'Packard trucks can. Three tons – twelve miles [19 km] an hour'. A copywriter for Maxwell (later Chrysler) asserted more whimsically: 'Life holds many big days. Two stand out prominently – the day a man marries and the day he buys an automobile.'

Road networks expanded massively to meet the new demands made upon them. By 1914 Gulf Oil was distributing free maps to American motorists, showing the hard-surfaced routes suitable for cars. From 1916 onwards the Federal government offered 50 per cent subsidies for road-building, and by 1921 the United States had 387 000 miles (623 000 km) of surfaced roads. The Lincoln Highway, constructed between 1913 and 1927 to link New York and San Francisco, was the first fully paved transcontinental route.

In Europe, the Italian dictator Benito Mussolini set about building the first autostrada – at that stage, a three-lane undivided highway – in his country in the 1920s. Later, German planners came up with the idea of the dual-lane carriageway, incorporating a stretch of it in a new road between Cologne and Bonn that opened in 1932. When he came to power, Adolf Hitler quickly spotted the strategic importance of

COP CAR This London police car has a rear-window blind which the driver can operate from the steering wheel to display a message ordering a driver to halt.

already prominent. Initially Britain imported most of its cars from France, but by 1914 there were some 200 British firms manufacturing vehicles. In particular Rolls-Royce, founded in 1904, had shown what could be done at the luxury end of the market. Its 1906 Silver Ghost set an endurance record – running some 14 000 miles (22 500 km) without a breakdown – which stood for half a century.

WRAP UP! Clothing manufacturers developed an extensive range of ingenious headgear to protect the hairstyles and complexions of Edwardian lady motorists.

But it was the United States that became the world's first motorised society. The first motoring association, the American Motor League, had been founded in Chicago in November 1895 – 11 days before its first European counterpart, the Automobile Club de France. The American Automobile Association was founded in 1902. Licence plates were required in Massachusetts from 1903. In the same year, a car built by the Packard Motor Company, Detroit, made the first transcontinental crossing – in 61 days (by 1909 the time was down to 21 days). In 1905 the Society of Automotive Engineers came into existence to encourage standardisation of parts among manufacturers.

Then in 1908 Henry Ford produced the first of his famous Model T's. His revolutionary aim was to turn out cheap and reliable vehicles which would convert the motor car from a rich person's plaything to the ordinary person's necessity – in Britain a 'Tin Lizzie' (Model T) cost £135 compared with more than £300 for most other cars. To this end, in 1913 he adopted the assembly-line production method, which he had first seen in action in Chicago meat-packaging plants. In so doing, he transformed not only the automobile industry but all kinds of manufacturing as his methods were adopted in the production of everything from vacuum cleaners to domestic irons. Demand for the Tin Lizzie shot up. By 1925 half of all the cars in the world were Model T's.

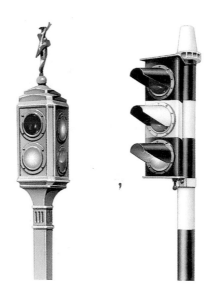

STOP – GO! Electric traffic lights reached London in 1926 (far left and near right) having been pioneered in the USA (centre left and right).

such highways and ordered the rapid construction of a 4350 mile (7000 km) network of autobahns across Germany, starting in 1934. In 1940 the Pennsylvania Turnpike was completed in the United States, a dual carriageway which traffic could enter or leave only via interchanges.

LIFESAVER

London introduced its first motor-ambulance service in 1905 – to ferry victims of motor accidents to hospital. Until then the police had relied on commandeering private vehicles. The police did not get their own cars until 1920, when the Flying Squad was established. Motorcycle patrols began the following year.

One worrying set of statistics was the toll of road deaths. As early as 1903-7 these had averaged 400 a year in the United States alone. In 1905 the *North American Review* noted that in just five months more Americans had been killed by cars than in the Spanish-American War of 1898. Thereafter road fatalities in the USA rose steadily to an average of 1900 a year between 1908 and 1912, 12 500 a year from 1918 to 1922, 33 700 in 1931 and 39 643 in 1939.

Danger on the roads

Obviously, better safety regulations were needed. The French authorities had required local motorists to pass a driving test since 1893 in Paris and 1899 in France as a whole. Other countries were slower off the mark. In 1903 the British Parliament rejected proposals for driving tests, vehicle inspections and penalties for drunk drivers. By 1935, however, it was taking things more seriously. It introduced compulsory driving tests that year and a number of other measures during the same decade, including specialised traffic police, standardised traffic

signs, a Highway Code of traffic regulations, a 30 mph (48 km/h) urban speed limit and 'cat's-eye' road reflectors.

The first electric traffic lights, using a red and a green light and a buzzer to warn motorists that they were about to change, had been installed in Cleveland, Ohio, in 1914. The New York authorities introduced a system using the now-familiar red, amber and green lights in 1918. Paris had a kind of traffic light by 1923; it was a large *Halte* sign on glass with a light behind that could be switched on and off and had a gong to warn drivers that it was about to change. A system similar to the New York one was installed in London's West End in 1926. Also in London, pedestrian crossings, introduced in the late 1920s and 1930s, reduced pedestrian fatalities by 20 per cent.

Meanwhile, motor cars were changing the shape of cities, especially in the United States. Suburbs continued to grow faster and spread farther throughout the 1940s as people took advantage of the new mobility that allowed them to live farther from their

places of work. During the 40s, the population outside the central city core grew by over 30 per cent in Buffalo and Chicago, 40 per cent in Cleveland, 50 per cent in Atlanta and a staggering 70 per cent in Baltimore, Dallas and Denver.

By the 1950s, the automobile represented the core of the American economy and was deemed essential to the American lifestyle. Motor manufacturers were the nation's industrial giants. A poll in 1951 showed that Americans made 80 per cent of their vacation trips by car, the average trip lasting 1400 miles (2250 km), spread over 12 days. The motel – a word first coined in 1925 – had become a distinctive national institution, and the latest automobile-related novelty was the drive-in cinema. By 1955, 57 per cent of American families living in cities with a population of more than 500 000 owned a car. In smaller cities and towns the proportion was a third as high again, and in the countryside almost four-fifths of all families owned a car.

New age, new styles

Car styles changed rapidly in the decades following the Second World War. The Volkswagen Beetle, originally designed in Nazi Germany, set new standards of cheap reliability, overtaking the Tin Lizzie as the

ROADSIDE REFRESHMENT Mammy's Cupboard in Natchez, Mississippi, has been refuelling travellers since 1947.

most popular car ever produced – more than 20 million had been sold by the early 1980s when production ceased in Europe. In 1959, the Austin and Morris Mini was a revolution in handy compactness. The oil crisis of the early 1970s put a premium on more compact family cars and encouraged Americans, in particular, to start to abandon their traditional 'gas guzzlers'. Around the same time, the Japanese entered the world auto scene as mass producers of cheap, reliable cars.

The same decades also brought more regulations. New York introduced traffic wardens – 'meter maids' – in 1960. The wearing of seat belts became compulsory in most countries. In Britain the Breathalyser, introduced in 1967, cut road deaths by 23 per cent within three months.

Car ownership continued to rise. By 1987 the USA and Canada both had a car for every 1.7 people. In Canada 80 per cent of all journeys to work were made by car, as were 85 per cent of all pleasure trips and 90 per cent of all intercity journeys. New Zealand ranked next in car ownership (one car for every 2.1 people) followed by West Germany and Australia (2.2), Switzerland (2.3), then Italy, France and Sweden (2.5).

THIS WAY Motorists cope with a barrage of signs on Route 66 from Chicago to Los Angeles. Congestion on the roads is an increasing, and global, problem.

MOBILE AUDIENCE Drive-ins, such as this one in Salt Lake City, Utah, reached the peak of their popularity in the 1950s.

While all this brought new freedom for millions of people, it also brought a new crisis. By the 1990s, better regulations meant that road deaths were falling in most Western countries, but several other problems abounded. Congestion was so acute that a single unusual event – even a predictable one such as a visit by a president or foreign dignitary – could bring the traffic across much of a city to a virtual standstill, creating the 'gridlock' dreaded by urban traffic planners.

Despite the mushrooming of multistorey car parks, there were often more car drivers wanting to park in city centres than spaces readily available to them. Out-of-town shopping centres or malls, with ample parking and a variety of handy superstores, became popular – but they conjured up their own nightmare vision of more and more green fields being swallowed up and coated with tarmac.

The sheer frustrations of driving, with its traffic jams and parking difficulties, induced the phenomenon dubbed 'road rage'. Traffic fumes, too, were a danger. By 1990, one in seven British children suffered from asthma or a similar respiratory problem. The Professor of Toxicology at London's University College suggested that it would be perverse to blame passive smoking while ignoring pollution from traffic fumes.

It seemed that the freedom of the roads which had done so much to open up new horizons to so many was beginning to turn sour. The age of the motor car was by no means over, and researchers were busy devising new generations of vehicles such as a 'cleaner' electric car, but it was abundantly clear that the whole question of transport, public and private, would have to be rethought to avert a catastrophic overload in the 21st century.

WHEN YOUR CAR WAS YOUR IDOL

In the age of the handy hatchback, it is hard to remember that motoring was an exciting novelty less than 100 years ago – as the English enthusiast Ralph Lee recalled:

'Eventually the great day arrived when I'd got enough money to be able to buy a motor car for myself. I particularly wanted a Peugeot – the baby Peugeot – a little cabriolet two-seater. I'd never seen one, but I'd seen pictures of them and learnt how they worked. Anyway, I heard of one for sale in Northamptonshire. I was living in Surrey and I bought this car and drove it home through London. And I'd never had a driving lesson, or driven a car. I'd learnt it all through books.

'The young enthusiast in those days regarded his machine as an idol. He liked to do everything himself, with his own hands. We'd think nothing of taking the engine to pieces and fitting new pistons, often in the garden because there was no garage, and when it rained you had to rush out and put the tarpaulin over it. I also remember oil everywhere . . . If you had a reasonable set of tools we could do everything yourself, unlike today. And that was half the fun. Sometimes you'd do a job on the car that wasn't really even necessary, just for the fun of it, or we'd take things to pieces, always trying to get another mile or two out of a gallon of petrol.'

HOME ECONOMY

IN 1900 ONLY AMERICANS WORE JEANS, ONLY ITALIANS ATE SPAGHETTI AND ONLY CRAFTSMEN AND SHOPKEEPERS WORKED WHERE THEY LIVED. IN THE 1990S, PASTA, SWEATSHIRTS AND THE INTERNET HAVE SURPASSED NOTIONS OF A NATIVE LAND. DIVERSITY, CHOICE, DETACHMENT AND MOBILITY ARE THE HALLMARKS OF 20TH-CENTURY LIFESTYLES, AND THE DIFFERENCES BETWEEN NATIONAL TRADITIONS IN DRESS, FOOD AND WORK PRACTICES HAVE, TO A LARGE EXTENT, DISAPPEARED.

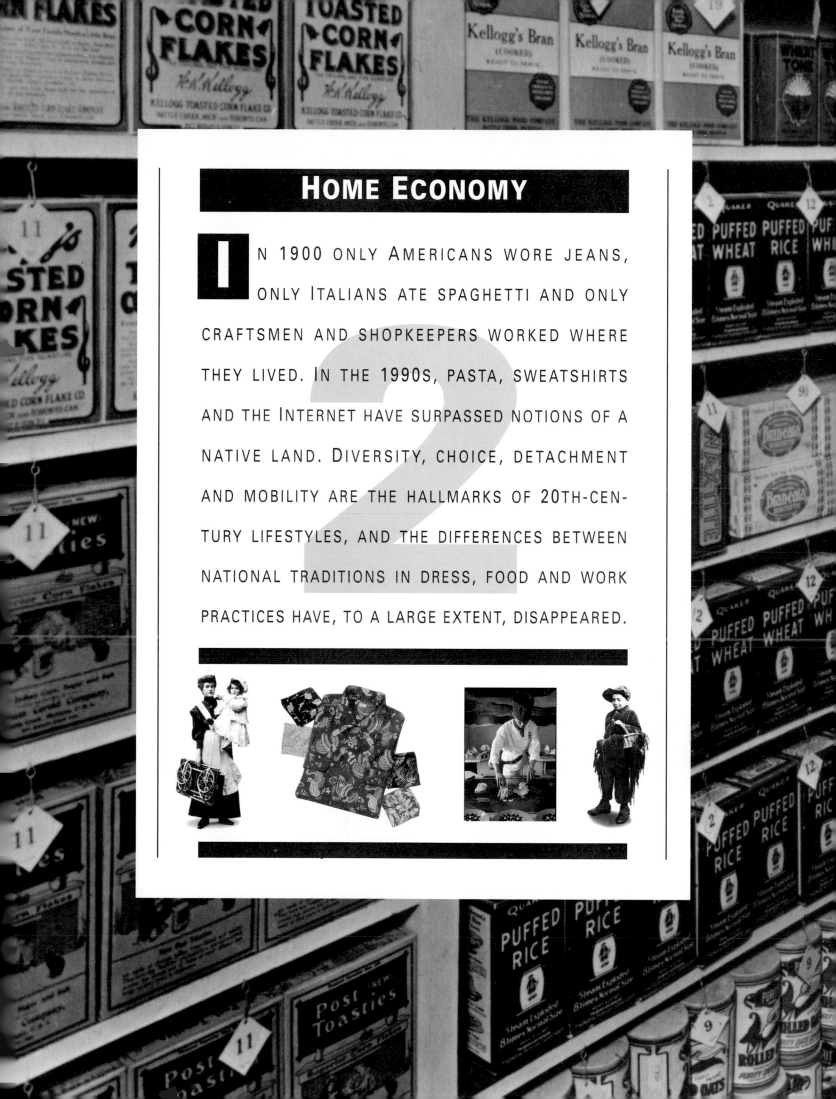

THE WAY WE WORKED

AS TECHNOLOGY HAS REDUCED LABORIOUSNESS AND INCREASED PRODUCTIVITY, IT HAS HELD OUT THE CHIMERA OF A WORKLESS WORLD

On Thursday, July 31, 1902, the people of Sydney were stunned by news of a coal gas explosion at the Mount Kembla coal mine. Gas had never been detected there before, so safety lamps had never been issued and miners worked by the light of naked flames. On the day of the disaster, 260 men were working underground. Ninety-four were either killed by the explosion itself or poisoned by the gas. It was the worst catastrophe in Australia's mining history. The next day's issue of the *Sydney Morning Herald* took grim consolation in the fact that: 'In this country we are not accustomed to these calamitous visitations, and industrial or other accidents on a large scale of tragedy are fortunately not so common with us as they are in the United States, for instance.'

The work of the miner was generally acknowledged to be filthy, exhausting and dangerous. At the beginning of the 20th century, such work was more typical than exceptional. Even in the advanced economies such as those of Australia, the USA and Britain, most work was still manual and most workers ended their day's labour both tired and dirty. Accidents were common on farms, in factories, on docksides and building sites, at sea and in the transport industries. Work involving fast-moving machinery brought with it the risk of cuts, scalping and accidental amputation. Work with toxic chemicals

PRIMITIVE POWER When the century opened, the economy of much of Europe still depended on the most basic technology, powered by wind, water or muscle.

HANDMADE In 1900 boatbuilding remained a traditional industry in Europe, dependent on a high level of craft skills.

meant the near certainty of contracting diseases of the skin or respiratory system. Miners, however, were untypical of the manual labour force as a whole in at least two respects. They were moderately well paid and usually strongly unionised.

Worlds of work – new and old

At the beginning of this century, it was reasonable to suppose that, if you trained long and hard enough to get 'a trade in your hands', this would keep you employed for the rest of your working life. As the century closes, however, it has become virtually certain that no skill, knowledge or expertise acquired in youth will last a lifetime in the labour market.

In 1913 almost half of all Americans were still living on farms and only a minority worked in manufacturing. Most of those who did were recent immigrants. Having no family farm or store to take over, they had to be versatile and adventurous. Fortunately, demand for industrial labour in the United States was expanding rapidly. Manufacturing might mean anything from rolling cigars by hand, like the trade-union pioneer Sam Gompers, to operating massive machinery for one of the nation's newly founded corporate giants such as US Steel (1901), Ford (1903) or General Motors (1908). A new sort of economy was clearly emerging, in which firms could grow big by making such novel products as rubber tyres (Firestone, 1901), cosmetics (Elizabeth Arden, 1910) and even chewing gum (Wrigley, 1911).

In Britain the economy was far more industrialised than in the US, with less than 10 per cent getting their living from the land. But in British industry, the level of traditional craft skills remained high, with a seven-year apprenticeship still the normal way of acquiring them. In well-unionised, highly skilled industries, such as printing or engineering, getting taken on as an apprentice usually meant having a father or other close relative in the trade. Among the less skilled, dockworkers had also learned to combine union strength and family networking to protect their jobs. Outsiders usually referred to all dockworkers simply as 'dockers'; but, as in most industries, the men themselves were acutely aware of distinctions between different types of work, each

of which required what they regarded as quite distinguishable skills, which in turn implied crucial differences of status and pay.

In France and Germany on the eve of the First World War, more than 40 per cent of the labour force still worked as farmers, fishermen or in forestry. But, thanks to Renault, France led the world in motor-car production. Germany had the leading electrical and chemical industries, headed by new firms such as Telefunken (1903) and I.G.Farben (1904). Italy was still overwhelmingly rural, less advanced industrially than Belgium,

Switzerland or Sweden, and on the same level of average living standards as impoverished Portugal. But even Italy already had Fiat, Olivetti and Alfa-Romeo.

Man and machine

In the most advanced economies, a marked decline in the number of workers in food production was already being accompanied by huge increases in productivity. In 1900 the average American farm worker produced enough food for seven people; by 1940 the comparable figure would be ten and by

MACHINE AGE Men work at lathes, connected by belts to a central power source, in an American machine shop, around 1900.

1950, it was 15.5. In 1901, the US Industrial Commission was told that it took 100 minutes to shell a bushel of corn by hand, but that a steam-powered machine could perform the same task in 90 seconds. A combine harvester could reap 1 acre (0.4 ha) of wheat 40 times faster than a man. A machine perfected by American A.K. Smith in 1903

OLD AND NEW Large numbers of women still worked in traditional jobs in domestic service (below). New occupations, such as those in business, brought greater independence for women, as well as hazards, as this 1906 cartoon (right) suggests.

could, in one continuous process, cut off a salmon's head and tail, split and gut its body, and drop the residue into hot water, constantly adjusting its operations to match the dimensions of each individual fish. Smith's machine displaced Chinese hand-labour in canneries on North America's west coast. A 1911 machine that could top, tail and core 96 pineapples a minute had a similarly dramatic impact in Hawaii. Doughnut-making was automated in the USA from 1921 onwards, and potato-peeling from 1925.

White-collar workers and women

Mass education, and the growing scale and complexity of commerce, combined to increase the employment in offices and shops of workers who could read, write and calculate. They were initially referred to as 'black-coated' but later as 'white-collar', a term first recorded in the United States in 1921. At work, as in the street, dress signalled status. Foremen were often distinguished by brown or grey warehouse coats and usually wore a collar and tie, and sometimes a bowler hat as well. The relatively clean working conditions of white-collar workers were a mark of their exalted standing above the ranks of the blue-collar masses still involved in manual labour.

Over the course of the 20th century, the proportion of white-collar workers would steadily increase until they formed the majority of the workforce, first, by 1956, in North America, and then in Australia and Britain and other western countries. The typewriter and telephone, technological marvels initially entrusted mainly to male hands, had become female instruments of labour by 1900. Telephone exchanges at first employed teenage boys as operators, on the grounds that they would be quick to learn and cheap to pay. But they were often slapdash and cheeky to callers. Women were soon judged to be both more reliable and much better mannered. Female 'typewriters' (the word was at first applied to the operator as well as to the machine) proved both faster and cheaper than men. Private secretarial schools proliferated to teach shorthand, typing and basic bookkeeping. By 1911, a fifth of the entire clerical labour force of London's financial district was female.

Retailing, teaching, nursing and pharmacy were other sectors in which women were strongly represented. Niche markets for the talents of the gifted female included graphic art, studio photography, music and the stage. Even in liberal countries, however, professions that were, in theory, increasingly open to women were often closed in practice. The 1901 census revealed that Britain numbered only 212 female surgeons and 140 female dentists among its tens of thousands of medical professionals. There were just six women architects, two accountants and not a single woman lawyer. Yet the number of males employed in the 'higher professions' was over 150 000. As late as 1950, Britain's professions would remain 92 per cent male.

In the industrialised countries, a number of the traditional consumer goods industries,

WOMEN'S WORK Scottish fishwives pose at the English port of Great Yarmouth in 1905. Their work was to gut herrings in freezing cold water and pack them into barrels.

such as textiles, pottery, hosiery and food processing, continued to recruit women by the million. But the largest single employer of female labour in Europe at the start of the century was domestic service. Working hours were, by definition, even longer than the

waking hours of those on whom they waited. Pay was low, but servants lived 'all found' and untaxed, and also usually benefited from tips from visitors, cast-off clothes and the occasional travel. They could also usually count on medical care being paid for by their employers.

Servants were both part of the family and not. Despite the enforced intimacy that came from living in the same household, it

HOMEWORK Much female labour involved the commercial exploitation of domestic skills such as garment-making. A campaign in 1906 drew attention to these workers' plight (right).

was not a situation that necessarily produced mutual trust. Some employers were constantly checking whether a housemaid had thoroughly dusted behind every piece of furniture. Honest Jean Rennie, a Scottish maid working at a Highland castle in Argyllshire, was puzzled to keep finding odd coins under cushions, and even under carpets, until she realised with horror that her mistress was deliberately putting temptation in her way to see if she would pocket the money for herself. Sexual exploitation by male employers was the greatest single 'industrial hazard' for a servant girl, but even some feminists favoured domestic service as a way for girls from poor homes to learn the manners and housekeeping skills of their 'betters'.

On May Day 1906 an exhibition, sponsored by the *Daily News*, opened in London to expose the evils of the 'sweated industries', which represented the most lowly level of employment in one of the supposedly most advanced industrial nations. Sweated workers, most of whom were women

bound to their houses by the claims of children or invalids, made clothes, trimmings, lace, packaging, artificial flowers, dolls, brushes and chains. Others, mostly Jewish immigrants, toiled in grimy workshops, often sleeping among the garments, boots or furniture they made. Their pay was paltry (1 penny for sewing an entire shirt), their hours were long (up to 16 a day), and their working conditions often harmful. One English girl, employed in packing cocoa powder, was recorded as handling 24 192 packets in an average week – for 7 shillings.

Starvation wages enabled retailers to make huge mark-ups. For making a silk blouse with a front and back composed entirely of small, hand-sewn tucks and insertions of lace, a seamstress would be paid under 1 shilling – less than one-twentieth of its retail price; and she had to pay for her own thread. As the Women's Industrial Council pointed out, every member of Britain's comfortable classes was complicit in this exploitation: 'To whom are shoes not sent home in boxes? Who does not buy matches, or tin tacks, or toothbrushes?... There is no person in this kingdom ... who does not partake in the proceeds of underpaid labour.'

Workers' rights and remuneration

Throughout the advanced economies, trade unionists joined forces with teachers and preachers in a crusade to ban sweated and child labour by law. In 1908 an International Conference for the Protection of Labour called for the total prohibition of night work for children. And in 1909, Britain's Liberal Government passed a Trade Boards Act establishing minimum wages for various sweated trades. Significant though legislation and propaganda were, however, the gradual reduction of sweated and child labour was quite as much the by-product of new technologies, which made machines even cheaper to employ than the cheapest hand labour. As a result, sweatshops have never disappeared completely. They were still commonplace in the 1990s in the manufacture of carpets in Pakistan or shirts in Thailand and Vietnam. Investigators also discovered thousands of children working in European countries such as Italy and Portugal, making shoes or garments. In

Australia and the UK, especially among ethnic minorities, thousands of children worked at home or in family-run catering businesses, not as employees but as assistants, at weekends or after school.

Laws – often provoked by strike campaigns – were most successful in regulating working hours and conditions in large-scale, heavy industries, where huge concentrations of grown men made it easier to form unions than in trades where workers were dispersed or deeply divided by gender, age or race. In the first decade of this century, major industrial confrontations were mounted by steelworkers in the USA, sailors in France, dockers in Germany, and miners almost everywhere. In Spain they struck for the right to be paid weekly, rather than regularly run themselves into debt while waiting for their wages. And in 1905, British miners at last got a standard eight-hour day – although this did not include the hour or more it might take them to travel to or from the actual coal face.

When governments and employers ganged up against them, unions responded by building their own alliances. In 1909, leaders of German and British workers met to compare conditions and to consult on common interests. Within Britain itself miners, dockers and railwaymen came together in 1914 to found a 'Triple Alliance', with a common committee for collective bargaining. Apart from limits on hours and the

UNION STRENGTH   The New South Wales union of Watchmen, Caretakers and Cleaners celebrates winning an 8 hour day, 1919. Right: A French publication of 1911 depicts workers and management in thrall to the strike-leader.

SLEEP-IN   Welsh miners snatch a rest during the bitter Tonypandy dispute of 1910. Three hundred police were sent from London to curb riots with their truncheons.

recognition of the right of unions to exist, organised labour also campaigned for higher standards of industrial safety and 'workmen's compensation' for industrial injuries. In 1900 a young American lawyer called

HEROES IN HELL

As the writer George Orwell (1903-50) observed, Britain's coal-based industrial economy rested almost literally on the shoulders of the miners, yet few appreciated the appalling conditions in which they worked. Orwell's first trip to a coal face in northern England in the 1930s left an indelible impression on him:

'Most of the things one imagines in hell are there – heat, noise, confusion, darkness, foul air and, above all, unbearably cramped space. Everything except the fire... overmastering everything else for a while, is the frightful, deafening din from the conveyor belt which carries the coal away. You cannot see very far, because the fog of coal dust throws back the beam of your lamp, but you can see on either side of you the line of half-naked kneeling men ... driving their shovels under the fallen coal and flinging it swiftly over their left shoulders ... It is impossible to watch the 'fillers' at work without feeling a pang of envy for their toughness ... They have got to remain kneeling all the while – they could hardly rise from their knees without hitting the ceiling – and you can easily see by trying it what a tremendous effort this means. Shovelling is comparatively easy when you are standing up, because you can use your knee and thigh to drive the shovel along; kneeling down, the whole of the strain is thrown upon your arm and belly muscles... But the fillers look and work as though they were made of iron... under the smooth coat of coal dust which clings to them from head to foot. It is only when you see miners down the mine and naked that you realise what splendid men they are... In the hotter mines they wear only a pair of thin drawers, clogs and knee-pads... You can hardly tell by the look of them whether they are young or old... No one could do their work who had not a young man's body, and a figure fit for a guardsman at that... You can never forget that spectacle once you have seen it – the line of bowed, kneeling figures, sooty black all over, driving their huge shovels under the coal with stupendous force and speed...'

Louis Brandeis exposed the callousness of a Boston laundry that not only refused to compensate a girl who had been scalped after her hair had become entangled in a mangle, but had deducted her wages for the rest of the day on which the accident had occurred.

Australia was widely regarded as a working man's paradise, and by 1900 most skilled men there had an eight-hour day and an average income even higher than Americans enjoyed. A Scottish Agricultural Commission in 1910 paid tribute to Australia as a country

CHILD'S WORK In 1900 in the United States, children still accounted for as much as a quarter of the labour force in establishments such as this cotton mill in the South, and they regularly worked a 13 hour day.

of 'abounding prosperity . . . (where) . . . work in towns is especially plentiful and attractive', although it urged newcomers not to be put off by the isolation and long hours of farm work, because in the outback a man could still hope to have his own place one day, rather than remain an employee all his life.

Working for the First World War

When war broke out in Europe in August 1914, the industrial agenda changed dramatically and in totally unanticipated ways. Both sides expected the conflict to be 'over by Christmas' and thought primarily in terms of mobilising infantry rather than industry. However, Germany had all but exhausted its military supplies as early as October 1914.

WOMEN AT WAR English munitions girls found that high pay and fixed hours compensated for the noise and dirt of factory work.
Right: A chimneysweep's wife keeps the business going while her husband is at the front.

Throughout the war, the Kaiser's empire struggled to supply its men for battle, breaking bottlenecks in manpower by drafting in workers from conquered Belgium and Poland, and even by releasing men from the army. Both sides achieved prodigious levels of output: Germany managed to build a new submarine every four days; and, in the course of the war, Britain and France produced 100 000 planes between them.

In Britain, where skilled, highly unionised engineers had long preserved their wages

and privileges by requiring seven-year apprenticeships to restrict recruitment to their trade, their exclusion of semiskilled labour was roundly denounced by politicians and Press as grossly unpatriotic. The whole complex, status-bound hierarchy of boilermakers, welders, riveters, turners and fitters was shaken to its roots by an invasion of American machine tools – manned by women. Salford slum-dweller Robert Roberts recalled the rapid reduction in his own father's standing: 'In his cups he was wont to boast that, at the lathe, he had to manipulate a micrometer and work to limits of one thousandth of an inch. We were much impressed, until one evening in 1917 a teenage sister running a capstan in the iron works remarked indifferently that she, too, used a "mike" to even finer limits. There was, she said, "nothing to it". The old man fell silent . . . The awe that many simpler souls had felt before the mystery of craft began to evaporate...'

Women not only invaded factories. They also took on dozens of other tasks that tradition, convention and vested interests had deemed beyond their strength and competence, such as driving buses, trams or tractors, and operating dock-side cranes. In 1917, a major masculine bastion crumbled when London Underground's new station at Maida Vale opened with an all-women staff.

Throughout Europe, 'the American system' – standardised interchangeable parts, manufactured in volume and put together

on an assembly line – was widely adopted to meet the insatiable demands of war. British Dominions, cut off from imports of British industrial goods, expanded their own industrial base. In Australia, annual pig-iron production almost trebled from 130 000 tons. In Germany, cut off by Allied naval blockade from natural nitrates dug in the Chilean desert, chemists learned to extract nitrogen from the air itself, revolutionising the production of explosives and agricultural fertilisers.

Manufacturing, marketing and management

With the return of peace, the democracies redirected their economies to the demands of the market rather than of the military. The United States led the way in treating the customer as king. In 1923 American automobile manufacturers hit upon a new marketing ploy that had profound implications for manufacturing itself – the annual change in the style of the model. They aimed to make existing vehicles outmoded simply by proclaiming them to be so, opening the way for sales of new, slightly (but quite visibly) different models. One far-reaching side effect

of such 'planned obsolescence', intended or otherwise, was to impose additional production and marketing costs on manufacturers, forcing smaller companies out of the market and preventing new ones from entering it. Even mighty Ford, which initially held out against the trend, was forced to capitulate in 1927, closing down entirely for five months to re-tool as it abandoned the Model T for the new Model A.

Increasing sophistication in manufacturing and marketing products was matched by an increasingly 'scientific' approach to managing the employees who produced them.

NEW FAD A Sunday-afternoon drive is so popular it creates serious congestion in 1920s St Louis, while advertisements (right) emphasise the luxury status of the car.

THE MAN WHO MADE AMERICA MOBILE

Henry Ford (1863-1947), a Michigan farmer's son educated in a one-room schoolhouse, changed the face of the United States, of the motor industry and of work itself. 'I will build a motor car for the great multitude', he proclaimed. The Model T 'Tin Lizzie' – 'stronger than a horse and easier to

READY TO GO Model T Fords are lined up for delivery to dealers. By 1925, when this picture was taken, the Model T was nearing the end of its life.

maintain' – was launched in 1908 and, over the 19 years of its existence, sold 15.5 million in the USA, 1 million in Canada and 250 000 in the UK – equal to half the world's entire output of motor cars. Over the same period, its price fell from $950 to $270.

Ford's genius lay less in his mastery of engineering than in his capacity for organising production. He did not invent the assembly line (which had originated in Chicago meat-packing plants), but he exploited its application to the full. Whereas once it had required 728 minutes to turn out a complete chassis for an automobile, the moving-line system established at Ford's 1914 plant at Highland Park, Michigan, reduced the time to 93 minutes. Eventually, the company would be turning out a Model T every 24 seconds. In the same year, when the average motor-industry wage was $2.34 a day, Ford announced he would pay a minimum $5 – and reduce the day from nine to eight hours, enabling him to introduce a round-the-clock three-shift system that maximised the use of his plant.

Ford achieved another major cost saving by dispatching cars to dealers 'knocked down' into their major components. Once the parts were at the dealer's, a competent mechanic could assemble a Model T in half a day. By 1913 every town in the United States with a population over 2000 had a Ford dealer.

The 'father' of 'modern management' and the first self-styled 'consulting engineer in management' was US tennis champion and rose-grower Frederick Winslow Taylor (1856-1915), pioneer of 'time and motion' studies, which aimed to eliminate wasted effort in the workplace. The essentials of 'Taylorism' were enshrined in *The Principles of Scientific Management*, which he published in 1911. Treating workers as living machines, Taylor's disciples extended their interests from employees to the working environment. In 1927, a team of engineers began an experiment at the Hawthorne works of the Western Electric Company in Chicago that was to have unsuspected but far-reaching consequences.

The team focused initially on the effects of lighting on productivity, and were puzzled to find that whatever they did to change the type, arrangement and intensity of the lighting, productivity rose every time a change was made. Baffled, the experimenters turned to an Australian psychologist at the Harvard Business School, Elton Mayo. By making even more radical changes in such matters

WORKS' OUTING Cadbury's, the confectionery manufacturers, adopted a 'human relations' approach to management. Here, its employees are treated to a day out in 1901.

as temperature, humidity, payment methods, break times and refreshment facilities, Mayo soon determined that what mattered was not the environment at all but the fact that the workers suddenly felt that somebody cared about them. The unusual degree of attention paid to the employees' comfort and concerns had so increased their solidarity and morale that they had come to feel that they really

QUICK-DRYING

Before 1914, Henry Ford offered customers a choice of colours. However, once he had established assembly-line production, all Model Ts were painted black – because it was the only paint that would dry fast enough to keep up with the line.

mattered. It was this that had translated itself into ever-rising levels of output. Mayo proclaimed a new doctrine – a 'human relations' approach that, focusing on the dynamics of informal groups, would combine efficiency with humanity. Unlike Taylor, who essentially regarded the worker as an isolated individual motivated solely by money, Mayo emphasised that the worker was a member of a group and was also motivated by such concerns as interest and dignity. A concern for 'human relations' became characteristic of management in 'progressive'

BOOTLACE BOY Children often sold goods on the street. This young boy was selling shoelaces in Paris in 1907.

ALL WORK AND NO PLAY At the turn of the century the USA, the world's most advanced economy, still relied on child labour for basic tasks such as picking cotton.

British companies, such as Marks & Spencer in retailing and Cadbury's in confectionery. The John Lewis retail chain pointedly referred to all its employees as 'partners'.

In those industries where workers were still exploited, it was largely left to journalists, unions and charities to expose the scandals. In hotels and restaurants, staff frequently worked 11-hour shifts spread over 15 hours, seven days a week. Many American states either specifically exempted hotels from observing the normal legal limits on working hours or simply omitted any reference to hotels in the relevant laws. A Consumers League survey of female office cleaners in New York found that only a quarter were US citizens, and that most could neither write nor read English; their potential for self-protection through organisation or recourse to law was therefore minimal. The long hours of harsh labour put in by sharecroppers' children on cotton plantations in the South were frequently ignored,

because children under ten were not counted by the US census, and therefore did not 'exist'. Street-corner paperboys, working through freezing nights and early mornings to supplement the family income, were similarly disregarded when it came to calculating the nation's wealth – and responsibilities.

A world without work

The First World War left Germany humiliated by occupation and, like neighbouring Austria and Hungary, wracked by hyperinflation. Italy, ill-rewarded for its wartime sacrifices, fell prey to a fascist experiment that promised a short cut to modernity by recalling the grandeur of ancient Rome. 'Victorious' Britain, after a brief export boom led by re-stocking and reconstruction in Europe, did not see unemployment fall below 10 per cent for 20 years. France, thanks to the return of its lost provinces, Alsace and Lorraine, experienced an industrial renaissance but was tarnished by political and financial instability:

ECONOMIC CRISIS   In the 1930s, job-seekers crowded employment exchanges. Normal commerce came to a halt (right).

between May 1924 and July 1926 alone, no fewer than 11 French governments succeeded each other. Underdeveloped eastern Europe remained severely depressed.

No European country experienced the surging, confident growth enjoyed by North Americans. Even this was short-lived, however, as the Wall Street Crash of October 1929 ushered in a decade of depression. A collapse in confidence amongst investors, bankers and exporters plunged the world into an economic blizzard between 1929 and 1932. By 1932, 30 million were unemployed worldwide and even more on short hours and diminished wages were constantly unnerved by the fear of unemployment. In America and Australia, more than a quarter of all workers were unemployed in 1932-3; in Denmark, Norway and Germany, a third.

For the majority of the unemployed, whether in Manchester, Montreal or Madrid, Berlin, Baltimore or Brussels, the daily routine remained depressingly the same. Those who hadn't given up got up in the morning and met their former workmates. They exchanged rumours of work; lined up for the chance of a job; lined up for state handouts; lined up for charity handouts; lined up for free soup, free bread and free apples. The sociologist E. Wight Bakke, who published a study of 'The Unemployed Man' in 1933, meticulously recorded the reactions offered by workless men to his enquiries. 'You've heard tell that the worker today don't get no satisfaction out of his work,' claimed one sheet-metal worker. 'Well let me tell you something. He gets a lot more satisfaction out of it than he does living without it on unemployment benefit.' Bakke also reminded his readers that work not only filled time and generated incomes, but through the latter 'gives a measure of a man's worth . . . In an earlier day, when money was not the key to most of life, money did not drive men on to exceptional effort, nor the lack of it to drink.' In the so-called 'command economies', run on communist or fascist lines, programmes of public works and rearmament were introduced to ease the unemployment situation. In Germany, the hyperinflation of the 1920s and the economic collapse that had put 6 million out of work by 1932, prepared the way for a Nazi electoral triumph, spearheaded by the simple slogan 'Work and Bread'. Thanks to the building of *Autobahnen* (motorways) and state-funded rearmament, Germans did at least get these.

Working for the Second World War

The mood of the people in 1939 was very different from 1914. In Britain, the government prepared for a long haul. Learning from the previous conflict, when unrestricted volunteer recruitment had stripped the war economy of skilled men, the authorities created a category of 'reserved occupations' – firemen and seamen, farmers and miners, draughtsmen and drivers. As 5 million men were drafted into uniform, women were mobilised to take their place. Fashion was put on hold 'for the duration', as the phrase of the day put it, and 300 000 women left the

HYPERINFLATION   In 1923 Germany's currency collapse made 5 million mark notes common (inset) and obliged shopkeepers to keep cash in tea-chests rather than tills.

textile and clothing industries. Some 147 000 women went into transport services; 220 000 went into chemicals, making drugs, dyes and explosives; 480 000 performed clerical tasks in the hugely expanded bureaucracy that directed the nation's production and consumption; and no less than 2 million went to work in factories making planes, tanks, bayonets, bullets and bombs. Thousands more women worked to feed the industrial labour force, as the number of factory canteens rose from 1500 in 1939 to 18 500 by 1945. On the

FEMME FATALE 'Rosie the Riveter' symbolised American determination to mobilise its women for war work. British workers (below) enjoy the camaraderie.

land, the harvest was brought in by 90 000 members of the Women's Land Army, and by 220 000 prisoners of war, 80 000 adult volunteers and 70 000 schoolchildren.

In the United States, millions of black workers left the fields of the South to work in the factories of the North. Women, too, joined the labour force; 'Rosie the Riveter' became a national icon; eager Boy Scouts worked alongside their grandfathers to dig 'Victory Gardens'; and the nation's real economic output, allowing for inflation, increased 150 per cent between 1939 and 1944. Even by 1942, the USA was producing more arms than all its enemies added together. Factories that had worked 40 hours a week now hummed with life for 90. US

output of shipping increased seventeenfold. And, despite the fact that war production was accounting for some 40 per cent of total output, civilian consumption also rose by over 10 per cent.

The mobilisation of national effort proved more complete in the embattled democracies than in totalitarian Germany where, due to the forced conscription of 14 million foreign workers, POWs and Jews, it was not thought necessary to summon German womanhood from the higher demands of 'Kinder, Küche, Kirche' (Children, Kitchen, Church) until 1943. Thanks to the extraordinary administrative gifts of economic supremo Albert Speer, German war production reached its peak in 1944; it then fell rapidly as Allied saturation bombing took its toll and as the contraction of the Reich's frontiers deprived it of forced contributions of labour and resources from conquered regions.

In Japan the mobilisation was more complete, with children in their early teens producing munitions. And the destruction was even greater. When Japan surrendered, the

RULED OUT

In 1976 the German firm of Keuffel and Esser manufactured their last slide-rule. Recognising that, after 350 years, this basic calculator had at last been made redundant by electronic devices, they presented it to the Smithsonian Institution in Washington, USA, as a museum piece.

country was on the verge of starvation. The following year, industrial production was a mere 10 per cent of what it had been just a decade previously.

Work for all

Thanks largely to the far-sighted generosity of the Marshall Plan to finance economic reconstruction, Western Europe was kick-started into recovery. Germany's 'economic miracle' tripled the country's economic output between 1950 and 1960. By the 1960s, unemployment was no longer a problem, and there was even an acute labour shortage, remedied by an influx of 'guest workers', especially from Turkey and Yugoslavia. In

ON THE BUSES Postwar employment policies created labour shortages in Western Europe in the 1950s. Some companies, such as London Transport, began to recruit staff in the West Indies.

Britain, hospitals and transport systems came to rely on newcomers from the Caribbean and South Asia.

Throughout the industrialised world, a rising proportion of women, notably married women, were recruited into the expanding labour force. In the USA, female labour, which accounted for 27.9 per cent of the total workforce in 1947, rose steadily to reach 38.1 per cent in 1970. But neither in treatment nor opportunity did women make much progress relative to men. They usually got jobs that were less secure and responsible, and when they did get equal work, they seldom received equal pay for it. The few who did manage to succeed in business or the professions generally got stuck on the lower rungs of the ladder. Women lawyers were sidelined into repetitive matrimonial or property work, women doctors into public or mental health. Most felt an additional pressure that seldom burdened their male colleagues – to organise the care of their children, either by professionally trained carers, or informally by relatives and neighbours.

For a quarter of a century after 1945, most firms in the advanced economies grew and prospered, and so did their employees. Increasing rewards from work were

NEWCOMERS Turkish 'guest workers' in Germany in the 1970s were not eligible for citizenship.

not, however, necessarily matched by increasing satisfaction at work. As a Detroit automobile worker told a researcher: 'The things I like best about my job are quitting time, pay days, days off and vacations.'

Industrial researchers began to notice that some industries (motor manufacture, docks), regardless of which country they were in, seemed more 'strike prone' than others (railways, chemicals). Confrontation

FACE OF THE TIGER The rapid growth of the 'Tiger economies' of the Far East was fuelled by an abundance of well-educated, youthful labour.

HIGH-TECH Robotic technology, which can perform complex tasks, replaces human workers in this Australian factory.

arose more frequently where workers were employed in close proximity on similar jobs, but lived in relative isolation from other workers and their own managers. Where workers experienced job variety and lived scattered throughout the community confrontation was far less common than in one-industry settings, where grievances generated at work during the day could become the staple of conversation among neighbours and workmates in the evening.

In Japan they seemed to manage the human side of industry better. By the 1960s Western management experts increasingly

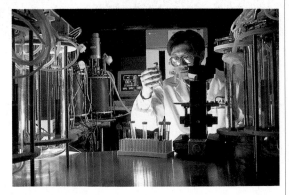

ENGINEERING THE FUTURE Biotechnology, which has been at the leading edge of industrial advance from the 1980s onwards, has provided jobs for highly skilled workers.

admired Japanese manufacturers, who seemed to combine high output, high quality and high worker satisfaction. The Japanese employee was held up to the world as a model of diligence, loyalty and skill.

An era of uncertainty

The confident expansion of the advanced industrial economies was severely jolted by the 'oil shocks' of 1973 and 1979, which decisively ended an era of cheap energy. At the same time, new computer-based technologies, offshoots of the Cold War 'Space Race', began to corrode old assumptions and practices, first in manufacturing and then in the service sector. As early as the 1960s, industrial analysts had predicted that 'cybernation' would wipe out the jobs of millions of process workers performing repetitive industrial tasks, and then eliminate entire layers of middle management.

General Motors installed its first industrial robots in its North American factories in 1962, but by the next decade Japan, the major manufacturing nation most dependent on oil imports, was far outstripping its rivals in levels of automation in its efforts to ditch energy-intensive processes and cut labour costs. Japan, which had built its postwar recovery on steel and ships and motor cars, relocated these industries offshore in Sao Paulo, Brazil, or Sunderland in northeast England where land and labour were cheaper. In Japan itself, meanwhile, industry eagerly launched into non-polluting,

knowledge-intensive, high value-added fields, such as biotechnology.

In what was now being called the post-industrial era, new jobs depended not on manipulating materials but on information. In 1950, some 17 per cent of the American workforce could be classified as information workers – clerks, teachers, lawyers, accountants and so on. Thirty years later, the figure was over 60 per cent, the single largest occupational category was that of clerk, and there were more people employed full-time in universities than in agriculture. Of the 20 million new American jobs created in the 1970s, only 5 per cent were in manufacturing; 90 per cent were in the information or service sectors. The trend was similar in other Western nations. Whereas the US labour force as a whole grew by 18 per cent between 1970 and 1978, the number of public officials grew by 76 per cent, bankers by

PLAYING MANY PARTS

Most parents have wanted to see their children set securely in a solid 'trade' or 'career' and feared for the fate of those who turned out to have creative, artistic, political or entrepreneurial ambitions. Many celebrities, however, abandoned seemingly solid beginnings. Poet Allen Ginsberg was an accountant, singer-composer Elvis Costello a computer programmer and crime-writer Agatha Christie a dispenser in a pharmacy. Ex-lawyers include Lenin, Gandhi, Castro, Otto Preminger, Hoagy Carmichael and Rossano Brazzi. In making their way in the world such restless souls have often had to take work where they could find it. Many have become familiar with the shovel: singer Rod Stewart used one to dig graves, while model Jerry Hall shifted manure at a stables. Groucho Marx cleaned theatrical wigs and Cyndi Lauper cleaned dog kennels. Ho Chi Minh, George Orwell and Warren Beatty were all once dishwashers, while Benny Hill, Matt Monro and Sean Connery were milkmen. Danny de Vito and Chuck Berry both worked as hairdressers. Bing Crosby, Walt Disney, Rock Hudson, William Faulkner and Conrad Hilton were employed by the US Postal Service. Rudolf Valentino, James Cagney, Kirk Douglas, Peter Finch, Dustin Hoffman and Yves Montand were all waiters; and Eddie Cantor, Ramon Navarro, William Bendix and Jack Lemmon were singing waiters. Ex-salesmen include Ralph Lauren, Gene Hackman, Steve Martin and Frank Zappa.

FINANCIAL FRENZY From a London bank to the Tokyo Stock Exchange, the international nature of financial markets in the 1990s puts intense pressure on those who work in them.

83 per cent, and health administrators by a staggering 118 per cent. The number of engineers rose by less than 3 per cent.

By the 1980s, Western nations had more than Japan to worry about. Mere mini-states, like Singapore, were now vying to become serious industrial competitors. Employers responded with a war on fixed costs, replacing permanent workers with part-timers, subcontractors and the self-employed, for whose security and welfare they took minimal responsibility. Workers at all levels, who might, only a generation before, have looked forward to a lifetime of steady advancement in return for being a loyal 'company man', found themselves squeezed out by younger, cheaper colleagues or smarter machines.

By the 1990s, it was the managerial class and the knowledge-based service industries that were experiencing large-scale layoffs. In just five years in the early 1990s BP, one of the most capital-intensive, wired-up corporations in Europe, cut its labour force from 117 000 to 60 000. 'Downsizing' cut a swathe through the ranks of whole sectors, such as banking and insurance, that had once been proverbial for security of employment. And those who retained their positions often did so at the price of being expected to work harder and harder.

THE WAY WE DRESSED

AFFLUENCE HAS BROUGHT FASHION WITHIN THE REACH OF THE MASSES AS THE NOTION OF STYLE HAS BEEN REPEATEDLY CHALLENGED

In January 1913 the American poet Robert Frost gate-crashed a party to celebrate the opening of London's Poetry Bookshop and was quite astonished when a total stranger turned to him and said:

'You're an American, aren't you?'

'Yes. How did you know?'

'Shoes.'

Frost was wearing 'wingtips', a distinctively American style, in which the soles protruded beyond the upper part of the shoe. Seen close up, they were an instant giveaway – even in Bohemian circles.

In general, however, by the first decade of the present century, the nationality of the

WORK WEAR   Clothes that would provide bodily protection were still the number one priority for manual workers like these Lancashire coal miners of 1920.

educated and propertied classes of advanced Western countries was no longer instantly detectable from a distance. American gentlemen approximated to the English ideal, wearing well-tailored jackets and trousers in a dull-coloured matching cloth. American ladies, like their English counterparts, took their cue from Paris.

What ordinary people wore was still much affected by their nationality, class, gender, and whether they lived in city or country. During the course of the century, these traditional and taken-for-granted influences would be undermined by the application of mass-production techniques to the clothing industry and by the influence of Hollywood films, TV programmes and magazines. These forces internationalised fashion and challenged the conventional boundaries between rich and poor, town-dweller and countryman, and even male and female.

Paradoxically, the dissolution of time-honoured distinctions was accompanied by the creation of new social groupings – hippies, yuppies, punks and 'power dressers' – who took their sartorial cues from each other, and were intent on distinguishing

'TODAY EVERYTHING HAS TO BE MODERN'

In 1909 an East Prussian village pastor named Mosziek published a transcript of a 70-hour interview with one of his parishioners, 69-year-old Frau Hoffmann. The former maid had much to say on the subject of dress:

'Who would have thought it possible a few years ago that workers' children could go around so well dressed! ... Today, if you don't have a shirt, you're stupid and lazy ... Nice things are cheap today ... Just stand on the corner and watch the wenches go by: they're all dressed up. And not one of the girls has a skirt made from a single piece of cloth. In a pinch they wouldn't be able to make a swaddling band from it. Around here you don't see folk costumes any more; up in Lithuania in the isolated villages you can still see them ... The shoulder collars with tassels as communion coats are completely out of fashion; the same goes for head finery – the black silk kerchiefs with a bow. Today everything has to be modern ... Velvet and silk aren't so expensive any more and are really beautiful. They rustle so nicely. As long as they're working at home or in the factory, the girls go around in a plain long dress; but as soon as they get off work, they change ... we old people don't care much about such things anymore; but still, everyone likes to get new shoes at Whitsuntide.'

themselves from mainstream society, rather than dressing, as their grandparents had, to signify their role and rank within it. Fashion changed from being a declaration of status to an expression of self. It ceased to be the prerogative of the elite and became the right of the masses.

Who wore what

In 1900 the upper classes on both sides of the Atlantic were distinguished not only by the quality of their clothes but also by their quantity and variety. The trousseau of an upper middle-class girl would include, at a minimum, a dozen each of petticoats, chemises, bodices, camisoles, drawers and nightgowns, all hand-sewn, lace-edged and monogrammed. Silk stockings could be bought ready-made from a store and were available in five sizes and 300 different shades. The wardrobe of this comfortably-off newlywed's mother might include such exotic and expensive items as a silk kimono from Japan, cartwheel hats decorated with osprey or ostrich feathers from Africa, and dresses trimmed with exquisite broderie anglaise from Switzerland or delicate lace edgings from Belgium or Ireland.

Different occasions, places, seasons and times of day all required different modes of dress. Even a single weekend in the country might require a trunkful of outfits and accessories to meet the requirements of travel, recreation, socialising, formal dining and church attendance. The support of a lady's maid – preferably French, or at least pretending to be – was essential for the proper packing and care of such garments, not to mention the arrangement of her mistress's hair into elaborate coiffures.

AT THE RACES **The social elite in the USA at the turn of the century regarded elegant attire as essential at sporting events, which were also occasions for display and courtship.**

For gentlemen, the rules were less elaborate but no less strict or subtle. Except in high summer, dark colours and heavyweight materials were the order of the day in informal settings such as a spa or seaside resort, or on informal occasions, such as a weekend house party. Transgression of the dress code through ignorance of it could expose a culprit to mortifying censure. When King Edward VII's assistant private secretary, Sir Frederick Ponsonby, attempted to accompany his royal master to a picture gallery while wearing a tailcoat, he was witheringly rebuked by the sovereign with the observation that: 'I thought everyone must know

NATIONAL COSTUMES In the militarised societies of Germany and Austria-Hungary, officers invariably wore uniform, even when they were off duty. Below: in those same societies, the peasant majority reserved their traditional finery for Sundays, festivals and weddings.

that a short jacket is always worn with a silk hat at a private view in the morning.'

When Keir Hardie, Britain's first Labour Member of Parliament, entered the House of Commons in 1892 he did so wearing a working man's cloth cap – scandalising the public, press and parliamentarians alike. Nevertheless, among the working classes, having the resources to uphold rigid dress conventions was a mark of status. Only little boys and the very poorest of the poor went bareheaded outdoors. People too poor to afford formal mourning clothes still sewed black patches and armbands onto their garments. Only the most insensitive would commit the social sin of attending a funeral in brown boots or not wearing a black necktie.

Uniform codes

One of the differences between the liberal democracies and the more authoritarian states of central and eastern Europe was the prestige accorded to military uniforms. In Britain, officers of the regular forces readily changed into 'mufti' as soon as their official duties were completed for the day. In the German, Austrian and Russian empires, by contrast, the exalted standing of the military encouraged the wearing of uniforms by civilian bureaucrats as well. In the Kaiser's realm, even university professors were proud to don the uniform of a reserve officer in the militia in preference to academic robes. In both types of society, democratic and authoritarian, military-style uniforms were also worn by the employees of organisations that wished to project an image of reliability and discipline, such as railway companies and the postal service.

Almost everywhere a distinction in dress between city and country was still strikingly evident. English gentlemen reserved their tweeds and brogues strictly for the country. In European countries with large peasant populations, the town-country divide was honoured in the elaborately embroidered costumes worn for religious festivals and family celebrations. Even in countries as advanced as France or as small as Belgium, regional identity was clearly preserved in peasant dress. In Alpine Germany, Austria and Switzerland, the origins of men and women from neighbouring regions could be distinguished from the different weave of their woollen stockings, the cross-stitch on their jackets and aprons or the pattern of pleats in their headdresses.

As the English socialist writer George Orwell observed in the 1930s, it was possible

CLOTH CAP The flat cap was worn by the working classes in Europe and the USA. The straw 'skimmers' in this 1911 English soccer crowd suggests an early season match.

before 1914 to classify the social status of any inhabitant of the British Isles, instantly and at a glance, simply by what he or she wore. Headgear alone was sufficient for males. 'Toffs' and 'nobs' wore a shiny silk 'topper'; the respectable middle classes a stiff 'bowler', or, more daringly, a soft 'trilby' or the German 'Homburg' favoured by the dandyish Edward VII. Working-class men wore a peaked 'cloth cap', which had made its first appearance in the mid 19th century as a sporting cap worn by the better off for activities such as shooting and fishing.

Dress denoted distinctions of status within classes as well as between them. In industrial Lancashire, the mass of mill girls still clattered to work in clogs and shawls, like their mothers and grandmothers before them, but a 'forward miss' who took the tram to work in a shop or office might well risk provoking hostile stares from her neighbours by wearing a hat and coat. In the rural United States, the carpenter's bibbed overall was widely adopted by farmers, who could wear them over thick pants and 'union suits' of underwear in the freezing winters and over nothing at all in sweltering summers. With the aid of the ubiquitous Singer sewing machine, farm

CATALOGUE SHOPPING North America's scattered population kept in touch with fashion through movies and mail order.

wives could readily run up rough approximations to 'store-bought' items or ones ordered through the Sears' mail-order catalogue.

Breaking the boundaries

Edwardian formality was occasionally challenged by such provocative fashions as the 'hobble' skirt, which restricted its wearer to a pace of 9 in (23 cm) and was the height of

MOVING ALONG   A postcard mocks the 'hobble' skirt, which was replaced by loose, flowing lines (far left).

fashion in 1908-10, or the exotic 'harem' trousers, inspired by the stage costumes of Diaghilev's brilliant 'Ballets Russes', which hit Europe in 1909. The real assault on convention began in the 1920s, although only the wealthy young could afford to outrage their elders with raccoon coats or extravagantly cut 'Oxford Bags', which ballooned out to 30 in (76 cm) around the bottom. French tennis star Suzanne Lenglen scandalised Wimbledon with her short skirt and bare legs – and around the world newspapers reproduced pictures of her doing so. 'Sportswear', originally developed for specific games such as cricket, tennis or polo, began to be worn casually on informal occasions and by far more people than actually played sport. The really rich could afford to play their days away. Aspirants to affluence could at least try to look as though they did.

In 1922 Paris designer Jean Patou exhibited the first-ever 'sportswear collection'. 'Plus fours' were seen off the golf course, and garishly patterned loose sweaters were favoured by the young of both sexes. The craze for

TREND-SETTER   Britain's style-conscious Prince of Wales encouraged the wearing of casual fashions, such as this boldly patterned Fair Isle sweater.

SHOCKER French tennis star Suzanne Lenglen stunned Wimbledon crowds in 1922 with the shortness of her skirts – but was still obliged to wear stockings when playing in front of royalty.

day-long rambles in the countryside developed, under German inspiration, into a fad for more strenuous hiking holidays, during which the hiker wore such informal garments as shorts, short-sleeved shirts and French-style berets. Clothes that were loose and comfortable symbolised the social and personal freedom demanded by a generation liberated from prewar conventions. Britain's youthful Prince of Wales, a skilled exponent of the foxtrot, was frequently photographed in holiday mood wearing jazzy sweaters and elegant, full-cut slacks.

By 1926 a more definite 'look' had begun to emerge as a small proportion of rich, young women opted for a 'boyish' style – flat-chested, slim-hipped, with short, 'shingled' hair. The ideal female silhouette was radically simplified. Fussy trimmings were banished from garments, which might now be made from previously unfashionable textiles such as knitted jersey or, more daringly, from 'male' fabrics, such as tweed or corduroy. This revolution was led by the Parisian designer Coco Chanel, who made it 'chic' to dress like the poor in black or beige or grey, adopting the workman's cap or scarf as an accessory. High fashion, henceforth, did not necessarily imply luxury.

This trend was paralleled among members of the European middle class, who had recently been impoverished by wartime taxes and who affected to despise 'glamour'. Chanel initiated a revolution of accessibility, and thus did for women's dress what Beau

Brummell had done for men a century before, abandoning flamboyant fussiness in favour of a bold simplicity dependent on line, cut and quality. In 1926, the American edition of *Vogue* magazine shrewdly recognised that Chanel's deceptively simple 'little black dress' was destined to acquire classic status as the couture equivalent of the Model T Ford.

Among the young, stiff corseting was abandoned in favour of the elasticated brassiere, which gave a new freedom of movement. For the first time in centuries, hemlines rose to mid-calf and then almost to

SHIP TO SHORE

The 'blazer' originated as a striking blue-and-white uniform jersey designed for the crew of HMS *Blazer* in honour of a visit by Queen Victoria in 1845. Later, the name was transferred to the brightly coloured jackets worn by oarsmen, cricketers and other sportsmen. By the 1920s, a well-cut blazer had become acceptable dress at semiformal occasions, such as a summer garden party.

the knee. Female footwear, now exposed, became a fashion item in its own right as shoes replaced boots. Hats, although greatly diminished in size, did not decline proportionately in price. A 1931 advertisement for Galeries Lafayette, in London's Regent Street, portrayed a dress of wool and crepe de Chine, selling at 55 shillings, to be worn with a velour cloche hat, priced at 56 shillings – just 2 shillings less than two weeks' unemployment pay for a man with a wife and two school-age children.

Make-up was no longer the prerogative of actresses and prostitutes, though reactionary British males, like the journalist St John

Ervine, writing in *Good Housekeeping* magazine, denounced plucked eyebrows and pointed, painted nails ('bloody talons'). He feared that the country was sliding towards the standards of the United States, where 'even children of ten have their rougepots and lipsticks'. Before 1914 a respectable wife might have employed a touch of rouge to remedy the fading bloom of youth. A decade later, the same sort of woman was quite likely to be using subtle face powder and nail polish and even, on special occasions, lipstick and scent. By 1930 a survey conducted among

ACCENT ON YOUTH The svelte lines of Coco Chanel's classic 'little black dress' favoured the young and the slim.

DREAM FACTORY   Hollywood supplied images of glamour (below), eagerly absorbed by a female labour force often working in unglamorous surroundings (right).

Good Housekeeping readers in the UK would reveal that fewer than one in a dozen used no make-up at all, although it would not be generally adopted until the 1950s.

Hooray for Hollywood

Before 1914 chambermaids dreamed of looking like a duchess, 20 years later they dreamed of looking like a film star. For the first time, cinema – in effect, Hollywood – exerted a major influence on the fashion industry. In the 1932 film *Letty Lynton*, Joan Crawford wore 26 different outfits in the space of 84 minutes. Although the main concern of studio wardrobe departments was to make the star look good, they also succeeded in

setting trends for the fashion-conscious. Costume designer Adrian distracted Miss Crawford's fans from noticing her large hips by riveting their eyes on her broad shoulders, which he enveloped in startling puffed epaulettes of tulle. By the end of 1932, 10 000 American women were strutting through salons in imitation 'Letty Lynton' dresses. When tough guy Clark Gable took off his shirt in *It Happened One Night* (1934) and revealed that he wore no vest, sales of vests plummeted.

The popularity of platinum blondes such as Jean Harlow and Mae West was good for sales of hydrogen peroxide. Their other prominent assets revived designers' interest in décolletage. German film star Marlene Dietrich, by contrast, personified a far more severe sensuousness and could make even tailored trousers look sexy.

NONCONFORMIST   Marlene Dietrich asserted a paradoxical femininity by favouring mannish dress, but few women followed her example.

Film-making was a new industry, with no traditional recruiting ground. Many early film-makers had gained their first business experience in the garment trade, and attached great importance to high standards of costume as one of the hallmarks of a quality film. In the silent era particularly, sumptuousness had to be conveyed visually. Producers favoured iridescent, diaphanous or flamboyant materials, like satin, crepe or fox fur, which looked good on the screen. The wealthy could afford to indulge their fantasies by having clothes made in imitation of those worn by the stars. By 1937, the less well-off in America could buy cheap copies retailed at one of 400 Cinema Fashions Stores. Or they could save up for garments made with new substitutes, such as rayon, sold as 'artificial silk' ('artificial' in the 1930s carried the sort of connotations that 'hi-tech' would in the 1980s).

Although Joan Crawford's freckles were re-touched out of her publicity photographs, the sun-soaked climate of California made tanning fashionable, entirely reversing the Edwardian emphasis on a 'milk white' complexion, which had been the clearest evidence that one did not do outdoor manual work, like a peasant. The growth of factory and office work, however, meant that even paid employees had acquired the pallor that had once been the prerogative of their employers. In Europe, 'sunbathing' was encouraged by German scientists on health grounds, particularly as a way of tackling deficiency diseases. The cult of sunbathing was further reinforced by the passion among the rich for leisurely winter cruises in the Caribbean and Mediterranean.

Depression and deprivation

The harsh economic realities of the 1930s and 1940s set limits on the ability of the masses to indulge their fashion fantasies. The 1931 'New Survey of London Life and Labour' might observe that Kensington housemaids on their days off were virtually indistinguishable from their mistresses – but Kensington was a very affluent area, even by London standards. And George Orwell might remark that mass-produced cheap suits, from chain retailers such as The Fifty Shilling Tailors, had begun to blur class distinctions – but even he conceded that an underpaid clerk could only pass himself off

as better than he was for a little time and from a little distance. In the depressed regions of the North, in Wales and in Scotland, boots and clogs, shawls and overalls, remained the standard dress of working-class adults, and labouring men continued to go collarless except on Saturday nights in the pub and Sunday afternoons in the park.

The spread of fascism throughout Europe in the interwar period encouraged the wearing of uniforms by a higher proportion of the population, who found themselves enrolled in militias, youth movements and labour corps. Even women's garments began to be cut with square shoulders – a trend that was to be accentuated during the militarised 1940s. In Hitler's Germany, traditional *lederhosen* and other forms of peasant garb won official approval as emblems of 'Volkisch' authenticity. The Austrian peasant *dirndl*, a full skirt with a tight waistband, became a popular fashion in both the USA and UK among the younger generation. Most German high fashion remained derivative. German manufacturers, like the Americans, were notorious for conducting more or less open industrial espionage at the

THE CENTURY OF COUTURE

Parisian haute couture was invented by an Englishman, Frederick Worth, in the 1850s, and dominated the world of female fashion until the 1950s. Before Worth, fashion was what aristocrats wore; after him, it was what couturiers said they should wear. Worth pioneered the notion of the seasonal collection, but the formal staging of annual fashion shows before press and public did not become a regular event until the early 1900s. By that

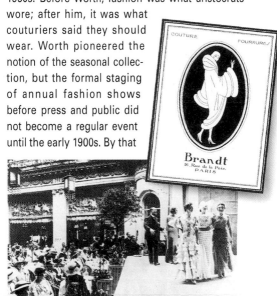

PARIS PINNACLE An outdoor show in the Bois de Boulogne in 1934 is well attended. The French capital set female styles worldwide for over a century (inset).

time, the French capital had 20 couture houses; by 1925, it had 72.

The Second World War dealt Paris a blow from which it only appeared to recover, while buyers and producers in the USA discovered and asserted their own native tastes and talents. Despite the success of Dior's postwar 'New Look', haute couture became increasingly marginalised. In the 1930s, Chanel alone had employed a staff of 2500; by 1985 the surviving 21 fashion houses would employ less than 2000 between them and serve only 3000 clients worldwide.

By 1975, made-to-order clothes accounted for less than a fifth of the direct profits of Parisian couture houses, and by 1985 less than an eighth. Salvation came in the shape of ready-to-wear clothing ranges – for both sexes – licensing agreements and non-garment products such as accessories, leatherware and spectacles. Lanvin, Nina Ricci and Chanel scented success elsewhere. Chanel 'No 5' alone was reckoned to generate global sales of $50 million. By 1981, the overall profits of the surviving Paris couture houses from clothes and licensing amounted to 6 billion francs – while fragrances brought in another 5 billion.

SUN AND SEA Changing notions of modesty and an increased emphasis on health encouraged a greater exposure of flesh in the interwar period. Tanning and exercise, along with beach holidays, became fashionable among the young.

annual Paris collections, employing teams of observers to memorise the garments they saw, and then rush back to their hotel rooms to make drawings of them.

For the respectable classes, who were neither very rich nor very poor, managing a family's wardrobe was an important part of a housewife's skill. Women's magazines devoted many pages to technical instruction in the arts of dressmaking and knitting, and frequently included free paper patterns as a promotional item to boost circulation. Although the wife of a bank manager

FOLLOWING FASHION The fashion-conscious kept up appearances during the Second World War by doing their own repairs and alterations (above), something taken for granted by Scottish crofters.

FASHION GOES TO WAR

TOMMY The British combat uniform in the First World War was influenced by experience in India, where *khaki* blended in with the landscape.

Mass-production tailoring was pioneered by the manufacturers of military uniforms, and the wearing of uniforms accustomed millions of conscripts to novel garments which they continued to wear in civilian life. T-shirts (named for their shape) were originally introduced in the 1890s as undershirts for American sailors. In 1914 the British firm of Burberry's Tielocken waterproof of 1910 was militarised by the addition of epaulettes and rings for hanging grenades, map-cases and binoculars; it became the standard officer's 'trench coat' and a postwar fashion classic. Second World War sailors keeping watch in freezing weather wore hooded coats of thick Duffel cloth which, instead of buttons, had toggles, which were easier to do up with numbed fingers.

In blitz-torn Britain, clothes rationing began in 1941 and lasted until 1952. Inspired by the slogan 'Make Do and Mend', housewives recycled curtains and blankets as coats and dresses. Woollen garments were routinely unpicked and reknitted. The muslin cloth used for wrapping cheese was unrationed, and so could be used for making underwear – as could illegally obtained parachute silk. British designers rallied round with a 'Utility' scheme of approved designs that, through skilful cutting, maximised the use of materials. At the end of hostilities, millions of men were discharged into 'Civvy Street' in a 'demob suit', which allegedly came in two sizes – too small and too large.

American manufacturers were subject to restrictions imposed by the War Production Board. Belts were to be no wider than 2 in (5 cm); cuffs were banned from coats, and attached hoods and shawls from tops. Unable to holiday in Europe during the war, wealthy Americans headed for Latin America and brought back some of the flamboyant styles of the sunny south. Others trekked to dude ranches on their own frontier and revived a taste for wearing denim jeans, checked shirts and elaborately tooled, high-heeled boots. Some of these items, along with 'sneakers' and 'bobby-sox', made their way across the Atlantic for the first time in clothes parcels for beleaguered Brits.

DEMOB British ex-airmen in demobilisation suits at the end of the Second World War.

could afford to go to a personal dressmaker for 'something special' for a big occasion, even she might still regard knitting sweaters and scarves as a source of satisfaction, and endless sock-darning as an unavoidable chore.

At the lower end of the middle-class spectrum, the wife of a bank clerk would pay even more painstaking attention to 'keeping up appearances', discreetly acquiring secondhand items at a 'bring and buy' in aid of a worthy cause. She would let out a straining waistband for her husband, run up a dress for her daughter, or revive a warm coat by retrimming its collar and cuffs.

The Second World War brought deprivation to most of the combatant countries. Frau Scholtz-Klink, head of the Nazi Women's Bureau, announced that 'German women must now deny themselves luxury and enjoyment'. And by 1941, the British were spending 38 per cent less on clothes than they had before the outbreak of war. American servicemen arriving in the UK were handed leaflets warning them that the British knew how to dress well, but that rationing meant that it was good form not to do so. For the first time, perhaps, fashion took its cue from the proletariat rather than the privileged. As millions of women took over men's jobs in industry, turbans and trousers could be worn with patriotic pride. Ingenuity was at a premium when it came to party clothes. A *Picture Post* reporter noted in November 1942 that at one London nightclub the guests included a girl in a silver lamé tennis dress and another in a gown made from pink-striped mattress ticking.

After austerity

The ending of hostilities produced a reaction to the austerities of wartime, although clothes continued to be rationed in Britain into the 1950s. Paris, eager to reassert its prominence in the world of fashion, responded enthusiastically to Christian Dior's striking 1947 'New Look', which rejected tight-fitting economical garments in favour of flowing lines that required an extravagant use of materials. Some of his dresses took up to 80 yd (73 m) of fabric. The USA welcomed the 'New Look', too. In 1949 Dior set up his first overseas operation, a warehouse in New York, selling 'off-the-peg' garments to trade outlets. The cutting-edge of innovation passed from

BRIGHTENING UP After the drabness of the war years there was a hunger in the USA for bold colours and patterns (below), which soon extended to men, who took to the Hawaiian shirt (right).

NEW LOOK Christian Dior's evening dresses in 1950 made extravagent use of materials and were elaborately decorated, in reaction to the austerity years of the Second World War.

haute couture to the 'ready-to-wear' business. The following generations of designers, such as Mary Quant, Cacharel, Kenzo, Calvin Klein and Karl Lagerfeld, aimed not to create expensive couture models that could be copied in cheaper versions, but models specifically designed for mass reproduction. German and Italian manufacturers proved particularly adept in developing what was referred to as 'middle-class couture'.

The 1950s confirmed the trend to female flamboyance, with slinky sheath evening dresses and bright cotton-print shirtwaisters for day wear. Shiny fabrics and dazzling floral patterns were a striking contrast to the dull, practical browns, greys and blues of the years of war and rationing. In the USA 'At Home' casual clothes, such as 'lounging pants' and flat-heeled 'mules', became popular with wives allegedly revelling in stay-at-home suburban security and glued to their newly acquired televisions.

Few European wives might have thought lounging pants becoming or even proper, but they eagerly embraced the concept of 'separates', abandoning the conventional dress in favour of blouses, sweaters and skirts, which could be worn in dozens of different combinations and glamorised by the new 'costume jewellery'. Stiffly structured brassieres with startling cone points,

pioneered by 'Sweater Girl' Lana Turner, and multilayered nylon petticoats, which could easily be washed at home and dried out in a few hours, gave added allure to the female form.

Such 1950s American male extravagances as tartan golfing trousers, Bermuda shorts and dazzling Hawaiian shirts failed to cross the Atlantic. But the Americans' refusal to be uncomfortable did at least challenge the strict conventions of English men's tailoring and promote a new trend towards a looser cut in materials of lighter weight. Over the following decades, this trend would be reinforced by the adoption of American-style central heating, which made it less necessary to wear cumbrous layers of heavy garments throughout winter. Underlying this shift of emphasis was an increasing acceptance of American informality. More profoundly,

FROM REVOLT TO STYLE A section of 1960s youth expressed their rebelliousness through psychedelic fashions. The cult model Twiggy epitomised a more acceptable style.

there was an unconscious recognition of 'the facts of life'. As 'mourning clothes' disappeared, specially designed maternity wear began to make its first appearance.

Youthquake

During the 1960s, the focus of fashion switched decisively to the young: even haute couture could only react. The sensational Courreges collection of 1965 was devoted almost entirely to clothing for the teens and twenties. In 1968 Yves Saint Laurent proclaimed 'Down with the Ritz! long live the street!', perceptively observing that girls no

TAKING FASHION TO EXTREMES

FROM REBELS, TO SUITED PERFORMERS, TO EXTRAVAGANTLY DRESSED ENTERTAINERS, POP STARS HAVE BEEN STYLE LEADERS FOR THEIR GENERATION

Elvis Presley led the way. Dressed in well-cut but casual jackets and trousers, he soon learned that falling onto his knees 'gospel-style' could be not only painful but embarrassing. So he had his trousers cut specially baggy in the crotch, with padding at the knees.

With the advent of *Hair* (1967) and *Jesus Christ Superstar* (1971), rock music and theatre increasingly converged. Performers who revelled in an ultra-theatrical style of presentation were the ones who grabbed the headlines. For Gary Glitter, presentation was performance. David Bowie drew on a succession of classic

traditional tartans, paisley patterns and items of formal clothing, sports gear or military equipment.

The career of the Beatles encapsulates two transitions. Before they became famous, they wore the standard rebel uniform of jeans, T-shirt and black leather jacket. After manager Brian Epstein had taken them in hand, they became as much known for their appearance as their music. Dressed identically on stage, they were clean-shaven, with neat, 'mop-head' haircuts. They wore collarless jackets, but the rest of their gear was conventional. Their white shirts and dark ties might have been worn by an office worker, and their trousers had crisp creases down the front. That was in 1963. By 1968 tailored, uniform gear was out. Each Beatle dressed differently – but in the same style: open-neck shirt and flared trousers, set off with an assortment of frills, velvet, furs, cheesecloth and satin. The message was clear: look as though you had begged rather than bought your ensemble – while hitchhiking from the Himalayas to Hollywood via Peru.

STYLE LEADERS Both Elvis Presley and the Beatles set styles of dress that could easily be imitated by their followers off-stage.

archetypes – pharaoh, medieval fool, pirate, spaceman, clown, harlequin and Japanese Kabuki actor. Not only did pop stars want to look both exotic and erotic, they also needed to look larger than life. Stiff shoulder pads, swirling capes, stack-heels and headdresses exaggerated their basic silhouette. Stylised make-up and tattoos dramatised the face and body. Jewels, sequins and Lurex created dazzling reflections from stadium arc lighting. Clothes were often worn in layers and ultra-loose to speed rapid costume changes and to conceal pads for absorbing sweat. These stage clothes made terrific photographs for posters and album covers.

In Britain, where for the majority of performers small-scale club appearances were more common than arena-style concerts, performers and audiences were much closer to one another. Detail could count, and humour mattered. As a result, performers created witty costume combinations that mocked or contrasted

POP ICON David Bowie represented a trend towards fantasy fashion.

A FRENCH-ITALIAN-AMERICAN-GERMAN CLASSIC

'Jeans' was how English-speakers, 150 years ago, referred to the trousers worn by Italian sailors from Genoa. 'Levis', however, perpetuate the name of their inventor, German immigrant Levi Strauss, who manufactured tough trousers at $13 a dozen pairs, for the miners of the 1848-9 California 'Gold Rush'.

For almost 100 years, jeans remained the distinctive garment of men doing rough, heavy, outdoor work, and as clothes they were 'non-fashion'. Then, in the depressed 1930s, they were worn by American college students, perhaps out of sympathy for the plight of the unemployed. By the 1950s, jeans were crossing the Atlantic as Europeans acknowledged in their own midst an American invention – the teenager. Even in Europe, teenage heroes were American – James Dean, Marlon Brando, Elvis Presley – and they wore jeans as emblems of defiance towards authority figures such as teachers or judges. Jeans were now antifashion.

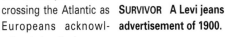

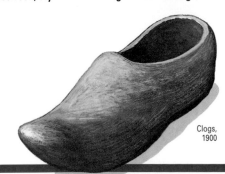

SURVIVOR   A Levi jeans advertisement of 1900.

In the 1960s, jeans won universal, unisex acceptance among the young, who usually wore them skintight and often faded. Torn, frayed and patched versions were favoured by those who clung to the antifashion notion of jeans – which, worn clean and neatly creased, had become high fashion.

In 1991, a jeans range was launched to accommodate the bulging waistlines and sagging bottoms of the middle-aged. They were called 'Dockers'. In name, at least, jeans had come full circle.

longer wanted to look like their mothers – but vice versa. Ideals of understatement and elegance gave way to celebrations of the bright and the bizarre. Pop groups like the Kinks dressed in velvet and sported shirts with huge frills at the throat and cuffs. Women took to wearing men's ties, leather blousons and heavy boots. Few may have adopted the sort of total look pop stars could afford – and needed in order to underline their special status. But many of their fans could save up for a single outrageous garment to enliven their more conventional gear.

By the 1960s, London was challenging Paris, appropriating to itself the concept of the 'boutique', selling cheap and cheerful clothes that disregarded all the so-called rules of good taste and many of the standards of good workmanship. 'Fake' was fine. Glitter was good. On the streets of the capital, at least, traditional British timidity gave way to the provocations of miniskirts and 'hot pants'. Even more shocking was the unanticipated emergence of the British male as a frustrated peacock, happy to deck himself in a puce velvet jacket and a frilly satin shirt, or to totter to a disco on platform-soled boots, swathed in an Afghan caftan. Even inhibited suburbanites experimented with 'polo necks' instead of the conventional collar and tie, and discarded clumping Oxfords and brogues in favour of elastic-sided 'Chelsea boots', slip-on moccasins made in Italy, or

MIX – BUT NOT MATCH   For these US punks, like their counterparts in Europe, the fashion rule was that there are no rules. The result was an instantly recognisable 'style'.

MEN'S SHOE TECHNOLOGY   In 1900 some European workers wore wooden clogs. In the 1990s, high-tech trainers with air-cushioned soles were fashionable. In between, styles went through several changes.

Clogs, 1900

Spats, 1920s

Corresponde
Sportsh
1920s-3

THE ULTIMATE GARMENT The comfort of the shell suit – derived from the athlete's track suit – made it popular with the unathletic of both genders and all ages.

'easy-care' Hush Puppy suedes from America. And, on holiday, they flirted with 'safari suits' as the jumbo jet began to make even far-off Kenya a fashionable destination by the 1970s.

Many fashion fads were popularised by showbiz personalities in the late 1960s and early 1970s. Sammy Davis Junior pioneered the collarless 'Nehru jacket', later adopted by the Beatles. Sonny and Cher made almost a trademark of their skintight, bell-bottom 'loons'. Nancy Sinatra's hit record 'These Boots Are Made for Walking' led her to invest in 250 pairs of the mid-calf vinyl 'Go-Go' boots – which had originated in France as a complement to 'hot pants'. Elton John teetered across concert stages on high-heeled, star-spangled footwear.

Fashion – farewell!

By the 1970s the notion that there might be a single fashion seemed virtually to have disappeared, and people were increasingly free to choose according to their personality and preferences. The self-mutilation associated with the extremes of 'Punk' limited its appeal to a very small, if highly conspicuous, minority. The 'power dressing' associated with the new breed of female executive portrayed in small-screen soap operas likewise remained a minority trend.

During the 1980s, the 'layered look' migrated from the campus to the catwalk, while 'athletic' clothing ceased to be the prerogative of athletes – as 'sweatshirts' and 'joggers' were worn to disguise flab rather than to display physique. A huge market emerged for 'trainers' of complex construction and staggeringly high prices. Some urban teenagers were said to buy a new pair every month, and by the end of the 1980s, 400 million pairs were being produced a year in the United States alone. The popularity of TV programmes that celebrated the sun-kissed lifestyles of Sydney, Miami or Los Angeles helped to take this fashion for informality among the young to its logical conclusion. To the despair of their parents, many young people believed that what was suitable for beach or 'barbie' was suitable for any occasion.

Under the patronage of the Princess of Wales, British designers made a splash on the front pages of the world's lifestyle magazines. Paris continued to regard itself as the home of couture, but it was Milan that most effectively managed to establish and exploit a link between high style and mass production. Italian designers' mastery of knitted fabrics had begun to establish their country's fashion credentials as far back as the 1950s. By the 1970s, the output of Italy's fashion and textiles business was worth more than its motor and electronics industries added together. And by the 1990s, the significance of Giorgio Armani was not so much that he had built a fashion empire, but that on both sides of the Atlantic the ambitious young of all classes and both sexes equated his name with style and were willing to pay for it. Jeans may have become the universal, unisex garment – but designer labels denoted status boundaries as tenacious as those of Edwardian England.

COOL CLOTHES Male style-setting of the 1990s inverts the norms of a century ago, taking its inspiration from the streets, not the salon. Footwear is a crucial accessory.

Brothel Creeper,
1950s

Chelsea Boot,
1960s

Trainer,
1980-90s

OUR DAILY BREAD

INCREASINGLY COSMOPOLITAN DIETS SUGGEST THAT, IN THIS RESPECT AT LEAST, THE GLOBAL VILLAGE IS NO LONGER A FICTION

British soldiers could remain steadfast in the face of almost any horror – except French food. That, at least, was the opinion of the poet Robert Graves, who served as an infantry officer with the Royal Welsh Fusiliers through the four bloody years of the First World War. On one occasion the supplies for the British front-line troops got muddled up with those of their French neighbours. The French stared sadly at a small mountain of tins of bully beef, 'hard tack' biscuits and plum-and-apple jam. The Tommies rejected, with contempt, the avalanche of fresh vegetables intended for conversion into stews and soups. On the other side of no-man's-land, the German soldiers no doubt munched on solid chunks of *wurst* (meat sausage) and black rye bread. While the senior officers of all three armies might have applauded the creations of a Parisian chef, the men under their command were completely loyal to their own distinctive national diets.

In food, as in fashion, Paris represented a peak of perfection but, outside the elite, few cared to imitate it. In the course of the century rising real incomes, international migration and the common experience of travel would change all that – with the eager encouragement of a massive industry devoted to the processing, preparation and promotion of food products and liquor. Italians would learn to drink whisky, the French to relish pizza, the conservative British to wash down pasta with wine, and the children of all

AT THE MARGIN The food reserves of a 1912 London slum family consisted of a little butter, some sugar and a nearly empty tin of evaporated milk.

made agriculture scientific and, in North America and Britain especially, mechanised. Even in these countries, however, the main motive power on farms was still supplied by the horse. Thanks to the advent of railways and fuel-efficient, steel-hulled, refrigerated cargo ships, foodstuffs were among the most widely traded of commodities. Britain, in particular, relied on imports to feed its people. The British commonly ate bread made from wheat grown on North American

FRENCH FARE A soup kitchen dispenses survival rations to the needy of 1903 (top), while Paris bank employees enjoy the use of a staff canteen.

three to eat American-style burgers and barbecues. Science, too, would play a fundamental though largely unacknowledged part in eroding traditional attitudes to food and patterns of eating, implanting a new orthodoxy of nutritional assumptions: that taste and enjoyment are not necessarily the best guide to healthy eating.

The people's diet in 1900

Food production was still the world's biggest industry in 1900, certainly in terms of the amount of manpower employed. Advances in chemistry, botany and engineering had

prairies, and meat raised in Australia or Argentina, washed down with tea from India or cocoa from West Africa, sweetened with sugar from the Caribbean.

Yet, despite advances in science and industry that might have seemed miraculous to previous generations, many of the poor in Europe and North America still suffered from malnutrition. This was largely a result of their poverty, but also partly a result of their lack of knowledge about nutrition. Malnutrition was common among the children of large families with a single breadwinner – who had to have the best of what food there was to keep up his physical strength. It was even more prevalent among their wives, who controlled the diets of both husband and children. Among the urban poor of northern Europe, potatoes and

bread accounted for the bulk of food intake. Proteins were largely taken from red meat, hard cheese and, less commonly, fish. Such a diet was also typical of the working class in big American cities. In 1914, the average family in Chicago's stockyard district (where there were many immigrants from Eastern Europe) spent over a quarter of their budget on baked goods, flour and meat, but only 4 per cent on vegetables (mostly potatoes and cabbage) and 2 per cent on fruit.

Among the world's industrially advanced nations, nutritional standards were probably worst in England, where the highly urbanised working population was so far removed from country life that they often lacked even an elementary knowledge of how food was actually produced. Frying was the most common method of cooking. Green vegetables were rarely eaten, and salads were virtually unknown. Canned milk was often preferred to fresh; fortified with sugar, it tasted better, especially to a child's palate, and it kept longer. 'Treats' consisted of dishes chosen on the basis of flavour more than nutritional value – kippers, pickles, syrupy-sweet canned fruit and sausages of spicy flavour and doubtful contents. Although more and more everyday foodstuffs, such as fruit, jams and tea, were sold in cans, jars or sealed packets, most commodities were still

SOLID STUFF German cuisine was varied and substantial for those families who could afford to eat well.

sold loose; this provided ample opportunities for accidental contamination and deliberate adulteration, especially by retailers. The dilution of milk with water was an almost universal practice.

Whereas many Britons puritanically regarded eating as a rather disagreeable necessity, for the French of all classes it was central to civilised existence, national pride and family life. A knowledge of gastronomy was by no means confined to the bourgeoisie. Even the poor knew how to make nourishing soups and hearty stews, often from ingredients that in Britain would probably have been unrecognised as edible. However, the 'traditional' peasant recipes of the different French regions so lovingly recorded by food-writers were almost certainly for dishes eaten on high days and holidays rather than as daily fare. Many of the poor could not afford to eat well. Jeanne Bouvier, a seamstress in Paris in the 1890s, began her day with bread and milk. At noon she bought a bowl of boiled beef and vegetables in broth, mopping up the broth with bread and saving the beef to eat in the evening with more bread. With a little

FARAWAY FOOD European grocers (bottom) sold goods from all corners of the world (left and below).

TINNED TREATS Manufacturers were quick to decorate cans with pictures of the supposedly mouth-watering contents (below).

FAIRS' FARE

The first soluble 'instant' coffee, invented by Japanese-American Satori Kato of Chicago, went on sale to the public at the Pan American Exposition at Buffalo in 1901. The St Louis Exposition of 1904 witnessed the debut of no less than three major novelties from catering suppliers. German immigrants living in south St Louis inaugurated a national passion by making and selling chopped beef patties under the name 'Hamburg Steak'. The sweltering heat gave Englishman Richard Blenchynden the chance to cash in by selling refreshing glasses of iced tea. And Syrian immigrant Ernest A. Hamwi sold wafer-thin Zabalia pastry at a fairground concession until a neighbouring ice-cream stand ran out of serving-dishes and was delighted to buy rolled wafer cones from him in which to serve their ice cream.

cheese and thin wine, this monotonous diet absorbed half her weekly wage.

The Germans were renowned as a nation of large, rather than discriminating, eaters. Most short-stay visitors found their diet of rye bread, beef, broth, beer, sausage and potatoes cooked in 20 different ways, filling but boring. They lamented the absence of tea, mutton and fresh sea fish. Those who stayed longer, however, discovered the delights of smoked eel, roast goose, asparagus omelettes, hare basted with sour cream, pickled cucumbers, paper-thin noodles, chocolate with whipped cream, and tarts and cakes in infinite variety. Mrs Alfred Sidgwick, the German-born author of *Home Life*, published in 1904, summarised the culinary difference between Britain and Germany: 'If you like cold mutton, boiled potatoes and rice pudding, most days in the week . . . to cook for you requires neither skill nor pains, while to cook for a German family, even if it lives plainly and poorly, takes time and trouble . . . In well-to-do English households you get the best food in the world as far as raw material goes, but it must be said that you often get poor cooking. It passes quite unnoticed, too.'

Lands of plenty

Posters aiming to attract European immigrants to the unfarmed lands of North America, Australia and New Zealand frequently featured pictures of families around tables piled high with food. It was a shrewd marketing ploy, and by no means misleading.

The peoples of these pioneering societies ate well, if not always wisely. The sort of breakfast served by the Union Pacific railway at North Platte, Nebraska, in the 1890s, before dining cars came into regular service, would have seemed like a foretaste of heaven to many a newly arrived immigrant: ham and eggs, fried oysters, fried chicken, sausage, fried potatoes, hot biscuits, corn bread and hot cakes, all served with syrup and coffee.

But American obsessions with health and hygiene were already exerting a powerful influence on the nation's diet. The militant vegetarianism preached by Dr John H. Kellogg and his brother, Will, gave birth to peanut butter and to cornflakes, the first of the cold, dry breakfast cereals, whose success rapidly inspired rival products such as Shredded Wheat, Grape Nuts and Force. Dry cereals required no preparation and were preferred by children to the hot, glucy oatmeal that left mothers with sticky saucepans to wash. The food value of the cereals was low, but the milk and sugar eaten with them made up for that.

A parallel health-inspired fad was the consumption of citrus fruits from California and Florida. Those who baulked at fresh fruit substituted stewed prunes to combat the supposed American national curse of constipation. Salads were another American preoccupation. Coleslaw had long been known wherever the influence of the Pennsylvania Dutch had penetrated. Lettuce was grown widely, to be eaten raw with sugar and vinegar, or wilted, with the same ingredients, plus hot bacon fat. The French-style compote of mixed greens dressed with oil, vinegar, salt and pepper, was initially known only in smart city restaurants or on the dinner tables of the well-travelled upper class of the East Coast. From such rarified circles the principles of sound salad-making were spread by that temple of stylish nutrition, the Boston Cooking School, source of the 'Fanny Farmer' cookbooks. The Puritan heritage of the average American housewife, however, often tended to make her equate simplicity with idleness rather than elegance. Thinking vinegar vulgar, she

substituted lemon juice. Tempted by ready-made mayonnaise, she used it to dress lettuce. She also spiked the mayonnaise with ketchup or chili sauce to produce colourful or spicy variants.

American methods of food retailing were pioneered in Britain by Irish-born Thomas Lipton, who absorbed its fundamental

JUST LIKE MOTHER BAKES

In 1910, 70 per cent of the bread consumed in the USA was still baked at home; by 1924 the figure had plummeted to 30 per cent. In 1930 the first pre-sliced loaves went on sale, in the US, and three years later sliced bread accounted for 80 per cent of all bread sold.

principles during a teenage sojourn in the United States and was free in admitting it: 'Every successful move I have made has been suggested to me by my observation of American methods.' Recognising that the working-class diet meant that four-fifths of a

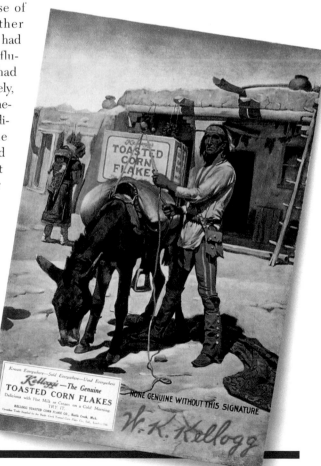

AUTHENTIC PRODUCT Reputable manufacturers emphasised the authenticity of their products to play on consumer fears of impurities in inferior imitations.

❝ FORTIFYING THE INNER MAN

Franz Rehbein (1867-1909) worked as an
itinerant farm labourer in northern Germany until he lost
a hand in a threshing machine and turned to journalism
instead. His autobiography reveals the major part that
was played by food and strong drink in the lives of the
machine-gangs who progressed from farm to farm
threshing the harvest:

'The machine master's first task in the morning is to
give all his men a shot of schnapps. Because of the short
night's rest, a little bad liquor has to revive your flagging
energy...Many farmers give the crew the worst possible
food...They reckon that where there is bad food the
crews will work as fast as they can in order to get away
from there fast. So it can happen that every noon for a
whole week or at least five days, you get the notorious
dumplings with gravy. When you consider that breakfast
and supper are always the same anyway – milk and bread
or beer and bread – then it's understandable how this
miserable slop finally makes your whole body feel sick ...

'I already mentioned the schnapps that every
threshing-machine worker drinks on an empty stomach
first thing in the morning. But this isn't the only time.
Rather, schnapps is given out at regular 2 hour
intervals...It is, so to speak, the life elixir of the
machine personnel...Besides, what else were we
supposed to drink? Granted, for the usual thirst, the
landlords handed out flat thin beer or buttermilk. As
long as the buttermilk is halfway fresh, it agrees well
with your stomach. But if it's old and sour...then you
can feel the effects right away when the seat of your
pants billows out violently...You also get an evil
slimy aftertaste in the mouth that not even chewing
tobacco can get rid of. Then you really long
for a drink that can clear out your throat...
and, unfortunately, the only thing available
for this is schnapps.' ❞

grocer's turnover came from the same dozen
or so basic items, he pared down the stock in
his shops to concentrate on bulk-buying
flour, tea, sugar, butter, eggs, lard, cheese
and other such daily necessities, passing on
economies of scale to the customer in the
form of lower prices.

Food – war's most decisive weapon

When the First World War broke out in
1914, neither side had prepared plans for
the maintenance of food supplies because
both expected the conflict to be bloody but
brief. After a year, however, the civilian population in Germany was experiencing an
alarming rise in the incidence of rickets,
tuberculosis and influenza. The lightning
conquest and exploitation of fertile Romania
in 1916 relieved the situation temporarily,
but by 1918 near-starvation had undermined the German nation's will to battle on.
In Germany's ally, Austria-Hungary, the situation was even worse, with outbreaks of
scurvy and deaths from hunger.

In 1916, Germany's campaign of submarine warfare had brought Britain within

RETAIL REVOLUTION Successful grocers in Britain, such as Sir Thomas Lipton (inset), used large display windows and dressed their staff in clean, white uniforms.

weeks of starvation, but the British Government was reluctant to introduce rationing. When this did become inevitable, it was introduced piecemeal, with a different impact in different parts of the country. 'War bread', made from flour with a high proportion of husk milled in, was, however, universally disliked as 'dirty'.

The experience of war stimulated scientific research into food-preservation techniques and the links between health and nutrition. British doctors at last understood that rickets was caused by a vitamin deficiency, while their Austrian colleagues still imagined it to be an infectious disease. In the interwar period, women's magazines sustained the nutritional crusade. In Britain *Good Housekeeping* magazine supported a 'Good Housekeeping Institute', which published a range of advisory pamphlets, staged public cookery demonstrations, and sent speakers to women's groups and girls' schools.

Novelty and nutrition

By the 1920s, improvements in refrigeration, transportation and communication were blurring regional differences in American cooking and fostering the emergence of a national cuisine. In 1928 home economist Christine Frederick was complaining that: 'I have eaten in Florence, Alabama, in Logan, Utah, in Mansfield, Ohio, and Penobscot, Maine. Is there any difference in the meals served in one locality from another? No. The customer will always sit down to the same old steak, or canned beans, bottled catsup, French fried or Adam and Eve on a raft. Where, I ask you, is the sweet potato pone of Maryland for a slice of which General Lee would walk a mile? Where is the genuine clam chowder of New England? Gone, or rapidly disappearing....'

One of the reasons for this standardisation lay in the fact that restaurant chains could be very profitable if they were organised on industrial lines and used commercially prepared foods that could be assembled by

unskilled, underpaid labour. In 1929, canned soup costing 3 cents a serving could be sold for five or even seven times as much. Leftover macaroni cheese, ham and remnants of so-called 'Spaghetti Italienne' could be rehashed into what the trade called 'work-overs' and sold under another name the following day. Public suspicion of these practices opened yet more avenues for the enterprising. Frank G. Shattuck carved a profitable niche in the market by promoting his chain of Schrafft's restaurants as suppliers of genuine 'home cooking'. This ploy was based on his

FAMILY FAVOURITES Some brands of convenience foods quickly became household names.

NOR ANY DROP TO COOK WITH

America's experiment with Prohibition, which was introduced in 1919 and not repealed until 1933, had a dramatic effect on the nation's eating habits, especially among the elite. French chefs emigrated in droves. Smart New York restaurants such as Delmonico's and Sherry's closed their doors, unable to offer fine food at relatively modest prices because they were no longer able to subsidise the meals by selling wines and spirits with high margins of profit. Redundant bars were turned into cafés or ice-cream parlours, and bar-tenders were replaced by soda-jerks. In California, the vineyards were turned to growing raisins. And at one teachers' college, an instructor managed to produce a volume on *French Home Cooking* that not only omitted wine from many of the recipes for which it would have been deemed essential in any French home – but even omitted to say that the wine had been omitted.

DO YOU COME HERE OFTEN? American sailors take their girlfriends to a soda fountain – Prohibition's respectable alternative to a public bar or tavern.

shrewd realisation that 'Mothers today . . . aren't particularly interested in pies. Their time is taken up with other things – movies, bridge parties, automobile rides. A young man contemplating marriage no longer asks whether a girl is a good cook; he wants to know whether she is a good sport.'

Technological changes in processing and packaging also had their impact on food in the home, as an account of the 'Grocery Revolution' in the *Ladies' Home Journal* enthused: 'Every day sees some ingenious new wrinkle [ploy] devised to lessen labour . . . You

don't have to clean up tea grounds; tea comes in individual bags, made possible by new packaging machinery . . . You don't have to prepare the morning grapefruit any more; if you wish you can get all the meat of the grapefruit in cans or glass containers ready for the hurried commuter's breakfast . . . There are few things except soft-boiled eggs that you can't buy almost ready to eat today.'

Department of Commerce surveys revealed that respondents still believed overwhelmingly that fresh foods tasted better and were more nutritious than canned goods – but canned goods were so much more convenient. Paradoxically, they were valued less in winter than in summer, when social and other activities such as gardening left the housewife with less time for lengthy food preparation. Should she be so pressed that she even forgot to shop for her canned goods, she could always find salvation in such handy recipes as Emergency Cream of Tomato Soup – one cup of diluted condensed milk, plus three tablespoons of catsup (ketchup).

In the 1920s, American-style 'convenience foods' began to penetrate Britain, although they made little headway in mainland Europe. During the First World War, many women had swapped the long hours and confinement of domestic service for well-paid, if noisy, factory work. The result of this change in occupations was a postwar shortage of servants, which in turn obliged many middle-class British housewives to do far more of their own cooking than they had previously done. They welcomed the short cuts represented by products such as custard powder and sandwich spreads. The range of canned goods, previously confined to soups, fish, corned beef and Californian fruits, increased enormously, the greatest demand being for crab and for peaches.

In London and a few other big cities, cocktail bars, and even milk bars, were established, but in the long run these failed to become part

of the British scene. The idea of 'self-service' grocery shops, pioneered in California, was likewise accepted only slowly. On the other hand, foods such as American-style breakfast cereals and canned baked beans were eagerly welcomed. Tempting advertisements for Heinz canned soups positively taunted the housewife – 'Would you buy a plump

young chicken just to make soup? Would you make soup with rich cream? Would you take new peas, choice asparagus and expensive mushrooms and put them into soup? Perhaps – if you were a millionaire! But that's just what Heinz do.'

Giant firms like Crosse & Blackwell and Heinz quickly came to dominate the food trade. Tate and Lyle had a virtual monopoly on sugar-refining. United Dairies controlled London's milk supplies. Marsh and Baxter's cured 40 per cent of Britain's bacon. The Anglo-Dutch Unilever combine swallowed up Chivers, Lipton's,

CUSTOMER CARE High wage costs in the US encouraged the development of labour-saving self-service in groceries (left). In France the customer was still helped by an assistant.

MacFisheries and the Home and Colonial Stores chains. The high streets of the nation were still populated by 80 000 grocers, 40 000 butchers, and 30 000 each of bakers and greengrocers; but small shopkeepers were being reduced to the role of an agent, selling the branded, packaged goods supplied by big firms, rather than blending their own teas, curing their own hams, or weighing out butter produced on a local farm.

Scraping by on bread and scrape

Dr John Boyd Orr's assessment of British diets in 1936, published as *Food, Health and Income*, caused considerable alarm – with its contention that half the population still did not have a diet adequate for optimum growth and health. Orr's findings were confirmed indirectly by British army recruitment figures: in 1935, 62 per cent of would-be volunteers were rejected on medical grounds. In areas of high unemployment, such as South Wales, diets were deficient not merely in the vitamins and minerals needed for sound bones and teeth, but even in the calories needed for body warmth and physical energy. In *The Road to Wigan Pier*, George Orwell summarised the survival

A NOTRE SANTE

During the 1932 Los Angeles Olympics, the French national team successfully managed to gain exemption from Prohibition by claiming that wine was an essential part of their national diet. The team won several medals, including four for cycling and three golds for weightlifting.

BREAD LINES The unemployed queue for handouts in New York's Times Square in the early 30s. Left: Many survived on soup, bread and coffee with the occasional apple.

strategies of the unemployed: '... a luxury is nowadays almost always cheaper than a necessity ... For the price of one square meal you can get two pounds [900 g] of cheap sweets. You can't get much meat for threepence, but you can get a lot of fish and chips. Milk costs threepence a pint [600 ml]... but ... you can wring forty cups of tea out of a quarter-pound [115 g] packet.'

As the nation slowly pulled out of the Depression, the situation began to improve. Sir William Crawford's 1938 account of 'The People's Food' suggested that the typical Briton still had very conventional tastes. The vast majority of those who could afford to do so ate a full cooked breakfast; only a small minority accompanied it with coffee rather than tea. Even a third of families in the poorest social category managed to start the day with a hot meal. More than half of all families still had a substantial hot midday meal at home, consisting of meat and vegetables, followed by a cooked dessert, usually a pudding. In the evenings another cooked meal was eaten, except by the poorest, who

BREAD INTO DUST In the Midwest USA, long-term erosion caused by inappropriate farming practices, compounded by natural disasters, stripped topsoil from the land.

were more likely to make do with bread and jam, cakes and biscuits.

During the Depression, the poor in America were said to have 'starved in the midst of plenty'. There were bread lines and soup kitchens, localised hunger and malnutrition even among the rural poor. But there was no indication, in mortality or other statistics, of an overall deterioration in the health of the nation. Even in Southern milltowns, the poorest workers still ate better than their counterparts 20 years previously. Research by anthropologists revealed that

cultural attitudes as much as material factors determined food preferences. A study of the rural poor in southern Illinois reported that taste and economy were far less important than status. Fish and greens, for example, were disparaged as 'nigger foods'. What 'Riverbottom' whites aspired to was the canned salmon and hamburgers they associated with city folk. Another study of farmers in the south-east in 1940-1 revealed a strong preference for processed foods over home-grown ones, even though the latter were both cheaper and more nutritious.

Guns before butter

In the 1930s the average German family spent almost half its household income on food, with bread the single largest item. Between 1932 and 1938, as Germany pulled out of the depths of economic depression, bread consumption increased by about a sixth. The price went down a little, but the quality dropped as maize and potato flour were added to the regular bread grains of wheat, rye and barley.

A rudimentary form of rationing was introduced as early as 1936. During the war, bread was further bulked out with bran and was generally sold a day old because this meant that the bread required more chewing and went farther. Average German meat consumption in the 1930s stood at about 110 lb (50 kg) a year, markedly lower than in the USA at 125 lb (57 kg) and the UK 140 lb (64 kg); and over half of that was in the form

WAR-TIME FOOD RATIONING

A SCARCITY OF SOME BASIC FOOD ITEMS IN EUROPE DURING THE SECOND WORLD WAR LED TO RATIONING FOR WHOLE POPULATIONS

Crossing to the USA immediately after the end of the Second World War, the journalist Alistair Cooke noticed that the British 'GI brides' aboard his ship were quite unable to finish even the breakfasts served to them because their stomachs had shrunk so much, thanks to more than five years of food rationing.

Britain's experience in the First World War of a badly improvised and unfair scheme of rationing provided valuable lessons for the second global conflict. A sophisticated system of allocating 'points' values to coupons enabled the Ministry of Food's 50 000 officials to manipulate demand for particular items according to their availability. Fairness did not mean absolute equality. Desk workers got lower allocations than labourers. Miners got extra cheese rations for sandwiches because there were no works canteens underground to provide them with hot food. The scarcity of fats and the need to fill up with vegetables forced most Britons to adopt a healthier – if to their taste more boring – diet than they would freely have chosen. Although the better-off could cheat by getting black market whisky,

GET BY ON LESS 'Standard' rations usually represented a target, not a guarantee. Combatants, and even PoWs, usually ate better than civilians, and peasants usually managed to conceal food for their own use. The inhabitants of big cities were generally worst off.

fruit or canned goods, the standard allocations of basic commodities meant that the poorest sections of the community actually ate better than they had during the depressed 1930s.

A similar pattern of positive discrimination was followed in other countries. In the German-occupied Netherlands adults got the same bread and potato rations as children aged 4 to 14, while 'heavy workers' got 50 per cent more and 'very heavy workers' double. (Biscuits, rice and oatmeal were reserved for infants.) The disparity was even more marked with regard to meat, with 'very heavy workers' qualifying for four times the standard allocation of nearly 4$\frac{1}{2}$ oz (125 g) per week. In France, engine drivers and miners were favoured above even the 'very heavy worker' category. Before the war, the average Frenchman drank about 28 fl oz (800 ml) of wine a day; by 1943 the standard ration was 35 fl oz (1 litre) a week – but miners and engine drivers got three times that amount, just as they got three times the standard ration of fats, twice the standard bread ration and more than four times the meat ration.

Propaganda and technical advice were recognised as essential weapons on 'the kitchen front'. Lord Woolton, Britain's food controller, was a persuasive broadcaster, though even he had a hard time promoting the ingenious recipe for meatless 'Woolton pies', or persuading country folk to revive 'traditional' recipes using rooks or nettles, or getting anyone to try strong-smelling whale meat.

UK	Meat 1$\frac{1}{4}$ lb (550 g)	Butter 3$\frac{1}{2}$ oz (100 g)	Sugar 8 oz (225 g)	Cheese 2$\frac{3}{4}$ oz (75 g)	1 egg	Bread not rationed · Potatoes not rationed
Germany	Meat 13 oz (375 g)	Butter 7 oz (200 g)	Sugar 8 oz (225 g)	Cheese 1 oz (25 g)	$\frac{1}{2}$ egg	Bread 5 lb (2.25 kg) · Potatoes 9 lb (4.1 kg)
USSR	Meat substitute salt/dried fish 10$\frac{1}{2}$ oz (300 g)	Butter 2$\frac{3}{4}$ oz (75 g)	Sugar 2$\frac{3}{4}$ oz (75 g)	Cheese rarely available	Eggs not rationed	Bread 8 lb (3.5 kg) · Potatoes 5$\frac{1}{2}$ lb (2.5 kg)
France	Meat 4$\frac{1}{4}$ oz (120 g)	Butter 2$\frac{1}{2}$ oz (70 g)	Sugar 4$\frac{1}{2}$ oz (125 g)	Cheese 1$\frac{3}{4}$ oz (50 g)	Eggs not rationed	Bread 4$\frac{3}{4}$ lb (2.1 kg) · Potatoes 2 lb (900 g)

FAIR SHARES   In England, the poorest families were better fed after the imposition of wartime rationing than during the 1930s.

of pork. Germans also consumed only half as many eggs and half as much sugar as Britons and Americans did – but roughly twice as much cabbage and potatoes, and three times as much wine. During the war, meat consumption fell to just 35 lb (16 kg) a year – but that was still more than twice as much as the average Frenchman or Pole. Average figures, however, are misleading. German soldiers usually ate much better than civilians, and 7 million designated 'heavy workers', a fifth of the labour force, also received extra rations. Ruhr miners, for example, got double the allocation of bread. Less favoured categories ate a third less than they had in the previous decade. Propagandists urged consumers to accept shortages cheerfully. When lemons became unobtainable, they argued that only German-grown nutrients really benefited the body of a pure-blooded German and that patriots should therefore be glad to consume home-grown rhubarb instead of foreign citrus fruits.

In postwar Germany, unprecedented prosperity, foreign travel and immigrants from Turkey, Yugoslavia, Greece, Italy and Spain, combined to revolutionise eating patterns. The 'economic miracle' of the 1950s was accompanied by a *Fresswelle* (wave of guzzling), as the nation attempted to bury memories of wartime hunger under an avalanche of food. By the early 1970s, medical statistics

RICH REWARD   Germany's postwar economic recovery was celebrated by a general indulgence in the sort of fatty foods unobtainable in wartime.

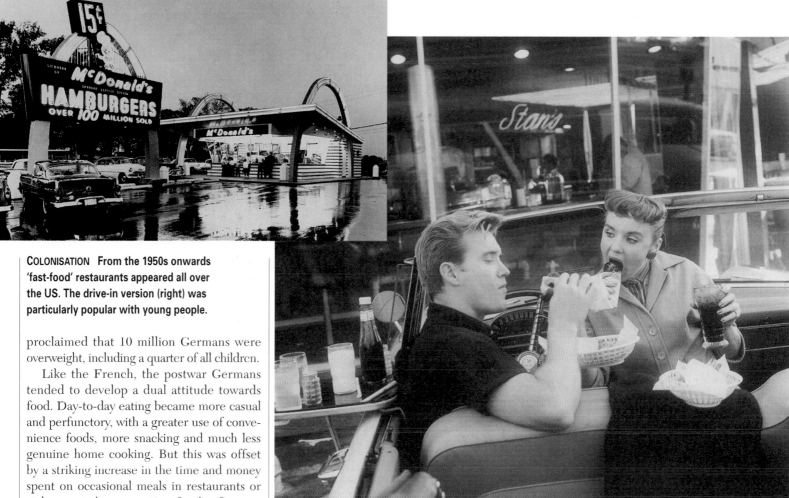

proclaimed that 10 million Germans were overweight, including a quarter of all children.

Like the French, the postwar Germans tended to develop a dual attitude towards food. Day-to-day eating became more casual and perfunctory, with a greater use of convenience foods, more snacking and much less genuine home cooking. But this was offset by a striking increase in the time and money spent on occasional meals in restaurants or at home at dinner parties. In the German port city of Hamburg, diners could sample not only the fare of the *Gastarbeiter* (guest worker) nations, but also Argentinian, Tunisian, Thai, Indian, Chinese, Swedish, Japanese and Portuguese cuisine.

Wine consumption in Germany rose from 12 bottles (7 litres) a head per year in 1960 to 46 bottles (26 litres) by 1990 – although this was still just a quarter of average French

or Italian consumption. In one respect, however, tradition held firm. Germans remained the world's second most enthusiastic beer drinkers (252 pints/143 litres a year), outclassed only by the Belgians.

The last bastion

The French, too, experienced wartime hardship and postwar austerity – but the term is relative. French women's magazines assumed that their readers were willing to take a great deal of time and trouble over preparing meals. The Christmas 1945 issue of *Elle* magazine suggested how to make a turkey last five days – as turkey stuffed with chestnuts, turkey giblets with carrots and celery, turkey croquettes, turkey risotto and turkey soufflé. Few British housewives could have risen to making a soufflé – or would have dared to set a risotto in front of their husband. But the problem was largely theoretical: in

the Britain of 1945, it was extremely hard to acquire a turkey in the first place.

The resurgence of France in the 1950s and 1960s was matched by a gastronomic renewal along largely traditional lines. The French were slower than the British and Germans to accept the products of modern food technology, such as frozen 'TV dinners'. Fine food had been an essential element of national identity and pride since the 17th century and the publication in 1651 of La Varenne's *Le Cuisinier Francois*. In the early 20th century, the advent of the motor car enabled 'gastro-nomads' to drive from province to province, celebrating the delights of French regional cookery and publishing their findings in guidebooks, and the Larousse dictionary was complemented by a *Larousse Gastronomique* from 1938 onwards. The *Guide Culinaire*, published in 1903 by master-chef Georges Auguste Escoffier (1846-1935), was a central text for trainee chefs three-quarters of a century later.

Escoffier, chef to the great hotelier César Ritz, was essentially modern in his outlook. He conceded that the traditions associated with his eminent predecessor, Antonin Careme (1784-1833), with their elaborate sauces and ostentatious presentation, might still be appropriate for an ultra-formal state banquet, but argued that they were quite unsuited to the atmosphere and practical requirements of the fashionable hotel or successful restaurant. Escoffier reorganised kitchen routines along production-line principles, anticipating the 'time and motion study' approach which the American management theorist F.W. Taylor would apply to manufacturing. By the 1950s Escoffier's revolution had run its course and was to give way to what the high priests of food-writing, Henri Gault and Christian Millau, dubbed 'nouvelle cuisine'.

In 1964 a group of French chefs returned from the Tokyo Olympics impressed by Japanese cooking and its simplicity, lightness, healthiness and artfully aesthetic presentation. These principles were the hallmark of a new orthodoxy. Rich, heavy, flour-based sauces were abandoned in favour of dressings made with herbs, ginger, vinegar or lemon juice. Cooking times were reduced to reveal 'forgotten flavours'. Steaming was rediscovered, to become the favoured method of cooking delicately flavoured seafood and vegetables. The truly excellent restaurant presented its patrons with a short menu, offering dishes prepared from the freshest ingredients available from

EAST MEETS WEST Westerners have accepted Japanese cuisine (right) as a mark of their sophistication. Some, however, still prefer to eat in a traditional French brasserie (below).

GLOBAL GOURMETS

THE PEOPLE OF THE WORLD'S AFFLUENT NATIONS CAN CHOOSE FROM AN EVER-EXPANDING VARIETY OF NATIONAL AND CROSS-CULTURAL CUISINES

INSPIRATION Traditional national dishes, such as *escargots* (snails, top left), spaghetti (top right), raw fish (bottom left) and sausages and sauerkraut (right), have become increasingly popular outside their countries of origin, not only in restaurants but also for cooking at home. Meanwhile, 1970s nouvelle cuisine (above), which stressed light cooking and elegant presentation, made use of a diversity of ingredients from around the world.

C ritics have called the process Coca-colonisation – the Americanisation of popular tastes and lifestyles. Since 1945, the expansion of American-based food-service chains has been awesome, giving the world such global products as Burger King (1954), Kentucky Fried Chicken (1955), Pizza Hut (1958) and Haagen-Dazs (1959). The traffic in food fashions, however, has not been all one way, and in some countries individuals have been influential alongside the big corporations.

After the Second World War, French cuisine retained its cachet among the elites of the English-speaking world. British celebrity cook Fanny Cradock aimed her first bestseller, *The Practical Cook* (1949), at servantless, would-be gourmets still hampered by strict rationing, and in 1950 the doyenne of British food-writers, Elizabeth David, seduced her startled readers with *A Book of Mediterranean Food*. Americans, under the tutelage of Julia Child, who had trained at the refounded Cordon Bleu school in Paris, responded more eagerly after seeing her prepare *boeuf bourguignon* on Boston's educational TV channel in 1963. Child's *Mastering the Art of French Cooking* (1961) sold 1.25 million copies by 1974. By then, Americans were revelling in a range of choices once undreamed of, even in a nation built on the concept of affluence.

The first restaurant to serve uncompromised Japanese food in the United States opened in New York in 1963. Hollywood's first Thai restaurant opened in 1969. By the 1970s, American demand for instant noodles and soy sauce was so great that Japanese manufacturers had set up plants to manufacture them in the USA. From 1971 Americans and Britons went to Florence to study Italian cooking – in English. By 1973 American readers were willing to contemplate *Cous Cous and other Good Food from Morocco,* and in 1977 they could purchase the first US edition of the classic *Larousse Gastronomique*.

for polenta or paella. But, of course, there were limits. Garlic and hot peppers were toned down in mass-market products. A range of 'authentic' Mexican foods was reassuringly 'adapted to suit Canadian tastes'. In London, Anglophile Americans eager to sample 'pub grub' drew the line at 'steak and kidney pie', and publicans obliged by substituting mushrooms.

The craze for jogging and fitness focused the minds of the baby-boomer generation on the links between diet and health. Foods that had for centuries been looked on as natural and normal were suddenly regarded as noxious. Concern over cholesterol caused the consumption of dairy products, eggs and whole milk to fall. The American Heart Association announced that in 1987, heart and blood-pressure diseases killed nearly a million Americans – more than cancer, accidents, pneumonia and influenza combined.

The food industry, guided by its usual instinct for self-preservation, caught on quickly and churned out newly packaged versions of conventional items that claimed to be low on calories, sodium, fat, cholesterol or caffeine, and high on protein, fructose, calcium and fibre. Slimness came to signify

SPOILED FOR CHOICE   In the 1990s Californian shoppers could enjoy an opulent adventure in a luxury superstore (above); in Britain, discount superstores offered value for money on a bewildering range of products.

the market on that day. The preserved products created by modern food technology were regarded as anathema. The leading chef also changed his location and status – from imperious master of the kitchens of an international hotel to proprietor of his own restaurant in a provincial town.

The new French openness to foreign influences was signalled in 1972 by the publication of an iconoclastic journal – *Neo-Restauration* – which looked abroad for new models and ideas, even to the USA and, more incredibly still, England. Far from despising self-service, fast-food and motorway service areas, the new magazine actually dared to celebrate 'cuisine à la franglais'!

Ironically, just as France's centuries-old defences against Anglo-Saxon culture crumbled in that most sacrosanct area of national life, cuisine, the Anglo-Saxons at last began

to imitate European styles of cooking, not just in hotels and restaurants, but even in their own homes. In Britain, the crusade was led by the food-writer Elizabeth David, a dedicated partisan of French provincial cooking. Continental travel by coach and car gradually exposed the British middle classes to French, Italian and Spanish dishes and this, together with eating in the burgeoning number of Indian and Chinese restaurants that were opening up, accustomed them to the possibility of substituting pasta for potatoes and eating rice as part of a savoury rather than a dessert course. In the United States, Jacqueline Kennedy introduced a French chef to the White House.

Increasing cultural awareness sparked an interest in 'ethnic' cuisines. The influx of Filipinos, Vietnamese and Koreans into Australia, for example, introduced new influences. All over the Western world, people no longer merely ate Italian food, but Tuscan, not Chinese, but Szechuan, not Arab, but Lebanese. On supermarket shelves, pitta now jostled for space alongside ingredients

THE PRICE OF A BOTTLE

In 1970 it was estimated that one in 15 adult French males drank more than two litres of wine a day, and three times as many drank more than a litre. Two thirds of the nation's mentally handicapped children were born of registered alcoholic parents.
Delinquency, ill-health and road accidents, caused by excessive alcohol consumption, were reckoned to cost the French state three times what alcohol raised in taxes.

healthy living – and as desirable in men as in women. According to advertisers, it really was possible for men to be as 'Lite' and 'Lean' as what they drank or ate. The result was a wonderful marketing paradox – millions of people spent more money on food that promised to give them less.

FROM CRADLE TO GRAVE

OUR GREAT-GRANDPARENTS SWORE TO MARRY 'UNTIL DEATH US DO PART' – WHICH OFTEN OCCURRED LONG BEFORE EITHER HAD REACHED OLD AGE. LIFE EXPECTANCY HAS INCREASED DRAMATICALLY DURING THE 20TH CENTURY AND SO HAVE LIFE'S EXPECTATIONS – PERHAPS BECAUSE THE CERTAINTY OF AN AFTER-LIFE IS LESS WIDELY SHARED. HEALTHCARE AND EDUCATION ARE NOW REGARDED AS RIGHTS RATHER THAN BENEFITS, BUT POVERTY REMAINS.

TO LOVE AND TO CHERISH

CHANGES IN MEDICINE, MORALITY AND TECHNOLOGY HAVE COMBINED TO FACE THE FAMILY WITH UNPRECEDENTED CHALLENGES AND DILEMMAS

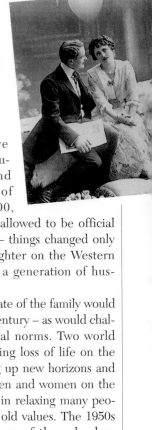

TRUE LOVE A British postcard gives an idealised view of middle-class courtship – a protracted business at the start of the century.

Many moralists at the beginning of the 20th century feared for the conventional family, even predicting its demise. In France, self-appointed crusaders formed themselves into bands for its defence – such as the League for Public Morality and the Central Society against Licence in the Streets. The Archbishop of Paris waged his own war against trends that he, like many others, saw as a threat to family values. Among other things, he inveighed against the couturiers of the world capital of style for producing 'indecent and provoking fashions' – a cry that would be repeated many times during the course of the century against a succession of fashions that would make those the bishop disapproved of look tame indeed.

In the United States, where the divorce rate in 1900 was the highest in the world, individual states, alarmed at this record, began to make divorces more difficult to

THE POOR MAN'S RICHES A Berlin working-class family, with attendant grandmother, pose in their one-room home in 1907. Privacy was almost unknown to slum-dwellers.

obtain. Some American commentators spoke out against a new breed of young women who wanted to be educated, take part in vigorous sports, ride bicycles, smoke, wear make-up, vote, go out to work and live apart from their families. The doomsters claimed to see all too clearly where such trends would lead: an erosion of the ideals of premarital chastity and monogamy – and they may not have been entirely wrong. The psychologist Lewis M. Terman, working in the 1930s, found that of the American women he surveyed 90 per cent of those born before 1890 were virgins at marriage. For the next decade, 1890-1900, the proportion slipped to 74 per cent. Among those born between 1900 and 1910, 51 per cent were virgins when they married; of those born between 1910 and 1920 the proportion fell to just 32 per cent.

In fact, family life by the late 20th century would probably have confounded the most far-sighted commentator of 100 years ago. Gay then still meant happy. 'Test tube babies' and 'surrogate motherhood' were not even the stuff of science fiction. The notion that children might move to 'divorce' their

parents would have seemed not just revolutionary, but beyond belief. In the eyes of French law in 1900, women were still not allowed to be official guardians of children – things changed only in 1917 after the slaughter on the Western Front had decimated a generation of husbands.

Unease about the state of the family would grow throughout the century – as would challenges to its traditional norms. Two world wars, causing devastating loss of life on the one hand, but opening up new horizons and freedoms for servicemen and women on the other, had their effect in relaxing many people's adherence to the old values. The 1950s brought the golden age of the suburban nuclear family, especially in North America; the 1960s inaugurated its deconstruction as young 'baby boomers' – born in the postwar 'baby boom' of 1947-57 – questioned many of its assumptions. In Catholic southern Europe, the extended family retained its hold, but even there more and more families were uprooted from their networks of relatives in the search for work, while young people increasingly broke free from the family embrace to set up on their own.

By 1977 a Gallup poll found that almost half of all Americans believed family life had deteriorated in recent years. The next year, a White House conference on the family generated not consensus but a heated debate which revealed how contested the whole notion of 'normal family life' had become. Social scientists noted that many 'conventional' families now consisted of remarried parents with children from previous relationships.

Family values

Foreign visitors to Britain around 1900 frequently commented on the national passion for family life. The aged Queen Victoria was revered beyond even the vast territories of the British Empire as an icon of motherhood, whose immediate

offspring united the royal houses of Germany, Denmark and Russia. But while domestic bliss arising from the marital state was celebrated in sentimental ballads and memorialised in albums with photographs of weddings and christenings, the realities of family life were more complex.

Victoria had nine children. By the end of her reign in 1901 the average British family had only three or four. One-person households were still rare, but single women were common. One in six women remained unmarried throughout their lives. More girls than boys survived infancy. Women, less vulnerable to industrial accidents than men and not liable to be killed in colonial wars, lived longer. More important still was the huge

exodus of young single men to the 'empty' lands of the Empire, such as Australia or Canada. In the Catholic countries of mainland Europe many such 'surplus' women might join a religious community. In Britain they were destined, according to their class, for domestic service or a subordinate position in the home of a married sibling.

In rural areas such as Ireland and much of continental Europe it was still common for extended networks of kin to live in a single home. In old-established industrial communities, although relatives no longer inhabited the same homes, they still often lived in the same tenement block, courtyard or street and supported each other with gifts and help. In new industrial communities, in mining or logging camps, by contrast, even nuclear families were a rarity and many single males lived in lodging-houses or dormitories.

In the families of the comfortable classes on either side of the Atlantic there was usually only one breadwinner. A grown-up son frequently lived under his father's roof until he had established himself in a chosen profession. During this time the father would

FOR THE ALBUM A cheerful, relaxed group from 1900 (left) contrasts with the carefully composed 'informality' of Queen Victoria's brood (below).

 MARRIAGE AND FAMILY PROPERTY

Emilie Allais came from a landowning peasant family in a remote valley of the French Alps. When, in 1928, she proposed marrying a penniless working man, Jean Carles, certain members of her family were horrified – but she stuck to her guns:

'Things would have been easier if my father had been alone. But there was the family; my father wasn't the worst of the lot because he loved me; I think he truly wanted me to be happy, and he sensed that what I wanted was not wrong. But one of my uncles stepped in as well, a tough man who had no reason to put on kid gloves with me. It all came down to family property; that was the fundamental question, but no one dared talk about it openly. I remember a conversation with my uncle. . . .

' "You're letting your feelings run away with you; the man's a good-for-nothing. We've had inquiries made, and if you are unable to keep a level head, with all your education, we will do it for you."

'I was beside myself at such manoeuvres and I got tough.

' "What?" I said. "You have negative information? If you do, you must show it to me."

' "We have no information to give you, all we have is advice, and it's advice that you are going to follow."

'The more he added, the more transparent the scheme became. They didn't have any information; if they'd had the slightest knowledge, they surely would have used it. It was unworthy of my father; in a sense, he too had allowed his brother to use him. I stood fast, and once more I said no.'

customarily pay his son an allowance to finance personal indulgences – in return for which he expected the son's continued obedience. After his death parental control might still be exercised by a matriarch. Franklin D. Roosevelt's mother controlled his personal finances even when he was president. The working-class or peasant family was far more of a collective enterprise. The contributions of offspring, in cash or labour, were the best hope such families had of raising themselves above subsistence.

After Armageddon

The impact of the First World War on every combatant nation was profound and enduring – but not universally negative. The absence at war of millions of men obliged a corresponding number of wives to take on the role of head of the household, handling its budget, disciplining its members and representing its interests when dealing with figures of authority – the doctor, the teacher, the priest or the policeman. When the warrior returned to resume his accustomed place in such a household he could no longer be 'the master' in quite the same old way.

The major impact of the war, however, was the immense loss of life, with junior officers having the highest death rates of all in combat. Drawn mostly from the educated classes, they were often eldest sons, destined to take over the family firm or farm. The bright futures once imagined for a million such enterprises lay cold in Flanders clay or beneath the icy waters of the North Atlantic. Grey-haired, grieving parents stared at a blank tomorrow. Spinsters faced the prospect of a lifetime without a partner. In Germany alone there were a million 'surplus' women.

In France, which had lost 10 per cent of its male population, various policies were launched to repair the demographic disaster. Laws passed in 1920 banned all publicity for birth control and prohibited the sale of contraceptive diaphragms. A *médaille de la famille* was instituted to celebrate the fertility of mothers producing four or more children. In Italy, the Fascist dictator Mussolini, who came to power in October 1922, aimed to raise an army of 'Eight Million Bayonets'. He made abortion a criminal offence and required all males in state employment, from teachers to postmen, to marry or face losing their jobs. Despite these initiatives, the size of families continued to fall in many countries.

Thanks to wartime service in the military, where the use of condoms had been encouraged to limit the transmission of sexual infections, knowledge of birth control was far more widespread among the working classes after the war than it had been before. Fear of unemployment caused many to postpone marriage and limit their families to one or two children.

As families had fewer children, each child became more precious, the focus of affection, attention and anxiety. Local government authorities in Britain employed trained nurses and funded health centres to promote the new notion of 'mothercraft'. The child-rearing guru of the post-First World War years, the New Zealand-born Dr Frederick Truby King, preached the confident message that 'Breast Fed is Best Fed' – providing it was done according to a strict four-hour rota. Birthday parties, trips to the cinema, the purchase of comics and the giving of regular pocket money became commonplace among families who could afford such indulgences. The sharing of parental bedrooms with children became a badge of poverty, with implications of shame and degradation. Far fewer children were required to address their parents by formal titles. Mother's Day, first celebrated in the USA in 1907, reached Europe in 1923.

Decade of depression

Economic instability inevitably left its mark on family life. In the early 1920s, defeated Germany suffered its period of excruciating hyperinflation when, at its worst in November 1923, one US dollar bought 4200 billion marks. Later in the decade came the Depression. Between 1929 and 1933 average American incomes fell by almost half. Official statistics revealed that in 1933 at least 29 people died of hunger in New York City; in 1934 the figure was 110. The poorest American families were reduced to living in dilapidated freight cars, sewer pipes, tar-paper shacks and even in caves. Less spectacularly, in all countries afflicted by severe unemployment, families unable to pay their rent were forced to move in with relatives. In Berlin, comfortable apartments were left vacant as their occupants left for cheaper

PAYMENT IN KIND A German family use food to buy seats at a circus during the inflation of 1923. Economic hardship brought some families close but destroyed others.

authority of the father as 'provider' was inevitably undermined in situations where the wages of an employed son, or worse still a daughter, in effect paid for his cigarettes, beer and betting.

The family at war

The Second World War subjected families to new strains and terrors. Aerial bombing accounted for some 55 000 civilian dead in Britain and about ten times that number in Germany. In France the number of civilians killed by bombing was a little higher than in Britain. As many French people, however, died as a result of military operations, and almost as many more as a result of Resistance activities. Some 200 000 French people – more than all three other categories added together – died as a result of being deported

to Germany for forced labour or execution because of their race or political activities. Poland lost a fifth of its entire population during the war, Greece a tenth – more than half from outright starvation.

Invasion and defeat forced huge numbers of people out of their homes. Between 1939 and 1945 an estimated 40 to 50 million Europeans experienced what it meant to be a refugee. For millions their exile became permanent. If they eventually returned to their own communities they were highly unlikely to find their previous network of neighbours and kin undisturbed. Disruption

FACE OF POVERTY Children in a centre for migrant workers on Long Island (above) in the 1950s, echoing the 1930s Depression. A farmer's family in Alabama (right) faces debt and ruin in 1935.

lodgings in the countryside. In such circumstances, it was not surprising that people postponed marriages or having more children.

Divorce rates, on the other hand, declined during the Depression as families pulled together in their battle for survival. With less money to spend on going out, family members often spent more time with each other. Party-going declined. A local newspaper in Muncie, Indiana, pronounced piously that 'many a family that has lost its car has found its soul'. Many families sacrificed from what little they had to help out elderly relatives who had even less. In 1930, 60 per cent of elderly Americans had been self-supporting; by 1940, two-thirds relied on public relief, private charity or support from relatives.

Divorce may have declined but rates of desertion soared as men left their families to search for work and lost touch with them. In Britain, where unemployment pay was calculated in relation to a means test based on total household income, younger, employed family members left home, withdrawing their contribution, so that their parents could qualify for 'the dole'. The traditional

BLEAK OUTLOOK An Oklahoma farmer in 1936 contemplates burnt-up crops in drought-stricken fields.

of family ties was also caused by recruitment into the armed services and industry. Britain, with a population of under 50 million, registered 60 million changes of address during the war years. Some 4 million children, mothers, invalids and blind people were evacuated from major cities to country areas judged safe from bombing.

Death, danger, disruption and deprivation took their toll on those who survived as well as those who succumbed. In 1950 John Bowlby published a widely influential study of English children's reactions to wartime bombing – *Maternal Care and Mental Health*. This supported an emerging consensus among health-care professionals and social-workers that having a mother at home full-time was indispensable for the healthy development of the child. The absence of adequate maternal attention was identified as a potential cause of retardation and disorders ranging from bed-wetting and thumb-sucking to insomnia, truancy and antisocial aggression.

As prosperity returned in the 1950s people

set about realising their domestic dreams. In the USA marriage rates reached an all-time high; the age of marriage fell to a record low, and the population grew almost as fast as it did in India.

In France Charles de Gaulle called for '12 million beautiful babies' to be born in the decade 1945-55. The French got two-thirds

HOMEWARD BOUND Two American children at the dockside in Galway harbour wait to return home to the safety of the USA in 1940.

WHERE TO? A 1940s card game makes light of the trauma faced by British evacuee children and their German counterparts (below).

HOMELESS Defeat condemned millions of Germans to flee their homes. Exhausted arrivals rest in Berlin (above). An all-female convoy pauses in a wood (below).

of the way towards his target. Partly, no doubt, this was a response to the optimism and expansion accompanying postwar reconstruction. But many pregnancies were still unwanted. France's first birth-control clinic did not open until 1961. At that time, two-thirds of all couples were relying on withdrawal to avoid conception. Abortions were estimated to run at around 500 000 a year, many performed with the help of a medically unqualified friend, resulting in an estimated 20 000 maternal deaths a year.

Childbearing remained the priority for many American women in the 1950s. Almost one in three was having her first child before she was out of her teens. Two out of three women entering college dropped out before graduating – either to marry or because they feared that graduation might damage their marital prospects. The supposedly progressively minded politician Adlai E. Stevenson told the 1955 graduating class of the elite

Smith College that their mission in life was to 'restore valid, meaningful purpose to life in your home' and back up their husbands and sons as they battled their way in the world.

The Easter 1954 issue of *McCall's*, the US's most popular women's magazine, featured the lifestyle of an 'ideal' family living in a New Jersey suburb, whose routines revolved around family mealtimes, playing in the garden, shopping at the supermarket and beautifying the home. 'Togetherness' became the slogan for the decade and those who did not subscribe to it were likely to be condemned as immature, selfish, afraid of responsibility or quite possibly repressed homosexuals.

The paediatrician Dr Benjamin Spock's revered manual on baby and child care, first published in 1946, replaced routines with relationships as the key to success in 'parenting': 'Children raised in loving families want to learn, want to conform, want to grow up. If the relationships are good, they don't have

to be forced to eat, forced to learn to use the toilet.' *Housewife* magazine agreed – 'firmness is one of the least useful attitudes of a good parent and certainly not nearly as important as sympathy, understanding, patience and skill'.

TOP OF THE POPS

By 1973 Dr Benjamin Spock's *Baby and Child Care* had become the biggest bestseller ever written by an American. Translated into 29 languages, it had sold 23 445 781 copies.

But the suburban scenario soon spawned its own critics who charged it with fostering mindless conformity and undermining true community and family feeling. Fathers, commuting ever farther to work, saw their offspring only at weekends. While *McCall's*

ME AND MY DAD   The suburban ideal of 1950s America was a nuclear family, with executive father and a mother who brought up the children, did the housework and was always beautifully dressed.

celebrated the 'fifty-fifty' father who pitched in with bathing, feeding and playing with his children, a contemporary survey showed that, in reality, of 18 typical household chores husbands routinely undertook only three – locking up at night, clearing up outdoors and fixing broken things. Everything else was left to the wife, who was also expected to act as a glamorous and imperturbable hostess on the social occasions deemed essential to securing advancement in his career. Chasing better pay or a promotion also meant moving on to yet another new suburb in a new city before a family had ever really settled in where it was before. Each year during the 1950s roughly one-quarter of the entire population of the USA was involved in moving house.

Realities failed to match ideals. Between a quarter and a third of 1950s American marriages ended in divorce. Two million marrieds lived apart from one another. Pollsters determined that a fifth of all couples living together considered themselves unhappy in their marriages. Alfred Kinsey's pioneering

LOVE WITHOUT FEAR – MARIE STOPES AND FAMILY PLANNING

The initial passions of Marie Stopes (1880-1958) were fossil plants and the problems of coal mining. Born in Edinburgh, she studied for a doctorate in botany at the University of Munich. This helped her to become the first woman on the science faculty of the University of Manchester while still in her twenties. But a disastrous marriage, unconsummated after five years, caused her to redirect her formidable intellect to the subject of sex. The result was the publication in 1918 of two books, *Wise Parenthood* and *Married Love*, which advocated birth control as a means of freeing wives from the strain of excessive childbirth and of opening the way to sexual fulfilment.

In focusing on the quality of marriage, rather than on more abstract issues of poverty and overpopulation, Stopes differed from other birth-control campaigners such as Margaret Sanger, her contemporary in the USA. In 1919 she was appointed to the newly established National Birth-Rate Commission, which was to recommend policies to make good the losses of war. Marie Stopes' contribution was more distinguished for its bluntness than its liberalism – 'the simplest way of dealing with chronic cases of inherent disease, drunkenness or bad character would be to sterilise the parents'.

Stopes' first Mothers' Clinic was established in 1921 in Holloway, a poor district of north London. At first the Church of England opposed her work but her tireless efforts and impeccable scientific credentials made her difficult to dismiss, and by 1930 it had been won round to approval of contraception, though Roman Catholic opposition remained virulent.

Stopes' second marriage, to aircraft manufacturer H.V. Roe, was more successful than her first but did not prevent her from taking a succession of lovers, which made her continued involvement with family planning a somewhat mixed blessing for the burgeoning movement.

JUST YOU AND ME Single-parent families became increasingly common from the 1970s.

1953 study, *Sexual Behaviour in the Human Female*, revealed that a quarter of the married women interviewed in his sample admitted to having had extramarital intercourse. Perhaps the rest were too preoccupied with driving their children from one club or lesson to the next or simply too exhausted by their chores.

Women's lives, it turned out, were busier than ever. Despite the acquisition of a washing machine, refrigerator, vacuum cleaner and food mixer, the American housewife was actually spending more time on housework than her mother or even her grandmother had done. Rather than releasing women from household chores, new gadgets simply brought higher standards. Families expected more varied meals and changed their clothes more often. People were increasingly aware of the importance of hygiene, hence homes had to be kept cleaner than ever.

Equal rights?

There was increasing talk of equality between the sexes, but again reality lagged behind many people's hopes. In West Germany the new 1949 constitution proclaimed the equality of men and women before the law, but legal recognition of equal rights over marital property had to wait until 1957. It was another 20 years before wives were allowed to take a job outside the home without, in theory at

NEW MAN? Social expectations required more active parenting from fathers (below). A fanciful poster shows a pregnant father to encourage men to be more responsible sex partners (below right).

MOTHERHOOD: A CARAVAN OF COMPLICATIONS

Anne Morrow Lindbergh, wife of the pioneering aviator Charles Lindbergh, meditated on the rigours of modern suburban motherhood in her book *Gift from the Sea*, published in 1955:

'I mean to lead a simple life, to choose a simple shell I can carry easily – like a hermit crab. But I do not. I find that my frame of life does not foster simplicity. My husband and five children must make their way in the world. The life I have chosen as wife and mother entrains a whole caravan of complications. It involves a house in the suburbs and either household drudgery or household help which wavers between scarcity and non-existence for most of us. It involves food and shelter; meals, planning, marketing, bills, and making the ends meet in a thousand ways. It involves not only the butcher, the baker, the candlestickmaker, but countless other experts to keep my modern house with its modern "simplifications" (electricity, plumbing, refrigerator, gas-stove, oil-burner, dish-washer, radios, car, and numerous other labor-saving devices) functioning properly. It involves health; doctors, dentists, appointments, medicine, cod-liver oil, vitamins, trips to the drugstore. It involves education, spiritual, intellectual, physical; schools, school conferences, car-pools, extra trips for basket-ball or orchestra practice; tutoring; camps, camp equipment and transportation. It involves clothes, shopping, laundry, cleaning, mending, letting skirts down and sewing buttons on, or finding someone else to do it. It involves friends, my husband's, my children's, my own, and endless arrangements to get together; letters, invitations, telephone calls and transportation hither and yon.'

least, having to ask their husbands' permission and assure them that the job would not interfere with domestic duties.

The 1960s proclaimed itself a decade of sexual liberation. In 1962 Grossinger's resort in the Catskill Mountains of up-state New York ran its first 'singles only' weekend. In 1964 the first Brook Advisory Centre opened in Britain to give birth-control advice to the unmarried. Britain was creating its youth culture but in the USA the 'youthquake' was well advanced, with more than half the population under the age of 30 thanks to the postwar 'baby boom'. Radical attitudes which had once seemed the prerogative of ultra-liberal Scandinavia spread elsewhere. By 1969, 37

generally attainable. Their children, who grew up in the 1960s and 1970s, enjoyed unprecedented affluence and undreamed-of opportunities for education and travel – two potent parents of discontent. One no longer 'grew up' to 'settle down' or even 'get on' but to discover oneself and fulfil one's potential.

Most people paid lip service at least to the core ideals of the traditional family, but a few denied even these. In 1967 the British anthropologist Edmund Leach proclaimed in the prestigious BBC Reith Lectures that 'far from being the basis of the good society, the family, with its narrow privacy and tawdry secrets, is the source of all our discontents'. In 1970 Australian-born feminist Germaine Greer dismissed

TWO SHALL BE ONE Marriages between the races have helped to ease tensions in multi-ethnic societies like the United States and, increasingly, in many European countries.

mothers as 'the dead heart of the family, spending father's earnings on consumer goods'. The Germans were more enduringly attached to the sentimental trappings of family life. Asked in the 1980s 'what in life is

PARTNERSHIPS Danish homosexuals (above) celebrate their marriage – a legal formality still denied in many countries. A lesbian couple (right) march in a British Gay Rights demonstration.

per cent of all first children born in Germany had been conceived before marriage.

Divorce and even illegitimacy began to lose some of their traditional stigma. Far fewer couples felt pressed to remain tied together in loveless unions. But there were undoubtedly losses as well as gains. Rates of reported sexual crimes and family violence rose sharply, as did deviant behaviour among juveniles, from truancy to drug-dependency, alcoholism and prostitution. Those to whom much had been given wanted yet more. The couples who married in the 1940s and 1950s, having grown up through Depression and war, were largely content to make their goal the sort of family life their own parents had rarely been able to enjoy. Thanks to decades of more or less full employment, that goal was

about a third of marriages ended in divorce. As average family size dwindled owing to later marriage and the increased use of contraception, fewer children grew up with brothers and sisters – although more grew up with step-parents or half-siblings.

Ever-increasing mobility meant ever less contact with relatives beyond the immediate family. One estimate opined that only one American child in 20 saw a grandparent regularly, although, thanks to increased longevity, four out of ten American children now had living great-grandparents. The enlarged role of women in the work force made it increasingly usual for children to spend at least some of their preschool years in the care of a non-relative 'minder'.

Alarmists in the opening years of the century had believed that the family was entering an era of unprecedented transition. Perhaps by the close of the century it was.

CARE COSTS Crèches in Mississippi (above) and Paris (right) provide an essential service for many working mothers but remain beyond the purse of others.

most sacred to you?', West Germans placed 'Christmas with the family' at the top of the list, ahead even of living in a free country.

In 1960 seven out of ten American households still had a Dad who was a full-time breadwinner, a Mom who was the homemaker and their kids. By the mid 1980s, fewer than one in seven American families fitted this pattern. Throughout the industrial world 'families' had increasingly come to embrace single parents bringing up children without a partner, couples living together without the formal tie of marriage, or 'blended' families of remarried couples with offspring from previous relationships.

An unprecedented number of individuals were living alone, either because they were students or widowed or divorced or still unmarried – or simply preferred to. Gay men and lesbians found it increasingly possible to live openly as couples and in the Netherlands and Denmark won legal recognition of committed relationships. 'Paternity leave' became institutionalised in numerous West European states including West Germany from 1986.

Interethnic marriage was also becoming increasingly common and not only in the American 'melting pot'. By 1969 immigrants made up 5 per cent of the population of Western Europe. Intermarriages increasingly challenged boundaries not only of language and colour but of caste and creed as well.

Whither the family?

The family was changing profoundly. In North America and Britain, by the 1980s almost half of all children could expect their parents to divorce before they themselves had attained the age of majority. In Germany and France,

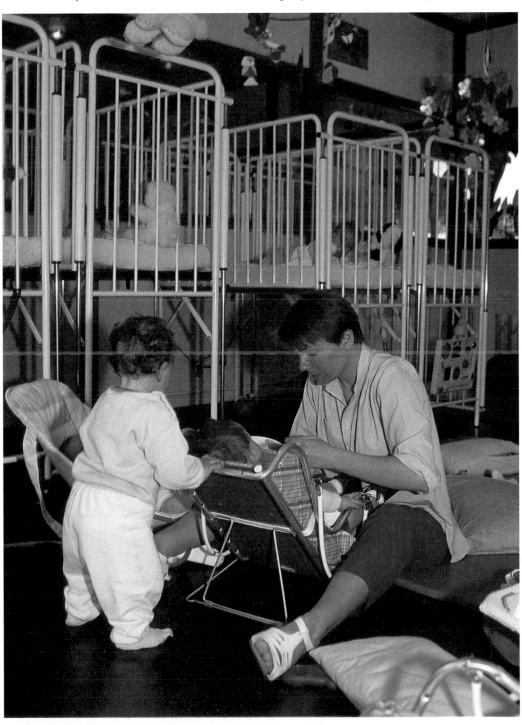

IN SICKNESS AND IN HEALTH

RISING STANDARDS OF MEDICAL CARE HAVE CHANGED OUR PERCEPTION OF HEALTH, FROM SEEING IT AS A BLESSING TO SEEING IT AS A RIGHT

Germany stood at the forefront of medical science at the start of the 20th century. Its medical schools were regarded as the best in the world – the German state made sure that they were also the most generously funded – and it boasted some of the most innovative medical scientists of the age. They included such figures as Paul Ehrlich, the inattentive scholar whose early teachers had regarded as a dunce but who went on to win the Nobel prize for medicine in 1908. His pioneering work in immunology (the study of immunity to disease) and chemotherapy (the treatment of disease with chemicals or drugs) laid the foundations for many later breakthroughs in the treatment and control of infectious diseases. He also discovered Salvarsan and neosalvarsan, used to treat syphilis before the discovery of antibiotics.

Medicine has been a field of heroic activity throughout the century. Already in the late 19th century scientists including the Frenchman Louis Pasteur and the German Robert Koch had studied the activities of bacteria and other microorganisms and dramatically expanded our understanding of what causes disease. The 20th century would see that process taken steadily farther – and people's expectations of a healthy life transformed accordingly as vaccines and other treatments were developed to control and even eradicate notorious blights. The BCG anti-tuberculosis vaccine, first developed in France in 1927, was a case in point. Thanks to BCG (Bacillus Calmette-Guérin, after the two French scientists who developed it), infant deaths from TB in Sweden fell from an average of over 400 per 100 000 between 1912 and 1921 to around 50 by the 1930s. The World Health Organisation, a United Nations agency established after the Second World War, carried the fight against disease a stage farther. It promoted health education and vaccination campaigns in countries of both the developed and developing worlds and had notable success against such threats as cholera, yellow fever and malaria. In 1977 it was able to announce that smallpox had been eliminated globally.

The results of such campaigns are all around us. In the Western world, people at the end of the century are unquestionably more healthy than they were at the beginning. On average, they live longer, grow taller and can expect more pain-free lives. Increased prosperity has struck at the roots of much ill health: poor hygiene and poor nutrition. National health schemes developed in most Western countries since the Second World

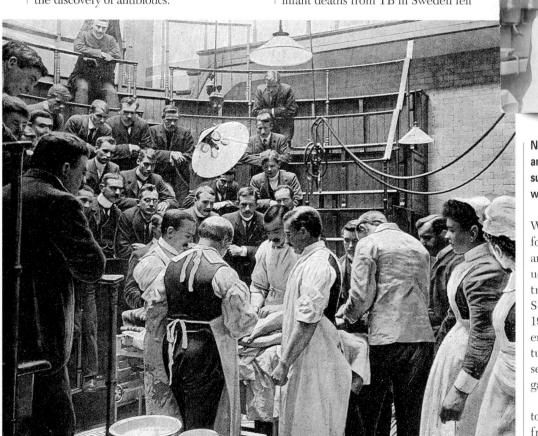

NO COVER The unhygienically bare heads and hands of these early 20th-century surgeons – English (left), French (above) – would horrify their modern-day counterparts.

War have brought wider access to up-to-date forms of treatment and health care. Medical and surgical science, meanwhile, have continued to open up new frontiers – from heart transplants, pioneered by the flamboyant South African Christiaan Barnard in the 1960s, to techniques such as keyhole surgery, enabling a surgeon, equipped with a viewing tube and remote-controlled instruments inserted through tiny incisions, to remove, say, a gallbladder, without cutting the patient open.

But ill health has also proved a slippery foe to fight. The diseases of dirt and deprivation, from typhoid to diphtheria, have yielded

BETTER HEALTH In 19th-century Europe, disease was often spread by shared drinking utensils. A dental hygiene class in the early 1900s (below) promotes better health care.

ground or even virtually disappeared in the Western world, but the diseases of affluence, from heart disease to cancer, have gained ground. Old diseases such as malaria, thought to have been controlled, have started to make a comeback; new diseases such as AIDS have struck down millions. As the 20th century draws to its close some people have even started to lose faith in the scientific basis of Western medicine, turning to various brands of alternative medicine instead, from homeopathy to acupuncture to aromatherapy.

Living at risk

Public health presented a mixed picture at the start of the century. Infant mortality was a major preoccupation in advanced countries, increasingly concerned at any wastage of a precious resource – their own populations. The statistics were not encouraging. In Britain in 1900 the number of infants dying within a year of birth was around 140 per thousand, more or less what it had been 60 years earlier in the 'Hungry Forties' – the decade of such disasters as the Irish potato famine.

The French had taken the lead in combating the problem. Contaminated milk had been identified as a major source of infantile disease, and so *gouttes de lait* (milk stations)

CONVEYING THE SICK

The first two motor ambulances to see regular service were French. In 1900 the French army acquired one, as did the town of Alençon.

were set up in Paris and other cities in the 1890s to ensure that mothers had a reliable source of uncontaminated milk. Later, figures such as the Parisian obstetrician Pierre Budin established the first child welfare clinics offering care and guidance for mothers

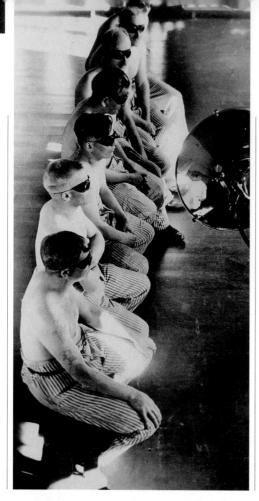

with babies. By 1907 there were 497 such clinics in France and 73 in Germany. The next year the New York City authorities put things on an official footing when they established a Division of Child Hygiene headed by a redoubtable champion of child welfare, Dr Josephine Baker.

For the rest, most people in the Western world in 1900 could expect to live a decade or so longer than their ancestors around 1800, though this had more to do with the engineer, builder, government inspector and farmer than the doctor. Thanks to steam-powered systems for distributing clean water and disposing of wastes, people were far less vulnerable to cholera, typhoid and other water-borne diseases than before. Improved housing and working conditions meant less risk of tuberculosis and respiratory diseases.

SHUT AWAY In 1930 German convicts with TB receive ultraviolet treatment (left). Isolation wards, such as this one in London in 1922 (below), were also used for TB sufferers.

More rigorous inspection meant less food infection, while better diets led to greater resistance to illness in general.

Hospitals, too, had improved. By 1900 there was a relatively high probability that if you died in hospital it would be from whatever you went in with, rather than from something you caught there or as a result of your treatment. Hospitals had ceased to be primarily prisons for the deviant and depositories for the dying and had begun instead to resemble agencies for curing the sick. Even so, they still catered primarily for the poor, who had no alternative but to trust them. The rich were usually treated at home. When Britain's King Edward VII was stricken with appendicitis two days before his coronation in 1901, he was operated on at Buckingham Palace, climbing onto the table himself, with Queen Alexandra there to hold his hand as he slipped into anaesthetic unconsciousness.

Medical practices were improving but, by the standards of the late 20th century, the

HOME OR HOSPITAL   A British mother in 1946 greets her new baby, born at home. From the mid-century onwards, hospital deliveries became the norm in Britain and the USA.

risks to life from both the environment and therapies remained horrific. Even young fit adults could be at grave risk from the simplest of injuries, as statistics from America revealed. As late as 1918, 46 per cent of all the fractures treated in the US Army led to permanent disability, usually from amputation; one in eight proved fatal. The only treatment for tuberculosis was still long periods of bed rest, good feeding and attentive nursing, usually provided in sanatoria, deliberately built in isolated places to prevent infected people from passing on their affliction. The cold, clean air of mountains was thought to be beneficial, so that many of the most famous sanatoria were clustered in regions such as the Alps.

PILL PUSHERS   In the 1900s expensive doctors' bills encouraged people to seek advice from apothecaries, and to trust the claims of the makers of patent medicines.

Other major areas of health, particularly mental health, remained clouded by primitive prejudice among the general public and the medical profession alike. Deafness, blindness, squints, dumbness, epilepsy, left-handedness and sexual precocity were all at times identified as signs that the person suffering from them was in some way mentally retarded.

Do-it-yourself

Doctoring could also be expensive. In the city of Manchester around 1900 the most common case heard before the local county courts was that of a practitioner suing a patient for non-payment of fees. These fees, combined with general ignorance about health matters, drove millions of people to self-medication. The barely literate poor throughout the industrial world were credulous readers of newspaper advertisements for nostrums that claimed to cure even life-threatening conditions such as syphilis. British males, anxious for their manliness, could have recourse to Therapion, a 'New French Remedy', whose makers claimed that it 'stimulates the vitality of weak men, yet contains besides all the desiderata for curing...discharges, piles, blotches and premature decay'. In poor districts opium-based compounds were widely used to keep troublesome infants comatose.

A DOG'S LIFE

In 1914, the year the First World War broke out, the French-born surgeon Alexis Carrel carried out the first successful heart surgery – on a dog.

There was also a widespread preoccupation with 'inner cleanliness', notably in Germany and English-speaking countries – the French were more preoccupied with the state of their livers. Weekends, when one could stay close to home and a lavatory, were favoured times for the purgation of adults with senna pods or cascara sagrada (the dried bark of the cascara buckthorn) and of children with liquorice powder or Californian syrup of figs. Even the better-off, whose more varied diet was less likely to lead to constipation, were susceptible to the obsession. In Britain, middle-class housewives in the interwar years were still being seduced into consuming

THE FOURTH HORSEMAN OF THE APOCALYPSE

After the most bloody war to date in human history came pestilence – possibly from a pig farm in Iowa. The great influenza pandemic of 1918-19 killed more people in 18 months than the Great War did in four years of unrestrained slaughter. A conservative estimate puts the figure at 21 million, about 1 per cent of the entire population of the world. In countries that had taken part in the war, many families who may have already lost a son in the slaughter found themselves confronted with yet more loss at home.

In the United States one person in four caught it and 550 000 died – more than all the nation's military losses in Vietnam, Korea and both World Wars added together. Spain, with a population less than a fifth as large as the USA, lost almost as many. In India a staggering 12 million died – one in 25 of the population. In sparsely populated Alaska one in 12 died, in the south Pacific one in five. And in Russia, torn by civil war, influenza deaths compounded the horrors of a four-year typhus epidemic which carried off 3 million.

The killer was a unique virus before which doctors were helpless. Unlike many maladies which prey on the old, the young, the feeble and the malnourished, the 1918 flu virus seemed almost to target fit young adults in the prime of life. After 90 men died in a day at an overcrowded military base, Camp Devens outside Boston, army surgeons opened the chests of the dead to find lungs corrupted to the consistency of 'redcurrant jelly'. American servicemen called it the 'Spanish Lady'. British Tommies knew it as 'Flanders Grippe'. In Japan it was 'Wrestler's Fever'.

White cotton masks were widely worn to protect against infection. In San Francisco they were made compulsory. But they were quite futile (although they did cause a sharp drop in deaths from measles, whooping cough and diphtheria). In New South Wales church services, auctions and race meetings were banned; theatres, billiard halls and library reading rooms were closed. One small town in Arizona made it a criminal offence to shake hands.

City life was crippled. In Philadelphia so many operators went down that the telephone system ceased to function; with 500 policemen in bed, the streets went unpatrolled. Gravediggers struggled to bury more in a week than they normally did in a month. But, by the summer of 1919, the great influenza pandemic – brief, global and anonymous – had passed as mysteriously as it had arisen.

FIGHTING FLU Clerks in New York in 1918 wear masks in an effort to avoid catching influenza.

the country's best-selling 'liver salts' by the promise that it 'gently cleans the bowels, sweeping away impurities that thicken your figure and coarsen your skin'.

A revolution in America

The United States at the start of the century was the richest country on earth, but it still suffered periodically from horrifying afflictions. Bubonic plague hit San Francisco in 1900, returned in 1907, when it also broke out in Seattle, appeared in New Orleans in 1914 and 1919 and erupted in Los Angeles in 1924. In 1905 more than 1000 people died in a single outbreak of yellow fever in New Orleans. Hookworm, meanwhile, was endemic throughout the impoverished South, as was pellagra – a skin disease caused by a deficiency of one of the B vitamins, niacin, found in yeast, liver and milk.

Things did improve. In 1900 the leading causes of death in the USA were tuberculosis, influenza, pneumonia, heart disease, and infant diarrhoea and enteritis. By 1922, the incidence of TB, flu and pneumonia had more than halved; the incidence of infant diarrhoea and enteritis had fallen by more than two-thirds; and deaths from diphtheria

---

APPLIANCE OF SCIENCE

The first iron lung, devised by Harvard Professor Philip Drinker and tested in 1928, incorporated two vacuum cleaners.

---

and typhoid had been all but eliminated. This transformation was due, at least in part, to a revolution in medical training. In the 50 years before 1914 an estimated 15 000 American physicians had been obliged to pursue postgraduate studies in the German-speaking world. As late as 1910 an investigation of 155 North American medical schools reported that only one – Johns Hopkins in Baltimore – was up to European standards. A $600 million programme was launched to put things right. Full-time professorships of clinical medicine were established at universities and by the mid 1920s America had medical schools that were as good as any in Europe.

Out of evil . . .

War or the threat of it helped to raise public awareness of health. Even in the late 19th century, the Germans and French, with their conscript armies, had been alarmed by the poor health of the recruits emerging from their growing industrial cities. In Britain, the puny physical shape of many of the recruits during the Boer War of 1899-1902 sparked an intense debate about 'national efficiency'. The first fruits of this concern in Britain included free meals in elementary schools and compulsory medical examinations of all their pupils. One of the few beneficial consequences of the First World War was its dramatic effect on standards of health education on both sides of the conflict. Across Europe and North America, millions of men were drilled not only to fight the human enemy but germs as well; the rules of individual and collective hygiene were a fundamental part of their training.

The First World War also led to advances in methods and organisation. The military concern with record-keeping accustomed doctors to making fuller and more regular records of their patients' case histories when they returned to civilian practice. They likewise got used to having the services of a professionally staffed laboratory at their disposal. Experience of transporting and treating wounded men would carry over into peacetime with better ambulance and emergency services for victims of industrial accidents. The widespread use of X-rays, to detect pleurisy and pneumonia as well as in

surgical cases, sharpened the expertise of radiologists. Blood transfusion became a routine procedure which no longer required the supervision of a highly skilled surgeon.

As artillery fire was by far the most common cause of casualties, leading to horrendous disfigurements and disabilities, surgeons focused their efforts on developing better reconstructive techniques and technicians on constructing better artificial limbs. The recognition of shell shock as an illness did much to raise the prestige of psychiatry. Venereal disease, which in peacetime had a

COMPACT CARE   This ingenious 1928 German sidecar ambulance was designed for use with a motorcycle.

PRICE OF GLORY   A casualty of the Russo-Japanese war of 1904-5 has a limb amputated in a Hiroshima hospital. The nurses on the right were probably seconded from Britain, Japan's ally.

seventh of the British army in India regularly out of action at any one time, was tackled by blunt 'education', the distribution of condoms and treatment with Paul Ehrlich's arsenic-based 'wonder drug' Salvarsan.

In the postwar period major companies built on this wartime progress by providing medical care for their employees and their families, believing that it raised productivity and morale and cut down malingering. The French railway system employed some 1500 doctors to care for a labour force which, with its dependants, numbered 600 000.

In this new age the prestige of medicine rose considerably. Patients came to expect more from their doctors, but they also held them in awe. In one British industrial town a local practitioner campaigned against the over-consumption of fried food by smashing families' cast-iron frying pans against the stone step when he made a house call. None dared say him nay, although every housewife immediately went out and got another one.

While the priest or minister became the butt of popular mockery in an increasingly secular age, the doctor was rarely derided. School curricula reinforced the heroic image of medicine by recounting the life stories of such titanic figures as Edward Jenner (pioneer of vaccination), Lord Lister (antiseptic

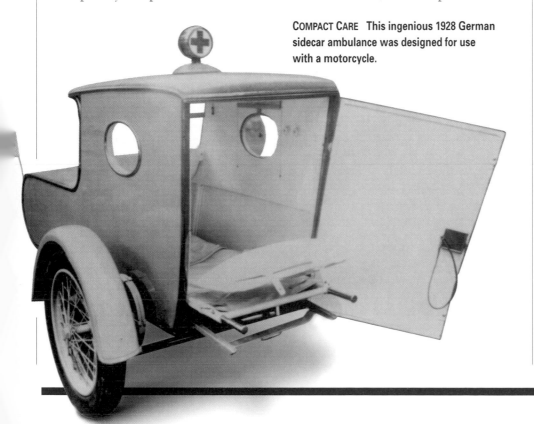

surgery), Florence Nightingale (nursing education), Robert Koch (bacteriology) and Louis Pasteur (microbiology).

The enhanced public standing of the medical profession greatly increased its political clout in such matters as nutrition, housing and working conditions. In capital cities leaders of the medical profession were earnestly consulted by government ministers and hobnobbed with celebrities. At the other end of the social scale, in rural communities, it was often the local practitioner who lived in the best house and was the first to have a telephone and motor car. These conveniences enabled him to cope with a much-increased case-load, and also marked him out as a person of consequence.

The advance of medical science

Outside Germany, medical research before the First World War had been almost exclusively in the hands of physicians and surgeons. During the 1920s, however, the German-style multidisciplinary approach, drawing on chemists and physicists as well as medics, spread to other countries. Dramatic advances in biochemistry and sciences such as bacteriology followed, producing a series of seemingly miraculous new treatments.

Insulin for the treatment of diabetes was first synthesised at the University of Toronto in 1922. The importance of this achievement was recognised at once and earned the researchers F.G. Banting and J.J.R. Macleod the 1923 Nobel prize for medicine. In Germany IG Farben, the chemicals giant, made a major breakthrough in 1932 with the creation of Prontosil, the first man-made

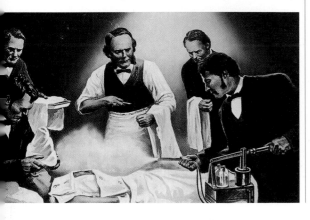

ANTISEPTIC   After seeing amputees die of infection, the 19th-century surgeon Joseph Lister pioneered the use of a carbolic-acid spray to combat postoperative infections.

LIFELINE   A US medical orderly in the Second World War administers plasma to a casualty. Since then, field transfusions have drastically reduced the death rate from major wounds.

drug capable of attacking bacterial infections such as meningitis, pneumonia and rheumatic and puerperal fever.

The most important medical revolution to emerge from the Second World War was the use of antibiotics – naturally occurring substances (in, for example, fungi) that are capable of destroying bacteria. These had been known about since the start of the century, and the most famous, penicillin, had been discovered by the Scotsman Alexander Fleming as early as 1928. But it was not until the mid 1940s that drug companies learnt how to isolate and prepare antibiotics in large quantities. The impact first of penicillin, then of streptomycin and other antibiotics was huge, taking the sting, so it appeared, out of such dreaded diseases as pneumonia and tuberculosis.

As medical experts seemed to be eliminating many of the scourges of earlier centuries, so any revelation of the limitations of their powers became that much more terrifying. Infantile paralysis – poliomyelitis – was an example. A viral infection which could paralyse or kill, polio was particularly virulent in attacking the very young, although older people could also get it. An Australian outbreak in 1937 was centred in Victoria and led the

TAKING THE CREDIT FOR PENICILLIN

As every British schoolchild knows, penicillin was invented by Sir Alexander Fleming. In fact Fleming, working at St Mary's Hospital, Paddington, London, discovered penicillin in 1928 quite by chance and regarded its bacteria-killing qualities as little more than an interesting curiosity.

A decade later two Oxford researchers, Australian Howard Florey and German-Russian refugee Ernst Chain, took a new interest in Fleming's discovery and, having produced meagre quantities of penicillin from a mould of brewer's yeast, used it successfully to treat child patients under threat of death from certain kinds of infection. They published the results of their treatments in The Lancet on August 28, 1940. Four days later Fleming turned up in Oxford, fired with renewed interest in his discovery.

The Second World War had recently broken out but, although Florey had proved the clinical efficacy of penicillin against germ infections, he was unable to synthesise it in large enough quantities for the military to use it in treating wounds. That was the achievement of the giant US drug companies, who brought it on stream just in time for the Allied invasion of Normandy and the Soviet advance into eastern Europe, thus saving tens of thousands of lives.

In 1945 Fleming, Florey and Chain shared the Nobel prize for medicine, though the Oxford team could scarcely bring themselves to speak to the bumptious and opportunistic Fleming.

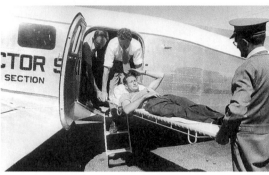

panic-stricken authorities in neighbouring New South Wales to take extraordinary measures of self-protection. Police reinforcements were rushed to patrol interstate crossings, aerodromes, stations and wharves. Children travelling interstate were isolated for 21 days on arrival at their destination.

The United States' most famous victim was its future president, Franklin D. Roosevelt. In the summer of 1921 the fit and active 39-year-old, who had run for vice-president the year before, was stricken with the disease while on holiday and for a time he was left nearly totally paralysed. Determined to recover the use of his legs – which, however, he never did – he spent several winters in Florida, swimming in the warm sea there, and became a regular patron of the mineral baths at Warm Springs, Georgia, where he later established a charitable foundation for the care of polio sufferers. He also returned to politics, though the stigma attached to disability was such that he had to disguise the full extent of his paralysis. For public appearances he had to be propped up, usually by his two sons, one on each side of him, as he imitated a kind of rolling walk to the podium or his seat.

Polio was again endemic in the USA in 1942-53, peaking at 33 344 cases in 1950. Effective vaccines, developed separately by the Americans Jonas Salk and Albert Sabin, ended this curse from the mid 1950s.

Beyond the bedside manner

By mid century doctors were more and more becoming mini-scientists. Their predecessors in 1900 had been proficient in diagnosing dozens of diseases, but had no idea how to cure many of them. In such cases, a doctor's chief skill had been to inspire confidence in the patient

GRIN AND BARE IT   A reluctant youngster from Buenos Aires receives an injection during a 1956 polio epidemic in Argentina.

MERCY MISSIONS   An English doctor on a house call in 1907 (top) and Australia's flying doctor service in action (above). Doctors were among the first professionals to make use of the century's improvements in transport.

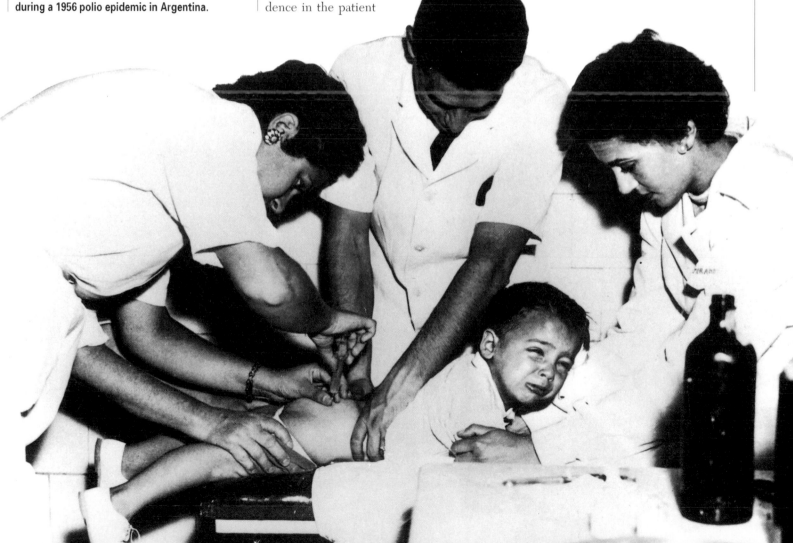

and then trust to the body's own repair mechanisms to do their work, assisted by an appropriate diet and careful nursing.

A convincing bedside manner had then been a basic asset in the physician's professional armoury, to the extent that a certain calculated theatricality was not only permissible but desirable – one was, after all, treating a patient not a disease. At the start of the century, a handbook for practitioners had advised them always to carry a thermometer, not merely to provide information on which to base their diagnosis but also as an 'aid . . . in curing people by heightening their confidence in you'. However, as science came to provide doctors with an ever-increasing range of antibiotics and other drugs, which really could cure illnesses, medical training tended to downgrade such sensitive social skills.

Paradoxically, this trend away from the use of psychological skills in medicine paralleled a growing awareness of the importance of psychology in its own right. At the start of the century, the Viennese physician Sigmund Freud had published his ground-breaking work, *The Interpretation of Dreams*. In the years that followed – against considerable opposition from conventional opinion – he developed his theory that certain forms of mental illness or neurosis are due to the sexual conflicts of early childhood which have never been properly resolved. Later, his former disciple, the Swiss Carl Gustav Jung, researched into such areas as character types, coining the terms extrovert and introvert in the process.

During the same period, a range of treatments was devised, and often discarded, for coping with more serious disorders such as schizophrenia and manic depression. Electric shock treatment was used in the mid-century, though it was later largely discredited. From the 1950s, drugs such as lithium for manic depression were found to be successful in at least stabilising the behaviour of sufferers.

A new age

The power of medicine as a social institution reached its apex around the third quarter of the century. In 1967 Dr Christiaan Barnard, leading a team of 20 surgeons, performed the world's first successful heart transplant operation at the Groote Schuur Hospital in Cape Town. The patient was a grocer, Louis Washkansky, with an incurable heart condition, and the transplanted heart came from an accident victim. In the event, Washkansky died 18 days later – from double pneumonia. Drugs administered to stop his body rejecting the heart had also destroyed his immunity mechanism. A second operation the next year was more successful with the patient surviving just over a year and a half. Twenty years later

MYSTERIES OF THE MIND   While Jung (above) and Freud probed the complexities of neurosis, the usual treatment for sufferers from serious psychiatric illnesses was incarceration. A US doctor in the 1920s stands with a patient diagnosed as insane (left).

heart-transplant patients were routinely surviving for five years or more and successful kidney, liver and lung transplants were becoming relatively commonplace.

Meanwhile, another seeming miracle had come in 1978 when the first 'test-tube baby' was born in Britain. An egg from the mother had been fertilised in a test tube using sperm from the father and then implanted in the mother's womb. Subsequently, *in vitro* fertilisation became increasingly common for infertile parents, though it raised a number of ethical problems which led some countries to ban certain forms of it: for example, surrogate motherhood when the fertilised egg is implanted not in the mother's womb but in another woman's.

Now, it seemed, doctors could both cheat death and manufacture life. They were intervening in people's lives in other new ways,

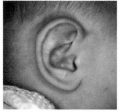

WE CAN FIX IT The deformed ear (above left) of this baby girl, born in 1995, was surgically corrected within days of birth.

too, thanks to some wholesale redefining of what sickness meant. Such conditions as alcoholism and drug abuse came increasingly to be regarded as treatable illnesses, rather than purely moral failings. Surgery could even be used, not merely to save life, but also to improve on it – with enough money, surplus fat, an undersized bosom or a sagging neckline could all be corrected.

Power over the public imagination was matched by power over the public purse. Expenditure on health came to absorb an ever-increasing portion of every advanced nation's spending. In the United States, allowing for population growth and inflation, it rose seven-fold between 1940 and 1975. By the 1990s, many Western European countries were spending more than 10 per cent of their gross national product on health care. The act of giving birth, for example, which still commonly happened at home around 1940, had become routinely hospitalised, involving teams of specialists using expensive hi-tech equipment. Thousands of babies' lives were saved as a result, but the increased cost was considerable.

The tide turns

In the end, medical science's very success helped to produce its own crisis. Doctors, surgeons and scientists continued to push back the frontiers of what was understood about health and disease and what could be done to alleviate or even banish suffering. From the 1960s, for example, thousands of people with arthritic hip joints were granted a new lease of pain-free life by the artificial hip-replacement operation. In the following decades a stream of new technology, from body-scanners to the use of lasers, transformed doctors' and surgeons' ability to diagnose and treat illness.

As the century drew to its close, the power of medical science to achieve seeming miracles had not abated, yet there was a definite crisis in healthcare in advanced countries. The

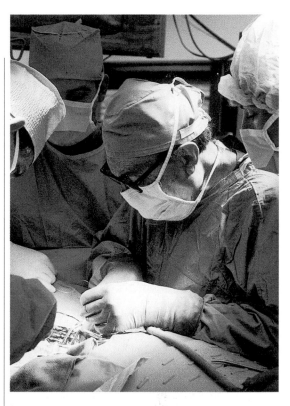

HEART MENDER By the 1980s open heart surgery had become a standard procedure.

sheer spiralling cost of it was a major concern for governments anxious to trim their budgets. People's very expectations of medicine could lead to a corresponding sense of disillusion or at least disappointment when it seemed to fail them. No cure for cancer had yet been found. The advent of AIDS, mysterious and seemingly inexorable in its onslaught, served as a brutal reminder that there were still very real limits to what doctors could do. The mere fact that many common diseases were no longer killers and therefore that people were living longer had opened the gates to previously rarer ailments: for instance, post-menopausal diseases such as osteoporosis, which had not been such a problem 100 years ago, simply because fewer women survived for many years after the menopause. At the same time, scientific advances could also yield disturbing results. Advances in genetics promised new ways of treating hereditary diseases from cystic fibrosis to muscular dystrophy, but they also raised ethical conundrums about how far we should go in tampering with the genetic codings of fellow human beings.

Even some of the achievements of earlier decades were being thrown in doubt. By the end of the century TB was once more on the increase, even in Western countries, and so, on a worldwide scale, was malaria, thought to have been largely contained by insecticides

MINOR MIRACLES Louise Brown (left), the first test-tube baby, celebrates her second birthday in 1980. Also in the 1980s, a young patient awaits an X-ray (above).

THE ALTERNATIVES From the traditional healer to moxibustion (right) – a Chinese treatment in which herbs are burnt on acupuncture needles – natural therapies now exist alongside Western medicine.

WATER BABIES These 1990s babies swim with eyes open and without fear. Some believe that 'natural' birth in a warm birthing pool lessens the trauma for a baby.

and antimalarial drugs. By the early 1990s the anopheles mosquito, the carrier of the malarial parasite, was becoming resistant to the insecticides, and in many parts of the world the parasite itself was becoming resistant to the drugs. In the mid 1990s a drug derived from the wormwood shrub offered new hope, proving effective against the newly resistant parasites. But this presented a commercial problem. The drug had been used for centuries in traditional Chinese medicine, so no drug company could apply for a patent on it. Without a monopoly, no company could be sure of earning sufficient profits to make it worth their while to produce the drug relatively cheaply and in large quantities.

Another significant trend across the Western world was the growing interest in alternative therapies. Some women were even willing to experiment with new techniques when giving birth – the birthing pool, for example, with the baby emerging not into the air as normally but into a pool of water kept at blood temperature.

In Britain alone around 5 million people were regularly using alternative therapies, from acupuncture to osteopathy, by the mid 1990s, and the number of practitioners was growing year by year. In part this represented a return to the notion of the medical practitioner as healer rather than scientist, treating the mind and body as a whole –'holistic medicine' was a popular catchphrase. It was also a reaction against the use of drugs which in occasional, well-publicised cases proved to have dangerous side effects. 'Natural' treatments, such as herbal or homeopathic remedies, were seen to be much safer. In fact, this was open to doubt. Some homeopathic remedies were known in certain circumstances to lead to digestive problems, for example, and a lack of regulation in some countries meant that woefully underqualified practitioners occasionally set up in the healing business, sometimes with fatal results. Nonetheless, the popularity of 'complementary' medicine continued to grow in advanced countries, and the

attitude of orthodox medicine, initially scornful, if not downright hostile, tended to soften as doctors recognised the benefits of the holistic approach. The century that had seen such astonishing advances in medical science, transforming the power of the doctor and surgeon to heal as well as diagnose, had also brought reminders of the limits of their powers and the possibility that healing, or at least the alleviation of problems, could be effected in other, subtler ways.

NEW LIFE THROUGH THE KEYHOLE

A report in the British *Daily Express* in 1993 records successful keyhole surgery on a Scottish boy:

'Wonder-boy David Taylor last night told of his joy at making British medical history. Pioneering keyhole surgery opened up an artery deep in his lungs. It saved him from having a heart and lung transplant. And if that had failed heart failure would have killed David in early adulthood or middle age.

' "Now I feel terrific to be the first boy in Britain to have had this operation", said nine-year-old David. It was carried out at Glasgow's Royal Hospital for Sick Children.

'A minute, deflated balloon attached to a tube was inserted into a vein in David's leg and passed through his circulation system into the lung artery. Fitted over the balloon was an expandable stainless steel sheath called a stent. When the balloon was in place it was inflated to expand the stent. Then the balloon was deflated and withdrawn, leaving the stent behind. It has widened David's artery by 75 per cent. And it can be expanded further as David grows.

'David . . . had the three-hour operation on Tuesday. He came round yesterday morning, telling mother Sandra: "I'm hungry, mum. I want some rice crispies . . ."

'His mother said he was "blue" at birth and then survived a heart operation when he was five weeks old. But the blocked lung artery still made the right side of David's heart work at higher pressure. Surgeon Alan Houston said: ". . . the stent should last for the rest of David's life." '

THE WAY WE WORSHIPPED

RELIGION HAS CHANGED MANY OF ITS FORMS BUT RETAINED ITS TRADITIONAL ROLES: TO INSPIRE, CONSOLE, UNITE – AND DIVIDE

On Monday, July 31, 1905, at 8.30 in the evening, Reverend R.J. Bowen began a service at Shell Beach mining camp near Ladysmith, British Columbia. About half the congregation of 200 or so were in little boats moored within earshot of the beach. Accompanied by the lusty singing of a

MAKING DO American worshippers gather for an outdoor meeting. New communities had to wait to gather funds before they could build 'proper' church buildings.

'Welsh Choir' and the reedy piping of a concertina, the congregation sang 'There is a Fountain Filled with Blood' and heard a passage of scripture which was clearly aimed at the younger members of the impromptu congregation: 'Remember Thou the Creator in the days of thy youth.' Then they listened to a sermon, sang two more hymns and dispersed after a blessing from Bowen. An eyewitness recalled: 'Everyone present seemed thoroughly interested in the proceedings . . . The singing was very moving.'

Ladysmith at the beginning of the century was a very new community. Like thousands of others in Canada, Australia and New Zealand, it was steadily building up a regular church congregation. A Church of England parish had been organised there in 1901 and services were held, in Ladysmith itself and in outlying communities such as Shell Beach, whenever the busy minister could fit them in. They were important events for many local people because they were proof that they were truly becoming a

proper community with all the usual trappings of a community – such as a church, or at least church services.

In Ladysmith itself, the services were at first held in a building which doubled as Parish Hall and Sunday School. A constant round of social events organised by the Ladies of the Guild served the dual purpose of fundraising, so that they could erect a proper church and a community building. These included a Strawberry and Ice Cream Social, a High Tea followed by a concert and dance, a Fancy Dress Carnival, a Sherry and Ice Cream Social (admission 10 cents) and moonlight boat cruises 'with musical accompaniment'. Another useful source of funds was a tennis court, where young businessmen played from eight until nine in the morning before starting work and the ladies played midmorning, when their chores were done.

Unfortunately, despite their best endeavours, the people of Ladysmith did not raise the funds they needed, for the time being at least. By 1909, they had $1538.05 for a new church which needed an estimated $4000 to build. In 1910 plans for a purpose-built place of worship were therefore shelved in favour of altering the 'temporary' buildings housing the Church School. A vestry, organ

DEDICATED LIVES Life in closed religious communities, such as that of the Shakers of Mount Lebanon, New York, has continued to appeal to a small minority of believers.

ONWARD CHRISTIAN SOLDIERS Army-style drills
and uniforms attracted city lads to Boys'
Brigades. The idea was to steer the boys
safely from childhood to young adulthood.

FLOWER OF FAITH The
perennial poppy symbolised
sacrifice and renewal to
millions of Allied troops
of the First World War.

loft, octagonal chancel and Gothic windows
would be added and the gasoline lamps
replaced with electric lights. A 'proper' St
John's was not finally dedicated until 1944.

Religion and community were firmly
entwined in 1900, and would remain so for
much of the rest of the century. Churches
of different denominations sponsored
choirs, Boys' Brigades and even soccer
teams. Religious organisations such as
the Salvation Army, founded in 1878 by
the Englishman William Booth, did pioneering work in bringing soup, welfare
and the Gospel to the urban masses.

In many parts of Europe this entwining
spread into politics. Catholic-Protestant
antagonism brought Ulster to the brink
of civil war at various points. In much
of Continental Europe sectarian rivalry
was less significant than struggles over
the relationship between the Roman
Catholic Church and the state. Fiercely
anticlerical feeling existed in France,
Spain, Portugal and Italy – especially
among men, who often still approved
of their womenfolk and children going
to church. Whereas in England the vicar
was frequently a figure of fun, in southern
Europe the priest could be an object of
hatred as well as respect.

In the US, denominational allegiance was
strong, and remained so. Protestants pre-
dominated overall in 1900, but with regular
congregations of 12 million there were twice
as many Roman Catholics as there were
members of the largest Protestant denomination, the Methodists. By the end of the
century Catholics, thanks to a high birthrate
and Hispanic immigration, remained the
largest single denomination and the Baptists
had displaced the Methodists as the biggest
Protestant group. America also had more
Jews than the rest of the world put together.

Despite differences and divergences
between nations and continents, definite
patterns were obvious.
Religious commitment and
participation were stronger in
rural areas and small
towns than they
were in big cities,
among women than
among men, among
the old than among the young. This was
true as the century opened; it would remain
broadly true as it drew to a close.

The Great War

At the start of the First World War the
British journalist and poet J.C. Squire
penned a sardonic ditty:

> *God heard the embattled nations shout*
> *Gott strafe England and God Save the*
>   *King.*
> *Good God, said God,*
> *I've got my work cut out.*

The war definitely did more for superstition
than for religion. Clergy on both sides of the
conflict urged their countrymen to arms as
a duty and prayed fervently for the blessings
of the Almighty on their efforts – only the

MAN-MADE MIRACLE? A cartoon offers a
mock-scientific explanation of how troops
might have been deceived into seeing
the 'Angel of Mons'.

Quakers stood out almost solidly against war
fever. Superstitions flourished among men at
the front who experienced daily the arbi-
trariness of sudden and terrible death at the
hands of a machine-gunner sweeping no-
man's-land experimentally, or a grenade
lobbed over at random from an opposing
trench, or even a shell from one's own side

falling short. Fatalism was the most common attitude, summed up in the belief that if a bullet 'had your name on it' you were marked to die. This curious notion may have been a garbled Christian version of a folk-belief, common among Indian or Turkish Muslim troops, that at the hour appointed for death a leaf, inscribed with the name of the soul in question, falls from the Tree of Life in Paradise.

The most extravagant myths were fostered by a popular press eager for sensation but bamboozled out of hard news by military censorship. One such was the story of the 'Angel of Mons' – variously an angel with a flaming sword, a squadron of angels on horseback, even ghostly bowmen from the field of Agincourt (not too far away), which had supposedly intervened in the Battle of Mons on the Allied side. After the Angel of Mons came the statue of the Virgin Mary in the town of Albert. Located atop the cathedral tower, the statue became a natural target for German gunners and a bombardment in 1915 left her hanging at a perilous angle, apparently suspended on the brink of self-destruction. The rumour began that whoever brought down the statue would lose the war – a myth that proved false as the tower was eventually destroyed by the British in 1918.

When the war finally ended, there was the need to remember. Despite the revulsion many ex-servicemen felt at what they had seen and been through, acts of remembrance at war memorials throughout the former combatant countries were treated with almost universal reverence. The inhabitants of tiny French hamlets would gather round the local memorial and, as the youngest child piped out the names of the fallen, murmur respectfully in ragged chorus '*Mort pour La Patrie*'. Nations erected memorials at battlefield sites on the Western Front associated with their troops – the South Africans at Delville Wood, Canadians at Vimy Ridge. Throughout the century millions who had little use for formal religion or its rituals continued to experience the annual act of remembrance as a moment each year when the realm of the sacred came close to their hearts.

SING OUT! In the Salvation Army, founded by William Booth (right), music and free prayer characterise worship.

Hitting the headlines

After the First World War, although politicians devoted far less time to discussing religious topics than they had done a generation before, religious leaders and organisations continued to pronounce on public affairs and the popular culture of the day. Birth control was denounced, for example, not only by Roman Catholics but, until 1930, by Anglicans too. In the 1920s, fashions such as jazz, the Charleston and short skirts were condemned from the pulpits of all denominations as incitements to immorality.

Individuals, too, made the news in their attempts to influence history. In Germany in the 1930s, a minority of Protestants broke away from the Lutheran mainstream to form a separate church, the Confessing Church, which was one of the few bodies of any

POLAND'S PAPAL PILGRIM

The foreign travels of the Polish Pope John Paul II have called forth astonishing scenes of fervour. In June 1979 he made a particularly moving trip – his first to Poland since his election as Pope, described here by a reporter for the British *Daily Telegraph*:

'Pope John Paul II, who left Krakow as an archbishop seven months ago, returned to Poland at the weekend as the first leader of the Roman Catholic Church ever to set foot in a Communist country.

'The 59-year-old Polish-born Pontiff stooped to kiss the ground after stepping from his Alitalia Boeing 727 jet in Warsaw's scorching sunshine.

'Then, as every church bell in the city and surrounding villages rang, he declared: "I come as a pilgrim . . ."

'The visit, subject of months of tough negotiations between Church and State, is an historic event for Poland's 30 million Catholics who have clung tenaciously to their faith, despite 35 years of Communist rule. . . .

'The formal opening was followed by an ecstatic welcome as the Pope drove seven miles [11 km] in an open float through the city streets [for a Mass in] St John's Cathedral in Warsaw's old city. . . .

'The crowd, estimated at between 900 000 and 2 million people, packed 20 deep against metal barriers all along the route. Plain-clothes police had to haul several of the marshals off the long red carpet laid out for the Pontiff from the tomb of the unknown soldier to Victory Square. The marshals, who were supposed to be holding the crowd back, dashed in front of the Pope and threw themselves at his feet, seeking blessings.

'Admission to the Mass was by ticket only, but one determined nun scrambled between a marshal's legs.'

description that dared to speak out against the Nazi persecution of Jews. One of its leading figures was the theologian Dietrich Bonhöffer, who became an active member of the German anti-Hitler resistance during the Second World War. He paid for this opposition with his life when the Nazi authorities found documents linking him to a failed plot to assassinate the Führer. He was executed on April 9, 1945.

Another priest who came to prominence in the interwar years was Father Charles Coughlin. Ordained a Roman Catholic priest in Detroit, Coughlin began broadcasting sermons and talks to children in 1926. As the USA plunged into Depression the Michigan-based priest's pronouncements became more and more political and ever more extreme. He lambasted Roosevelt's New Deal policies and made vitriolic denunciations of Jews, Wall Street capitalists and communists, all of whom he blamed for the Depression. In 1934 he launched a National Union for Social Justice which recruited 5 million members within two months, but his efforts to win a seat in the House of Representatives proved a fiasco. Undeterred, he continued to preach his message of hate until his magazine *Social Justice* was eventually banned from the mail for violating the 1917 Espionage Act; in 1942 the Church hierarchy belatedly ordered him to stop broadcasting.

The language of faith

In 1909, the American pioneer of black rights Booker T. Washington visited London's East End and watched a street preacher in action: 'He was a young man, fresh from college,

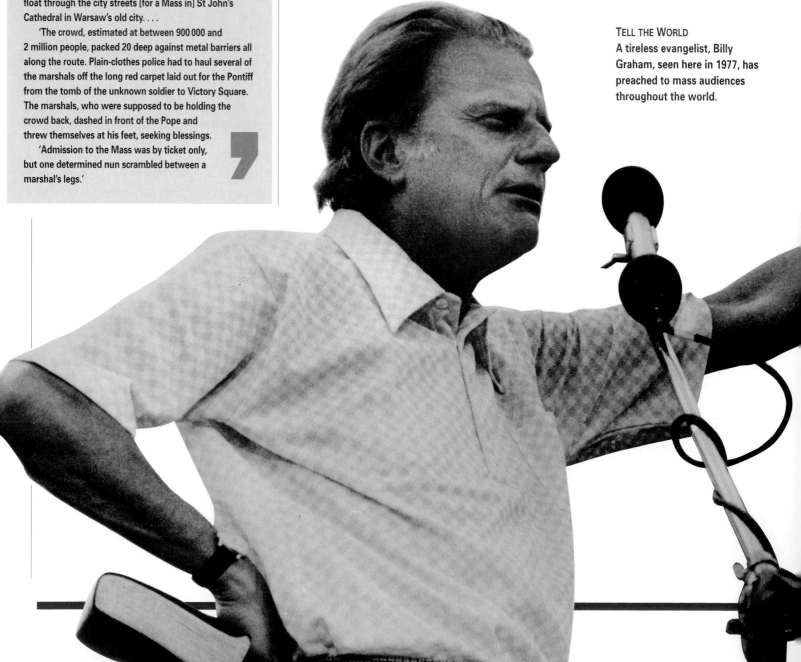

TELL THE WORLD
A tireless evangelist, Billy Graham, seen here in 1977, has preached to mass audiences throughout the world.

BORN AGAIN Two thousand converts are baptised by Jehovah's Witnesses at a lido in west London in 1951.

and he was making a very genuine effort . . . I observed that the people listened respectfully to what he had to say . . . It was only too evident, however, that he was speaking another language than theirs . . . After listening to this man I thought I could understand . . . the great success which the Salvation Army at one time had among the masses . . . it picked its preachers from the streets . . .'

Street preaching, when it was well done, was a vital way of recruiting for the churches at the start of the century. Later, radio and television offered powerful new means of evangelism, while the careers of gifted platform preachers such as the Southern Baptist minister Billy Graham were confirmation that live, face-to-face communication could still yield impressive results. He preached in his

REPACKAGING REVELATION

In 1989 an editor at a British publishing house told a journalist: 'It's just called "The Bible" now. We dropped the word "Holy" to give it a more mass-market appeal.' Another venture in Bible publishing was a Scottish-English version in which only the Devil spoke Standard (Southern, 'Sassenach') English.

first evangelistic campaign in 1946 and 50 years later was still rousing thousands at skilfully organised rallies. He has been the friend of presidents and has taken his message, based on a call to repentance and conversion, all around the globe, from Moscow to Buenos Aires, Paris to Singapore.

Outside the orthodox Christian mainstream the Jehovah's Witnesses, originally founded in the 1870s by the American Charles Taze Russell, perfected the technique of door-to-door evangelism armed with batteries of pamphlets and magazines. Denying the divinity of Christ and preaching the imminence of a final day of judgment, they spread remarkably from the start of the 1940s when they had just 106 000 members worldwide. By 1995, they had more than 5 million.

The language of faith, rather than the channels through which it was communicated, remained a preoccupation for many religious organisations. Most experienced a tension between traditionalists, who regarded their accustomed forms of Scripture and worship as inviolable, and modernisers, who saw an urgent need to reframe the Gospel message in the language of the present. In 1901 a proposal to publish the Gospels in modern Greek provoked such serious riots in Athens that the head of the Orthodox Church resigned and the government fell. At the end of the century, in post-communist Russia, Orthodox priests who tried using modern Russian instead of the almost unintelligible Church Slavonic in their services were treated with profound suspicion by their fellows.

Nonetheless, the importance of Scripture in both the Christian and Jewish traditions ensured that new translations of the sacred writings were

TV, SCANDAL AND THE GOSPEL

'Why should the Devil have all the best tunes?' asked William Booth, founder of the Salvation Army, who shrewdly saw how military-style brass bands could be used to draw crowds and drown out hecklers at the same time. A century later America's 'televangelists' applied the same thinking to the century's most powerful medium. Their priorities, however, were often rather different from those of the ruggedly upright Booth. A 1986 analysis revealed that America's top ten TV evangelists spent between 12 per cent and 42 per cent of their airtime appealing for funds. In 1987 Oklahoma-born Oral Roberts warned his supporters that God might 'call Oral Roberts home' if they failed to come up with $8 million. A donation from a Florida racetrack owner saved God the trouble.

TV saved Oral Roberts, but not some of his fellows. Also in 1987, a sex scandal caught up with South Carolinan Jim Bakker of PTL (Praise the Lord) Television. In the same year PTL, which had major housing and theme park interests, and $70 million of debts, was forced into bankruptcy. In 1988 Jimmy Swaggart, who had denounced Bakker as 'a cancer on the body of Christ', was forced to admit having visited a prostitute – after being confronted with photographs of the encounter. This spate of disclosures not only damaged all televangelists, guilty of sexual or financial impropriety or not, but brought an unexpected bonus to 'regular' churches which took the opportunity to distance themselves by claiming squeaky-clean standards of accountability and disclosure.

STAND BY YOUR MAN Jim Bakker poses with his wife Tammy. He confessed to adultery with a church secretary and payment of hush money.

undertaken. In the 1920s the German Jewish scholars Martin Buber and Franz Rosenzweig produced a masterly translation into modern German of the Jewish Bible – the Old Testament. Christian scholars used insights from the study of ancient texts to present the Bible in language that was fresh, and later 'non-sexist'. In 1946, after 17 years' work by 22 scholars from 44 Protestant denominations, the Revised Standard Version

SOLIDARITY A Polish Catholic confesses to a priest. Through decades of alien communist overlordship, the Church helped to maintain the strength of Polish national identity.

of the New Testament was published in the United States to replace the American Standard Version of 1901. Roman Catholic scholars in Jerusalem published the Jerusalem Bible in 1956, a translation into French that was later retranslated into numerous languages. The New Testament volume of the New English Bible appeared in 1961, selling a million copies in Britain in its first week.

A new pentecost

From the Albanian-born Mother Teresa working among the destitute of Calcutta to the Polish Pope John Paul II, the first non-Italian pontiff in nearly half a millennium,

HOLY FATHER Pope John XXIII gives the traditional blessing – *Urbi et Orbi* 'To the City and the World' – after his coronation.

the Roman Catholic Church has produced a crop of remarkable figures in the 20th century. But more significant probably than any individual was its Second Vatican Council which, from 1962 to 1965, transformed just about every aspect of its life. It was called by the most unlikely of revolutionaries, Pope John XXIII, elected as a *papa di passaggio*, 'interim pope', in 1958 when he was already 76. Until then he had never identified himself with reform movements in the Church, yet he was to unleash the most thoroughgoing changes Roman Catholics had experienced since the days of the Reformation and Counter-Reformation in the 16th and 17th centuries. His papacy lasted fewer than five years but they were enough to make him one of the best-loved popes of modern times.

In calling the Council, his avowed purpose was to 'bring the Church up to date'. In the process he had the rare honesty to admit that the Church needed new life – a 'New Pentecost' – breathed into it. Despite vehement opposition from some cardinals, who hoped to delay plans until the old man died, when they could be conveniently forgotten, he won his way, presiding before his death over the Council's first session in the autumn of 1962.

During its lifetime the Council abandoned the Church's traditional line of denouncing

members of other Christian denominations as heretics and instead offered the hand of ecumenical friendship. It also expressed its regret for the anti-Semitism of its past. Within the Church, the Council encouraged greater participation by lay people and approved the use of vernacular languages rather than Latin in the liturgy. Catholic clergy in the United States began to include some English prayers in their services as

INTERNATIONAL MISSION Known as 'Mother of the Poor', Mother Teresa was born in Albania, but dedicated her life to the poor of Calcutta, where she died in 1997.

SACRED CIRCLE Catholic bishops gather in synod at Rome. Roman Catholicism remains the world's dominant form of Christianity.

early as 1964. By Easter 1970 the entire Mass was being said in English, Italian, Spanish and other vernacular tongues – despite the opposition of ultra-traditionalists such as the French Archbishop Marcel Lefebvre (later excommunicated).

Horror and rebirth

For Judaism, the 20th century has been marked by two events: one appalling, the other the fulfilment of a long-held dream. The Nazi Holocaust cost the lives of some 6 million Jews in German-occupied territories

CHOSEN PEOPLE For Jews, Jerusalem's Wailing Wall (left) is a place of pilgrimage, prayer – and lamentation. Religious observance (above) lies at the heart of traditional Jewish family life.

between 1933 and 1945. The foundation of the state of Israel in 1948 fulfilled the Zionist dream of a return to the Holy Land which had emerged in the 19th century, partly in response to growing anti-Semitism in many regions of Europe.

Both events helped, in their different ways, to sharpen Jewish people's awareness of their identity. However, in many instances this was a cultural rather than a religious phenomenon. Even in Israel there were frictions between those who saw their religion as an all-embracing way of life – which affected everything from what they ate to how they dressed and worked – and 'secularised' Jews for whom their Jewishness was more a question of national or cultural identity. Outside Israel many Jewish religious leaders, including Britain's Chief Rabbi in the early 1990s, publicly lamented declining attendances at synagogues and the increasing numbers of Jews who were marrying outside the faith.

For all that, Judaism, which had suffered in mid century one of the worst traumas of its long and often troubled history, was in many ways stronger at the end of the century than it had been for hundreds of years. In the United States, the Jewish community

commanded a respect and authority out of all proportion to its numbers – nearly 6 million. The state of Israel, despite continuing conflicts with its Arab neighbours, was unlikely to disappear.

The spread of Islam

In 1900 the relatively few English-speaking people who knew what Muslims were generally referred to them as Muhammadans – a deeply offensive term to believers, since it implied worship of their Prophet, rather than of God. *Mohammedanism*, a standard survey by the eminent Sir Hamilton Gibb, published in 1949 by the Oxford University Press, did not change its title to *Islam* until a revised edition appeared in 1968. If the experts could display such insensitivity, what hope was there of greater understanding among the general population?

The long territorial separation of Islam and Christendom was ended by the unravelling of the European colonial empires and the growth of international migration in the years following the Second World War. By the 1980s there were at least a million Muslims in Britain, a population three times as large as the long-established Jewish community. Germany had perhaps twice as many Muslims as Britain. France had 4 million, making Islam the country's second religion, after Roman Catholicism.

While most Muslim migrants learned the languages of their adopted countries, only a small proportion of them became so culturally assimilated that they abandoned their religion or their identity as Muslims. More usually, they established mosques: at first in converted private houses then, as they prospered, in former churches or purpose-built premises. With foreign support, usually from oil-rich countries such as Saudi Arabia or Kuwait, they sometimes established specifically Muslim schools, segregated by sex, where children could pursue a full-time education with a curriculum organised on Islamic principles. By the 1990s Britain had almost 100 such schools. In 1996 a Birmingham primary school became the first state school to organise its religious education programme from an exclusively Islamic perspective.

A woman's place

In 1900 most religious bodies assumed that a woman's place was on her knees – either at prayer or polishing the floor of the church. Women were invariably more regular in their attendance at services, usually outnumbering men by roughly two to one. They organised

THE WORD Muslim girls in Western countries (left) have fought for the right to keep their heads covered. Study of the Qur'an (below) lies at the core of a strict Muslim education.

TO BE A BLACK PILGRIM

LATE CONVERT Malcolm X belatedly abandoned Black Muslim beliefs to embrace the universal non-racialism of orthodox Islam.

Malcolm Little (1925-65) saw his family home burned down by a Ku Klux Klan mob. At the age of 21, imprisoned for burglary, he converted to the Black Muslim – or Nation of Islam – faith, an American variant of Islam preaching strict personal discipline and the segregation of blacks from whites. Discarding his 'white slave name' in favour of the anonymous Malcolm X, he became a close lieutenant of the Nation of Islam's leader Elijah Muhammad after serving his seven-year sentence.

He was a brilliant platform speaker and won a devoted following among Black Muslims but his bitter invective against whites earned the hatred of many other Americans. When he dismissed the assassination of John F. Kennedy as a 'case of chickens coming home to roost', even Elijah Muhammad realised he had gone too far and suspended him from duty. Malcolm X responded by forming his own breakaway movement and decided to undertake a pilgrimage to Mecca – the *hajj*. This experience changed his life. The essence of *hajj* is the common submission of people of all races before the majesty of God. Adopting the name El-Hajj Malik El-Shabazz, the former Malcolm X converted to conventional Islam, renouncing his anti-white racism. Black Muslims denounced him as a traitor and threatened his life. Shortly afterwards he was shot dead at a rally. His posthumously published *Autobiography* made him a hero to black youth.

fund-raising events, arranged flowers and taught Sunday School. But the leading of acts of worship was a male prerogative. Only the Quakers and Salvation Army treated women as anything like the equals of men in such matters.

The admission of women to the ordained ministry in Protestant churches has occurred piecemeal – and at the cost of creating a major obstacle to the forging of closer links with the Roman and Orthodox churches. In 1958 the Evangelical Church of the Palatinate in West Germany and the Lutheran Church in Sweden both voted to admit women to ordination. In 1969 the Church of Scotland admitted its first woman minister. British Methodists voted to follow their example the following year.

In the world-wide Anglican community the struggle for women's ordination was particularly protracted. The first women to be admitted to the Anglican priesthood, Joyce Bennett and Jane Hwang Hsien Yuen, were ordained in Hong Kong in 1971. In the following year, 11 more were ordained in the USA. This step had, by 1977, provoked the

formation of a breakaway Anglican Church in North America, which claimed to be the true heir to the Anglican tradition. In England itself the General Synod voted to admit women to the priesthood only in 1992. The first ordinations took place at Bristol Cathedral in 1994.

FERVOUR Evangelical and Charismatic churches have evolved a style of liturgy emphasising involvement and spontaneity.

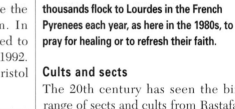

FAITH AND HOPE A scientific age still sees thousands flock to Lourdes in the French Pyrenees each year, as here in the 1980s, to pray for healing or to refresh their faith.

Cults and sects

The 20th century has seen the birth of a range of sects and cults from Rastafarianism to the Holy Spirit Association for the Unification of Christianity ('Moonies'). Within Christianity it has seen the growth of Pentecostalism and the Charismatic movement within the mainstream denominations, both emphasising 'speaking in tongues', healing and other miraculous phenomena. Spiritual hunger among the young and the disoriented found a diversity of outlets, such as transcendental meditation and the Hare Krishna sect in the 1960s, and the 'New Age' movement in the 1980s – a mélange of the occult, the holistic, the tribal and the oriental, which inspired its devotees to participate in drumming, dancing, dowsing, casting runes and sniffing trees.

Anyone tempted to view the 20th century as the era in which traditional, organised religion faded away in the industrialised world, however, should consider its continuing impact on politics and culture, social and sexual behaviour, and the solidarity of communities. Millions have continued to flock to Lourdes in southern France to pray for intercession by Our Lady on behalf of the

that organised religion has been failing to develop in other ways. Few may now become hermits but thousands choose to go on 'retreats' to pray and meditate. More people are perhaps meeting for prayer in each other's houses than have done so since early Christian times. If Catholic Croats, Orthodox Serbs and Muslim Bosnians resorted to 'ethnic cleansing' in the wreckage of a country that had supposedly been communist and secular for half a century, religion also proved a powerful force in sustaining Polish nationhood through alien occupation and atheistic rule earlier on in the century. If millions came to reject religion as divisive, irrelevant or simply boring, millions more continued to turn to it for succour and solace in this world, as well as salvation in the next.

CONVERSION AND CONTINUITY Members of the Hare Krishna sect celebrate their faith on the streets of Berlin (below) and Hindu women maintain their faith at a temple in London (bottom).

WISDOMS OF THE EAST

One of the features of the 20th century has been the willingness of Westerners – especially intellectuals and the young – to investigate, rather than dismiss, Asian religions and philosophies. This may have arisen partly from disillusionment with conventional Christianity, partly from the inspiration of spiritual personalities such as Gandhi and the Dalai Lama.

In Christmas Humphrey, a senior British judge, orthodox Buddhism found an eloquent spokesman, as did Sufism, a mystical strand of Islam, in the essayist Idries Shah. The Lebanese-American Khalil Gibran, a self-professed disciple of the English mystic William Blake, reached millions through his lyrical meditations on love and death, of which *The Prophet*, first published in 1923, is best known.

During the 1960s Hindu spirituality exerted a particular influence, most notably in the world of pop music and entertainment. The Beatles made a much-publicised pilgrimage to India to sit at the feet of the Maharishi Mahesh Yogi and absorb the principles of transcendental meditation. Saffron-robed Hare Krishna missionaries became a regular sight along the streets of Western cities. British singer-turned-businessman Adam Faith learned to 'centre' his life through yoga. American film star Richard Gere became a devotee of Tantric Buddhism.

The spiritual impact of these eastern currents was, however, probably less profound than their influence on music, costume design, fashionable decor and the cause of vegetarianism.

WE DO This mass marriage ceremony took place in 1982 for members of the Korean Reverend Moon's Unification Church.

stricken; in Portugal a major new shrine was established following a vision of the Virgin at Fatima in 1917. The black clergyman and civil rights activist Martin Luther King won the Nobel prize for peace in 1964; the Catholic nun Mother Teresa won it in 1979; the Dalai Lama in 1989.

Church attendance may be falling in the Western world, but this does not mean

A START IN LIFE

EDUCATION, AT ONE TIME THE PRIVILEGE OF THE FEW, IS NOW REGARDED AS A BASIC HUMAN RIGHT FOR ALL

The child was all-important. The aim of education should be to build on a child's existing interests, to stimulate, encourage and help them to develop. The teacher should not be a drillmaster, forcing pupils to learn by rote and imposing tasks. Rather he or she should be a mentor, working with pupils, helping them to find their own ways through the different fields of learning. The purpose of schooling was, as far as possible, to encourage children to grow and reach their full potential in every area of their lives. These were not the ideas of a 1960s radical, but of John Dewey, a respected American philosopher at the University of Chicago. He published his theories in two books that first appeared in 1899 and 1902.

As societies have been transformed during the 20th century, so has education, though practice has often lagged behind theory. A character in the Irish-born George Bernard Shaw's 1907 play *Major Barbara* confidently asserts that 'nobody can say a word against Greek; it stamps a man at once as an educated gentleman'. In most advanced countries in 1900, stamping was essentially what schooling was about: rote-learning in the classroom, Greek and other classical subjects for the (predominantly male) elite, basic literacy and numeracy for the masses. Portraits of monarchs or presidents and rituals such as regular parades around the national flag instilled patriotism. The social order depended on hierarchy and deference, and although there were many dedicated and inspiring teachers, and pupils who benefited from their lessons, most education systems were aimed primarily at buttressing that order.

Change was inevitable but came quite gradually. Among the visionaries was the Italian Maria Montessori, founder of the worldwide system for teaching young children that now bears her name. In 1907 she established her first Casa dei Bambini (Children's House) in Rome's San Lorenzo slum quarter. Scorning conventional classrooms which ranked children in rows, 'like butterflies mounted on pins', Montessori focused on providing children with concrete learning experiences which harnessed their curiosity. She used beads, rods, cylinders and slabs of wood of different sizes and colours to encourage the basic skills of coordination and perception fundamental to more complex learning tasks. Sceptics were confounded by the sight of infants as young as three, uncoerced and rapt in concentration on their

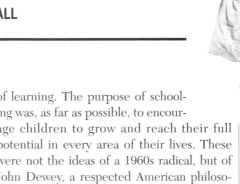

BOOK LEARNING Smartly uniformed middle-class German schoolchildren in the 1920s study a schoolbook. Old-fashioned drills and teaching methods were still very much the norm in the interwar years.

HELPING HAND In many countries, such as the Netherlands, the churches played – and still play – a key role in public education.

tasks for up to an hour at a time. Later, the interwar years saw a burst of small experimental schools set up by other reformers such as the Scotsman A.S. Neill and the Dutch Kees Boeke. They similarly focused on the need to fit the education to the child, rather than the child to the education. Though their short-term impact was limited,

many of their ideas would be picked up later by more mainstream reformers.

By mid century structural change was definitely on the agenda. Modern economies needed a workforce that knew more than just the basics of reading, adding and subtracting. In Britain, in the thick of the Second World War, the Education Act of 1944 made education up to secondary school level compulsory for all and reorganised the system so that it was available free in all state-maintained schools. After the war, the

French authorities raised the age at which children were permitted to finish their schooling from 13 to 16.

In education, as in most other areas, the 1960s and early 70s brought a ferment of ideas. In the universities of France, Germany and the United States, students demonstrated against the Vietnam War and the apartheid regime in South Africa, but they also demanded a greater say in the running of their own courses and institutions. German universities, for much of the century a bastion of conservatism, were overhauled following a decision of the Federal Constitutional Court in 1973 which allowed students an important decision-making role.

At the same time, those in authority were asking questions about the place and purpose of education in modern democratic societies. Deference was less important; adaptability and a supply of research workers and middle-grade specialists were much more important. New teaching methods

TOP OF THE FORM Prizewinners line up at a French primary school in 1947. A generation later, educational theorists often condemned school prizes as elitist and divisive.

PLEASE, MISS A German geography class and a French textbook – both emphasised patriotic pride in their nation's territory and heritage.

FENCING FOR HONOUR

Well into the 20th century, rapier duels (*Mensuren*) were a part of life at German universities. The British commentator William Harbutt Dawson described the practice:

'Virtually all the students' associations, except the theological, require their members to engage in a series of *Mensuren* . . . There is no danger in the exercise, though the weapons used frequently inflict severe wounds, which leave their mark for life. For safety's sake the hands, eyes, neck, and breast are protected . . . The face and skull are thus the parts really exposed to the cuts of the glittering blade. At every *Mensur* a medical student is present . . . He discharges his duty well, and many are the stories of the surgical feats which are performed in emergencies of this kind – of how nose-ends and ear-tips are gathered expeditiously from the ground and replaced so skilfully as not to betray the temporary excision. . . .'

were widely adopted, often along the lines detailed by Dewey, Montessori and other earlier reformers. The old two-track approach – one set of schools for the ruling class, another for the ruled – was increasingly abandoned or modified in favour of more 'comprehensive' education.

Them and us

Comments from the school inspectors' log books in the English industrial city of Salford around the turn of the century paint a dismal picture: 'Classrooms are insufficient – four for 450 pupils – and one is without desks'; 'The children are well behaved and under industrious if not very intelligent instruction'; 'The staff here must be strengthened at once, both in numbers and qualifications'.

Standards and conditions in 1900 varied across the advanced world. In Britain, one observer reckoned that after a generation of compulsory elementary schooling, a fifth of the working class was still totally illiterate and another fifth virtually so. Within the schools, classrooms were either, according to the season, fetid with the sweat of verminous juvenile bodies or freezing to all but the fortunate few who sweltered by the single stove. Apart from the basics of literacy and numeracy, slum children were taught stories from the Bible, history based on the lives of the kings and queens of England and geography which celebrated the fruitful bounty of the British Empire. They sang hymns; other than that, their contact with music was minimal, and

THEIR MASTER'S VOICE Kaiser Wilhelm II and his empress gaze down on schoolchildren in German East Africa. Teaching in such schools stressed the superiority of Western culture.

their contact with science or art or organised sport non-existent. Class-bound attitudes prevailed in England, where most elementary schools actively discouraged individual ambition, sure to be a cause only of disappointment or, worse still, of discontent. This was less true in Scotland and Wales, where schooling had long been honoured as the

path out of poverty and even the learned professions recruited from the working class, so that the son of a miner might indeed become a preacher, a lawyer or a doctor.

Across the North Sea in Germany, the scene was in many ways more encouraging, though also more rigid. Elementary schooling was compulsory for all, and for the mass of children this meant the *Volksschule* from which they graduated at the age of 14. Volksschule was free, with a curriculum tightly directed by central government. In its way, it provided a rounded education including a concern for body and spirit. As well as the basics of reading, writing and arithmetic, an

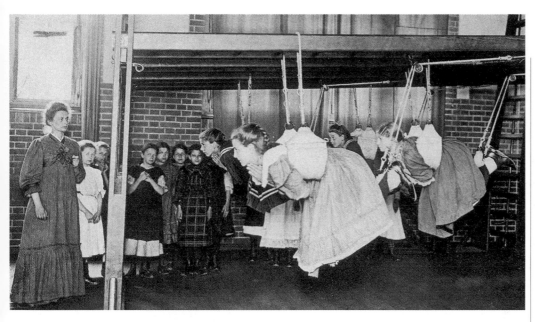

THEORY BEFORE PRACTICE German girls learn to swim without actually getting wet. Physical education for girls was often accepted only hesitantly.

another. The best a working-class boy could hope for was 'continuation school' which would further his vocational training. The German authorities wanted a disciplined, well-trained, able-bodied workforce – and by and large they got it, and kept it in its place.

For the children of the German upper and upper middle classes, meanwhile, progress through to secondary school and then university depended on the *Vorschule* (Preschool). This was fee-paying – keeping it out of the reach of the working class – and took children from the ages of six to nine. At nine, they had a choice of three kinds of secondary school, ranging from the *Gymnasium*, biased towards the classics, to the *Oberrealschule*, which placed more emphasis on 'modern' subjects – science, mathematics and modern languages. The *Realgymnasium* was a half-way house between the other two. Of the three, the Gymnasium, with its emphasis on the classics, was the most prestigious. All

important emphasis was placed on gymnastics and religion. Boys were trained for manual labouring jobs, girls for the domestic sphere. The education was practical – but strictly limited. Even in England, a bright working-class child could at least hope for a scholarship to the local grammar school (for boys) or high school (for girls), and thence maybe to the heights of a university education. In Germany, there was little chance of a child progressing from a Volksschule to a secondary school, let alone university. The cycles of the Volksschule and the various kinds of secondary school were deliberately kept out of step with one

TWO NATIONS Boys from Eton – Britain's most exclusive private school – make their way to a cricket match in 1934. London slum children have their lessons out of doors in a 1937 heatwave.

three kinds of school were limited to boys. The first secondary schools for girls had been set up comparatively recently, in the 1870s.

The new utopians

Of the prophetic educators working in the first half of the century, none was more influential than Maria Montessori. The first woman in Italy to graduate as a doctor, Montessori initially focused on the problems of children with learning difficulties. She was a professor at the age of 26, lecturing on hygiene, teaching methods and anthropology. Later, in her Case dei Bambini, she applied to average, but disadvantaged, children the methods she had developed to overcome the difficulties of the handicapped. The outstanding success of her methods set her on a 40-year globetrotting career of lecturing and advising that took her throughout Europe, India and the United States. Her core belief about human learning was summarised in the title of the last of her many books – *The Absorbent Mind*.

Another major influence on later progressive education was the example of a very small number of much-publicised experimental schools. Almost all of these were private, established in the aftermath of the First World War. Their founders were idealists who rejected what they regarded as narrow, nationalistic and authoritarian teaching methods which they blamed for the carnage of the war and the willingness with which millions had meekly gone to their deaths.

At the *Werkplaats* (workshop) in Bilthoven, near Utrecht in the Netherlands, Kees Boeke and his English wife Beatrice Cadbury (from the Quaker chocolate-manufacturing dynasty) decided to educate children using Quaker pacifist principles. The Boekes believed that children not only have a natural love of the

direct and the spontaneous but also desire order and method as well. The school proved highly successful and produced a number of offshoots. Boeke's British equivalent was A.S. Neill, who originally founded a community school at Hellerau, near Salzburg, before relocating at Leiston in Suffolk in 1927. The school 'began as an experiment and became a

CHILD'S PLAY The teaching method devised by Maria Montessori was widely adopted, as in this school (above) for the children of British munitions workers in the First World War.

demonstration'. Neill, greeted by the children of Summerhill with the chant 'Neill! Neill! Orange Peel!', made something of a speciality of dealing with 'difficult' children, many of whom were the offspring of wealthy Americans,

SELF-DISCIPLINE At Summerhill School in the mid 1960s, the charismatic A.S. Neill created a community in which children were encouraged to make their own rules.

who had been rejected as failures or disruptive by more conventional establishments. He spent hours with such charges giving what were called 'private lessons' but were in fact sessions of psychotherapy. Summerhill children were encouraged to evolve their own disciplinary rules through discussion and consensus and to enforce them through communal sanctions. Learning was regarded as essentially a matter of discovery rather than instruction.

The influence of these experimental schools was delayed in its impact by the onset of the world Depression of the 1930s, the huge disruption caused by the Second World War and the urgent need for straightforward reconstruction in the postwar decades.

Education for democracy

In theory at least, the United States had the most democratic education system at the start of the century. Though not all of their countrymen agreed, figures such as John Dewey firmly rejected the dual-track system accepted as natural in Europe. In a democracy, they maintained, there could be only one sort of school common to all. Separate provision for the children of the leisured and the labouring

BE PREPARED

**STARTING AS A SUMMER CAMP ON AN ISLAND OFF THE SOUTH COAST OF ENGLAND,
THE SCOUTS GREW INTO A HUGE WORLDWIDE MOVEMENT.**

During the second Boer War of 1899-1902 the South African city of Mafeking was besieged for 217 days by a large Boer force. When the city was finally relieved London went wild with delight, and the commander of the Mafeking garrison, Colonel Robert Baden-Powell, became a national hero overnight. Returning to England to become inspector general of cavalry in 1903, Baden-Powell was intrigued to find that his army handbook, *Aids to Scouting*, was being used to train boys in woodcraft. In 1904 he was asked to review the 21st anniversary parade of the church-based Boys' Brigade, whose members dressed in uniforms and learned basic army drill. Baden-Powell approved but began to think he could come up with something more appealing to the average boy, something to get him out of church halls and into the fresh air of the countryside, away from the squalor and temptations of city life.

The Boer War had revealed appalling levels of fitness among Britain's young men. The sight of slope-shouldered lads hanging around street corners while they waited for the pubs to open seemed to many not just a social disgrace but a threat to national security. Baden-Powell shared this view passionately, having a soldierly contempt for 'loafers' and 'shirkers' who were invariably, in his word, 'pale, narrow-chested, hunched-up, miserable specimens, smoking endless cigarettes'.

Believing that the thing to do was to catch boys before they had acquired idle or vicious habits, he organised a summer camp at Brownsea Island, off the Dorset coast, in 1907. For ten days boys, divided into patrols of Curlews, Ravens, Wolves and Bulls, crawled through gorse, raced through pine woods, cooked their own food, sang campfire songs and, exhausted and exhilarated, slept out under canvas. The huge success of this experiment inspired Baden-Powell to write another manual, *Scouting for Boys*. Published in 1908 in six weekly parts, it became the textbook of the world's most successful youth movement.

In writing it Baden-Powell drew not only on his experience as a military scout but also on his conduct of the siege of Mafeking, when he had used boys too young to carry a rifle to serve as runners, carrying messages and ammunition to the defenders of the city's perimeter. Such lads, characterised by a keen sense of duty, a willingness to volunteer, cheerfulness, resourcefulness, determination and 'pluck', became the model for Boy Scouts, who should grow up to be 'good citizens or useful colonists'.

In 1910, Baden-Powell retired from the army to devote himself full time to the Boy Scout movement and join his sister Agnes in founding the Girl Guides. By 1911 the movement had grown so fast that a rally could assemble 40 000 members in Windsor Great Park, to be inspected by King George V himself. In 1920 the first international Boy Scout Jamboree was held in London and 'B-P' was hailed as Chief Scout of the World. Half a century later there were Boy Scout organisations in 110 different countries.

WELL TURNED OUT The uniform, seen here in 1925, was a major expense for would-be Scouts.

classes lead inevitably, in Dewey's words, to 'a division of mental and moral habits, ideals and outlook . . . a plan of social predestination totally foreign to the spirit of democracy'.

The key to the US system was the neighbourhood high school. After 1910 US children did six years at elementary school from which they could graduate to junior high school for three years, then senior high school for another three. How much of this schooling was free and how much compulsory varied from state to state. How good the schools were also varied – in urban areas many were overcrowded and understaffed. Nonetheless, the ideal, even if it was not always lived up to, was that there should be roughly equal educational opportunities for all regardless of background or wealth. The greater social equality accorded to women in North America than to those in Europe meant that the education of girls was taken almost as seriously as that of boys.

In most European countries, the debate about dual-track versus single-track education did not really get started until well after the Second World War – and was still raging in many places at the end of the century. This largely revolved around the question of selection. By the postwar decades, the old class priorities were less important, but it was still taken for granted in most systems that children deemed suitable for higher education should be separated out at some point between the ages of around 11 and 15 and sent to special schools or put into special 'streams' where they would be prepared for university. The rest of the children would be given various levels of technical or vocational training.

FACES OF DEMOCRACY A science class in 1900 (below), high school girls dressed for their graduation 'prom' in 1922 (top), swearing allegiance to the flag in 1970 (right). The high school has been a cornerstone of American democracy in the 20th century. Below right, a graduate at New York University thanks his 'Mom'.

Sweden, which was largely spared the traumas of the mid century, had gone farthest in adopting progressive pedagogy into mainstream education between the 1930s and 50s and attracted eager pilgrims from Germany, France and Britain. In 1962 it became the first European country to abolish the distinction between 'academic' schools and 'non-academic' vocational ones in favour of a unified system. England started experimenting with non-selective comprehensive education in the same decade. Traditionally, pupils in the state sector had been tested around the age of 11, with those who did best being streamed into the academic grammar schools.

The object of comprehensive education was to keep pupils of varying abilities together in the same schools until a much later stage. It was believed that 11 was far too young for a definitive selection to be made. Keeping the pupils together for longer allowed those of less obvious ability more time to develop. Large numbers of local education authorities opted

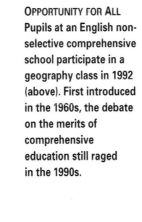

OPPORTUNITY FOR ALL Pupils at an English non-selective comprehensive school participate in a geography class in 1992 (above). First introduced in the 1960s, the debate on the merits of comprehensive education still raged in the 1990s.

for the new scheme, so that as early as 1970 nearly 50 per cent of children were receiving a comprehensive education. Around the same time, some education authorities in West Germany were introducing a similar scheme: the *Gesamtschule* (common school), a combined elementary and secondary school.

Co-education also became increasingly the norm. Most US high schools had taken both girls and boys since the start of the century. The same was true in most of Scandinavia – the Norwegians introduced co-education in 1896. In Britain co-education was common in primary schools but not in secondary schools until after the Second World War. In France the girls went to separate *lycées* (secondary schools), which until the Second World War taught a different curriculum from boys' schools; girls did not learn Latin or Greek and studied mathematics to a lower level. The curriculum for girls and boys was standardised after the war, but separate *lycées* continued until 1975.

Going to college

Education was opening up, and that applied to higher education as well. At the turn of the century American books on 'success' had generally told their readers that going to

five said they wanted their children to go beyond high school.

Universities and colleges were transformed accordingly. Long-established institutions, from France's super-elite *grandes écoles* to Britain's Oxbridge (Oxford and Cambridge) and America's Ivy League universities, continued to thrive, but a whole range of other institutions were either created or expanded. In Britain new universities and polytechnics – offering university-level courses in both technical and general arts and science subjects – broadened the options for those seeking higher education

PRIVILEGED POSITION? Despite efforts to broaden student recruitment, the universities of Oxford and Cambridge retained a mystique of exclusivity.

college was a waste of time, except for people who were already rich and did not have to worry about making a living.

By 1968 findings suggested that the opposite was true: it was calculated that those with elementary school education could expect average lifetime earnings of $196 000. A further stint at high school followed by attendance at university trebled that figure to around $586 000. By 1993, the average college graduate earned nearly 90 per cent more than the average high-school graduate.

Higher education expanded hugely across the advanced world, particularly after the Second World War. From being a hallmark of the elite and those in a handful of learned professions, such as medicine and the law, it became a passport to success in a whole range of careers, and increasing numbers of people aspired to it. By the late 1960s, the number of graduates per year in the USA had almost doubled since 1850 to around the 800 000 mark. By the late 1980s four US parents out of every

NIGHT OF THE BARRICADES

For several days and nights in May 1968 student riots erupted in Paris, triggered by many factors including dissatisfaction with the highly centralised French education system. The American Hans Koning was there:

'I remember sitting in a Paris Left Bank café on the evening of May 10, which was going to be the Night of the Barricades . . . Before it had got really dark, there was already a wild excitement in the air. You could almost taste it; it affected everyone. Waiters distractedly put coffees and drinks down and didn't bother to check the money . . .

'The fighting of the May 10-11 night was astounding. It was astounding to watch the students being unafraid of police with tear gas and CS gas, concussion grenades, nightsticks, pistols, helmets, visors, shields, grenade rifles, and the famous leaded capes. It was equally astounding to find their courage "rewarded", so to speak, by sympathy and even admiration not only from the radio reporters of the independent radio stations (Europe One and Radio Luxembourg) but also from the public at large . . .

'The students had made three demands: that the police get out of the Sorbonne, that the university be reopened, and that the arrested students and other demonstrators be released. They decided to try to enforce their case not "by writing letters to the papers" but by protest marches. That night, with the police barring their way wherever they went, they built their barricades where they found themselves stuck, in the Rue St-Jacques, the Rue Gay-Lussac, and some other narrower streets south of the Panthéon. . . . When dawn came, the last barricades fell to the police, and the remaining young men, and some young women, were dragged, often clubbed, into the police vans. An unknown number were taken into the hospital by volunteers who had to fight the police to get through.

'It was a cold morning. The streets were littered with stones, with debris of all sorts, burned-out cars, shoes, and lost pieces of clothing. A restless crowd of young people, probably mostly students too, filled the streets. It looked as if the police had won, but actually they had lost. The mood of the city and the country had turned against them.'

from the 1960s. Broadcasting technology lay at the heart of another British innovation – the Open University, established in 1969. It combined TV and radio programmes with more traditional materials sent through the post, such as specially written textbooks and even science experiments. By the 1990s some 75 000 students of all ages were enrolled in its undergraduate programmes

COME AS YOU ARE In recent decades student life, as at Frankfurt University here, has emphasised spontaneous self-expression.

alone. In all advanced countries, the old hard core of classical, literary and scientific courses was expanded to include new ones on subjects ranging from computer studies to sociology, psychology to politics.

New ways, old problems

In many ways, the innovative trends that marked education in the 20th century reached their high-water mark in the 1960s and early 70s. Old school buildings were giving way to light and airy modern ones. Inside the classroom the rigid barriers between teacher and pupil were giving way to a more relaxed relationship. Increasingly, it was realised that pupils should be encouraged and stimulated rather than merely drilled. Opportunities for higher education were blossoming for generations whose parents would have been lucky to complete a satisfactory secondary schooling. The post-Second World War 'baby boom' was by now feeding through to the universities and colleges, swelling their numbers to unprecedented levels. Students were a force to be

CONFRONTATION Student power showed itself in Paris in 1968 (top) and in anti-Vietnam demonstrations in America (above).

reckoned with, politically and in every other way. When student riots in Paris in 1968 came close to toppling President Charles de Gaulle, it was a telling symbol of the new-found power of Western educated youth.

It was a relatively short-lived heyday. As Western economies faltered with the oil

CENTRAL CONTROL

Before 1968 the French state school system was so closely regulated that a head could not even arrange an extra half-day holiday for a special local occasion without written permission from the ministry in Paris.

LUNCHTIME IN TOKYO Increasingly, advanced countries use their schools to improve child health through nutrition, exercise and medical check-ups.

crisis and rising inflation of the mid to late 70s, much of the confidence and sense of ever-expanding opportunities that went hand in hand with the educational revolution of the previous years began to break down.

LEARNING STYLES From the large class in a Russian school (below) to an Australian farm boy learning by radio (bottom), different situations demand different approaches.

Factors such as the high-tech revolution also meant that economies were now changing faster than ever. As well as providing children with a good basic education, countries had to organise themselves so that adults could retrain as appropriate to meet the new demands. In many countries education and training became a political battleground.

On the one hand, the reforming impulse continued. During the 70s the racial desegregation of schools had been a preoccupation in the southern states of the USA. In schools and campuses, people started re-examining history, literature, art and music courses for signs that they were 'sexist' or 'Eurocentric', marginalising the achievements of women, Afro-Caribbean peoples, Native Americans and other non-whites. The concern spread to other countries, many of them former colonial powers with ethnic minorities originating in their ex-colonies within their populations. During the 1980s such disputes were extended into a more general debate on 'political correctness'.

At the same time, there was soul-searching about standards. New teaching methods were often more imaginative than the old ones, but many commentators in countries where they had been tried felt that the pendulum had swung too far and that the basics of literacy and numeracy were being forgotten. A 1983 report of the US National Commission on Excellence in Education pulled no punches: 'If an unfriendly foreign power had attempted to impose on America the mediocre educational performance that exists today, we might well have viewed it as an act of war . . . We have in effect been committing an act of unthinking, unilateral educational disarmament.'

How countries responded to such crises varied markedly. In England and Wales a centralised National Curriculum started to be imposed for the first time in 1989, followed by national testing at the ages of 7, 11 and 14. Sweden at the same time was introducing a programme of radical decentralisation, devolving responsibilities away from central government to the regions. Questions abounded. Had comprehensive education been a failure? Should selection and the old 'academic' grammar schools and the like be reinstated? In England and Wales, children specialised young; around the age of 16, those aiming for university usually chose just three subjects to study for A-level, the key to university entrance. Their Scottish and French counterparts pursued a much broader curriculum up to the level of Highers in Scotland and the *Baccalauréat* in France. What one nation's children gained in breadth of learning, they lost in depth, and vice versa – so what *was* the correct balance? One thing was sure: education, the key to success in a rapidly changing world, looked set for many further transformations.

WORK – OR PLAY? The fascination of computer technology can both stretch gifted children and seduce reluctant learners, while economising on direct teacher time.

LEISURED SOCIETY

THE PROVISION OF PLEASURE TO THE MANY WAS TRADITIONALLY THE PROFESSION OF THE FEW – FROM MUSICIANS TO INNKEEPERS, JUGGLERS TO COURTESANS. MASS AFFLUENCE AND COMMUNICATIONS HAVE TRANSFORMED ENTERTAINMENT INTO THE WORLD'S FASTEST-GROWING INDUSTRY, SPAWNING THE CINEMA AND THE CD, JAZZ MUSIC AND THE JACUZZI, AND DEFINING THE CENTRAL PURPOSE OF WHOLE COMMUNITIES, FROM LAS VEGAS TO LAS PALMAS.

HOLIDAY TIME

THE 'LEISURE INDUSTRY' HAS BECOME A PROVIDER OF NOVEL EXPERIENCES, REFRESHING ENJOYMENTS – AND MAJOR EMPLOYMENT

The seaside has retained its appeal throughout the 20th century. From the cheerful throngs milling along the promenades and piers of Britain's Blackpool at the start of the century to the rows of roasting north Europeans lining the beaches of Spain and Greece in the 1990s, holidaymakers have kept faith with the seaside and its tonic virtues. Styles have changed, and the decorously clad bathers of 1900 would stare in amazement – and most probably outrage – at the bronzed flesh and skimpy attire of late 20th-century sun worshippers. But for millions of people in the developed world, holidays are still virtually synonymous with beaches and the seaside, as they were for the working and middle classes alike in much of industrialised North America and Europe at the start of the century.

In Britain, which had pioneered the seaside holiday in the 19th century, 55 per cent of English people were taking day excursions to the seaside by 1911 and 20 per cent were taking holidays there that involved staying overnight. Britain's Brighton and Blackpool had their transatlantic counterpart in Atlantic City, New Jersey, where visitors could stroll along 5 miles (8 km) of boardwalk, eating taffy (a sugary sweet) and buying picture postcards imported from Germany. Nearby Ocean City had been founded by Methodist ministers and was firmly against the sale of liquor, making it a favoured location for religious conventions and the family vacations of the ultra-respectable. Germans had a selection of Baltic resorts such as Binz, Lohme and Sellin on the island of Rügen; Belgians frolicked on the North Sea beaches of Ostend and Nieuwpoort-Bad. By July 1912 the French *Revue hébdomadaire* was able to assert that

MAIDENLY MODESTY Bathing beauties (right) dare partial exposure of the limbs. Bathing machines, hats and sunshades on the beach at Ostend (below) around 1900 reveal a preference for sea rather than sunshine.

'50 years ago the person who took a vacation stood out. Today a person stands out if he does not take a vacation'. Meanwhile, the super-rich of all nations patronised high-society watering spots from Newport on Rhode Island, to Deauville, Biarritz and Nice in France.

On the other side of the world, a visit to the beach became a basic feature of weekend life in New South Wales, Queensland and Western Australia from 1909, when work-places began to close on Saturday afternoons. For Australians the beach was as much an arena for strenuous exertion as sedate relax-ation. Under the eye of voluntary lifesavers the youth of the nation practised surfing and the 'Australian crawl' – which had been used by Pacific Islanders for centuries. Clerics inveighed against such hedonism and thun-dered against the moral mire of mixed bathing – but to little noticeable effect.

Blackpool lights

With their piers (where promenaders could inhale the health-giving sea air without get-ting their feet wet), their bathing machines, their bands and donkey rides, popular resorts in 1900, whether in Germany, Belgium, Britain or North America, all bore a certain resemblance to each other. Blackpool, how-ever, was pre-eminent in the enthusiasm with

THE SEASIDE – ENGLAND **The classic 1950s seaside family holiday, whether at Blackpool (below) or Southend-on-Sea (right), enshrined such rituals as the donkey ride and the wearing of silly hats.**

THE SEASIDE – FRANCE **High-fashion bell-bottom trousers emphasise the importance of elegance rather than family fun at Juan-les-Pins in 1930.**

which it embraced the holiday industry. Its corporation, uniquely in Britain, acquired the right to levy a local tax to spend on advertis-ing and publicity stunts. It also invested in facilities. It was the first town in Britain to have an electric tramway. Five years after the completion of the Eiffel Tower in Paris, Blackpool had built a rival tower of its own. In the same year, 1894, London's leading the-atre architect Frank Matcham had completed his masterpiece, Blackpool's Grand Theatre. Most resorts had one pier; Blackpool had three, the newest of which had not only a bandstand but no fewer than 36 shops. In 1912 the town took advantage of the new technology of electric power to inaugurate its famous illuminations, creating an attraction that extended its season well into the autumn. Blackpool's relentless drive paid off handsomely and continued to do so throughout the 20th century. By 1914 it had 4 million visitors each year. The figure reached 7 million in 1939, and topped 16 million as the Blackpool Tower celebrated its centenary in 1994.

The visitors came in droves from the tex-tile towns of Lancashire and Yorkshire, par-ticularly at the start of the century in 'wakes weeks' during July and August. Wakes were originally celebrations to mark the dedica-tion of a parish church, but they had become

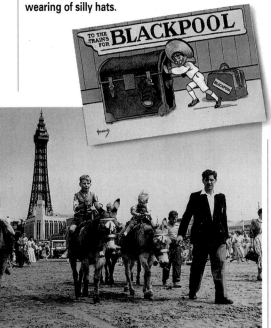

BE PREPARED   For these rich Berliners in 1908, travel meant bulky trunks to ensure you had appropriate dress for all occasions.

CAMPING OUT

In the summer of 1919 so many people flocked to Blackpool that many were forced to sleep on the beach and kindly bobbies allowed distressed women and children to pass the night in police cells.

secularised and extended into complete breaks in the collective life of tight-knit mill communities. What had once been a 'holy-day' was now a 'holiday' – a trend that would establish all across the industrialised world. Employers accepted a complete shutdown of their factories because it reduced disruption from casual absenteeism and gave them a time to arrange annual repairs and mainte-nance work. The seasonal exodus to the coast also meant the extinction of ancient preindustrial revels, invariably notorious for drunkenness and disorder. 'In place of the fair,' one man reminisced, 'we see hundreds

REST CURE   Patients at Baden-Baden in the 1930s pass long hours chatting or strolling to and fro – or watching others do so.

of people carrying boxes and bags on their way to the railway station for a few days at the seaside.'

Most took their spare clothes in ordinary household shopping bags or even brown paper parcels, tied up with string. 'Proper' luggage was an unattainable luxury for the humble. The one-week holidays were unpaid, a glorious spree painstakingly saved up for over the whole year in accounts administered by employee savings' clubs, unions, chapels, temperance societies and railway companies. The only manual employees in Britain who did have the benefit of paid leave were those who worked for unusually 'progressive' com-panies like Lever Brothers, the soap manufac-turers, or for some of the railway companies and a few town corporations.

Taking the waters

At the start of the century, inland spas were still popular among the wealthy of all nations. Britain's King Edward VII paid for his pleasures, medically speaking, by passing the entire month of August each year at Baden-Baden in Germany, taking the waters, abstaining from alcohol and restoring his once-powerful physique to face the onslaught of another 11 months of self-indulgence. Homburg was another German spa favoured by the king, who set a sartorial trend by wearing the elegant, rolled-brim felt hat named after it. Edward's prime minister, Sir Henry Campbell-Bannerman, preferred France and found his public duties sufficiently undemanding for him to be able to spend six weeks at Aix-les-Bains each summer.

Among the very wealthy, spas declined in popularity during the course of the century, partly as a result of medical scepticism, part-ly because of competition from exclusive warm-climate beach and yachting resorts such as Puerto Banus in southern Spain. Baden-Baden, which had 15 000 hotel beds in 1900, had just 4000 by 1990; the grand Hotel Kaiserhof had given way to a super-market. But, thanks to the generous German health insurance system, some 300 spas in Germany did continue to survive, attracting about 9 million visitors a year for an average stay of two weeks. Both patients and doctors in Germany believe in the effectiveness of natural remedies. Rest cures at spas are used

for rehabilitation (after heart attacks, strokes and so on), as well as for the treatment of chronic diseases. Research in Germany showed that after a rest cure, the patient's absence from work through illness, and the cost of their medical treatment, fell by 60 per cent.

PROWLING IN PARIS

The English writer Arnold Bennett lived in Paris at the beginning of the century, when it was the mecca of pleasure-seekers from both sides of the Atlantic. The high-minded were drawn by its artistic brilliance, others by the belief that 'on holiday there is no shame' and Paris was the best place to be shameless. His diary for February 17, 1906, records a Saturday night masked ball at the Paris Opera. A bachelor himself, Bennett recognised the characteristic type of predatory masculine vacationer, eager to make a conquest while passing through and requiring only evening dress to gain admission to the hunting-ground:

'We got to the ball at 12.45. Already an enormous crowd. Great cohorts of men in silk hats. I should say the men outnumbered the women by 5 to 1. The people who looked really well were the chorus girls etc. from the Opera who were thoroughly used to fancy dress and knew how to walk and how to dine. Outside these, and a few professional men, there was almost no fancy dress . . . There was, relatively, very little dancing. Not a single well-bred Frenchwoman there, so far as I could see . . . And the cohorts of men, all on the lookout for something nice, seemed to lurch from time to time in one direction or another . . . and sometimes even stampede. There was something undignified in these masses of masculinity . . . We left at 3.15. Many people had preceded us.

'I was a wreck on Sunday . . . However I wrote a brief account of the ball for the Standard, rather sardonic, and took it down to the office.'

A place to stay

In 1928 the English hotelier Sir Francis Towle observed somewhat despondently that great hotels were rather like battleships – they became obsolete every 20 years or so. The history of hotels in the 20th century has tended to confirm this maxim.

The typical major hotel of 1900 was notable for its spacious public rooms, its exclusive restaurant and its extensive banqueting facilities. Its staff would almost all have been natives of the country in which it was located, with the exceptions perhaps, in the most expensive establishments, of the manager, the maître d'hôtel and the chef. They might come from Switzerland, France or Italy, or at least have been trained in one of those countries whose hotels offered the most rigorous apprenticeship.

The guests, apart from a sprinkling of rich globetrotting Americans and British, would have come overwhelmingly from the country where the hotel was located, except perhaps along the Riviera where Monte Carlo and most notably Nice, with its Promenade des Anglais, were very much British 'colonies'. Wealthy guests in those days stayed for lengthy periods – usually weeks, often months, sometimes years. Many came as whole families. For both these reasons their rooms – or suites – were spacious and elegantly furnished, commanding fine views of seashore, lakes or mountains.

During the interwar period the layout and appointments of leading hotels began to

SUNSEEKERS In 1930s Monte Carlo (above), holidaymakers under a beach umbrella take a break from the new fad of sunbathing. In an age when international travel was still the prerogative of the few, decorative luggage labels (right) proclaimed their privilege for all to see. Horse-drawn carriages ply the seafront at Nice (below) before the First World War.

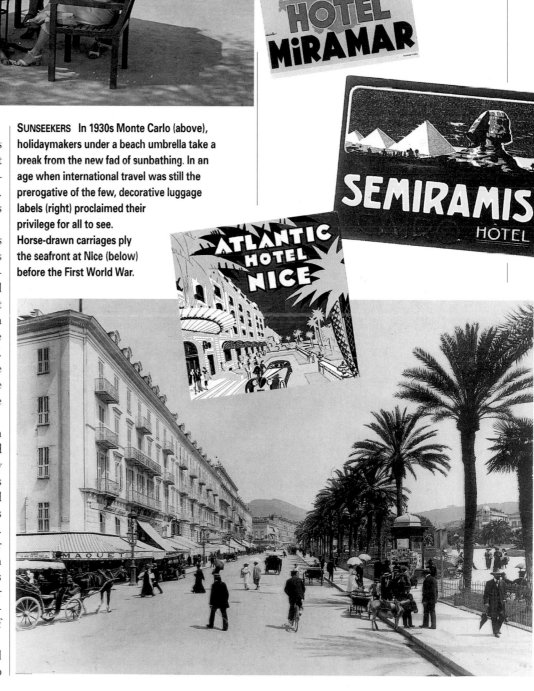

SIMPLY THE BEST Thomas Cook, inventor of modern tourism, created a business that was synonymous with calm competence from Jerusalem (above) to the farthest antipodes.

change in response to new patterns of travel and recreation. Elevators, central heating and en suite bathrooms were increasingly regarded as essential by the elderly and invalid – and by Americans, who additionally looked for telephones in their rooms and a newsstand in the foyer. The craze for new dances, such as the high-kicking Charleston in the 1920s, made a permanent professional band desirable. Thanks to the influence of Hollywood movies, wealthy socialites also wanted a cocktail bar and a night club. Young people wanted tennis courts and a swimming pool, both for the sake of genuine exercise and to give them an excuse to slip into newly fashionable sportswear.

The hotels of the late 20th century had changed again. The high cost of prime locations had encouraged the construction of narrow, multistorey buildings. The only ground-floor area likely to have grown bigger was the foyer, needed to handle a much higher turnover of guests, many of whom were travelling for business rather than pleasure. To cater for their demands hotels not only provided conference and meeting rooms, but also international telephone and fax links.

In their off-duty moments guests could browse in the shopping arcade, take a sauna, use the fitness centre or just relax in their rooms watching TV and consuming the contents of a refrigerated mini bar while an automatic trouser press restored their slacks to pristine condition. The vast majority of guests stayed only for a few nights, often just one. Their

rooms, if air-conditioned and abundantly equipped with gadgets, were usually compact. The large hotel had ceased to resemble a battleship, or even a luxury liner; it had become the terrestrial equivalent of the jumbo jet.

Packaged paradise

Modern package tourism, which until after the Second World War remained very much the domain of the British and Americans, is essentially the invention of one man: the Englishman Thomas Cook. He had begun it all in 1841 by chartering a train to take 500 fellow Baptists, neighbours and friends to hear a lecture against the evils of alcohol. Half a century later, at the time of Edward VII's coronation in 1902, Thomas Cook and Son was praised as one of 'the three most competent organisations in the world' – the

other two being the German army and the Roman Catholic Church.

Between 1900 and 1913 the number of Britons crossing the Channel each year rose from 650 000 to a million. By 1914, 150 000 Americans were arriving in Europe each year. American Express established itself in Europe to challenge Cook's for a share of this lucrative market. Cook's responded by looking for new business down market and launched a range of Popular Tours, for people 'prepared to travel abroad under less luxurious conditions than those of our Select Conducted Tours'. These provided second-class travel and accommodation and left clients to arrange their own excursions.

The First World War put the emerging travel industry into temporary eclipse, but it bounced back in the 1920s when people were eager to put the horrors of the recent past behind them. Surplus Army trucks were converted into charabancs to cash in on the demand for excursions. Their success inspired the manufacture of purpose-designed motor coaches, an innovation that was to transform tourism. Cook's used the new coaches to transport clients on six-day tours of the European battlefields. It also began to offer half-hour rides in converted Handley-Page bombers and made confident predictions about the future of air travel: 'Space will be annihilated, the cities of the world will be brought within the reach of all.' In 1927 Cook's arranged the first-ever escorted tour by plane – from New York to

TRAVELLER'S DELIGHT After the First World War, motorised coaches opened up new fast-paced excursions and touring holidays to a new breed of traveller.

SKY HIGH

AIR TRAVEL HAS MADE TOURISM A GLOBAL INDUSTRY WHILE ALSO REVOLUTIONISING DOMESTIC VACATIONS WITHIN LARGE COUNTRIES LIKE THE USA OR AUSTRALIA

Civil aviation began in Germany in 1910, using airships. By 1914 airships had carried 34 228 passengers the equivalent of four times round the globe without a single injury. The first scheduled passenger air service using planes was established in 1914 in St Petersburg, Florida. Passengers were flown – one at a time – 20 miles (32 km) across Tampa Bay.

Efforts to develop passenger services began after the First World War, when surplus military aircraft became available and discharged pilots sought employment flying them. In 1919 the first international services began – Paris-Brussels, London-Paris and Toulouse-Barcelona-Tangier. Cabins were unheated, unpressurised and noisy. As late as 1928 Britain's Flying Scotsman rail service could beat a plane travelling from Scotland to London. In America, where luxurious long-distance rail travel was widely available, there were no regular passenger air services until 1926. Then the Americans opted for a 'flying bus' approach, aiming to compete with the railroads in reliability and cheapness.

A London-Cape Town service began in 1932, a London-Brisbane and San Francisco-Hawaii service in 1935. Landing strips were rare, so flying boats were preferred. From 1935 onwards, however, more air strips were built and the Douglas DC-3 (Dakota) supplanted the flying boat as the workhorse of civil aviation. PanAm established the first transatlantic service in 1939,

JUNGLE JAUNT Airlines were promoting 'safari' holidays in Africa as early as the 1930s.

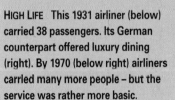

but this was suspended following the outbreak of the Second World War. When civil aviation resumed after 1945, air travel remained the prerogative of the rich.

The dawn of a new era glimmered in 1952 when TWA pioneered a new concept – Tourist Class. But mass air travel required a new type of carrier. Britain was the first to establish a regular long-haul jet service with its 1952 London-Johannesburg route, flown in De Havilland Comets. But a series of crashes led to the Comet's withdrawal from service. Boeing successfully filled the gap with its 707. First test-flown in 1954, the 707 could carry 219 passengers. In 1958 more than a million passengers crossed the Atlantic by plane, surpassing the number travelling by ship for the first time.

The 707 was superseded by the 747 'jumbo' in 1969. Capable of carrying more than twice as many passengers as the 707, the 747 brought long-haul flying within the reach of even modest budgets. Its internal cabin length of some 40 yd (37 m) was just about the distance flown by Orville Wright on his historic first powered flight in 1903.

HIGH LIFE This 1931 airliner (below) carried 38 passengers. Its German counterpart offered luxury dining (right). By 1970 (below right) airliners carried many more people – but the service was rather more basic.

HELLO, CAMPERS! Butlin's holiday camp at Skegness brought industrial management methods to the leisure business, providing a standardised product at a bargain price.

Chicago to see Jack Dempsey fight Gene Tunney for the world heavyweight title.

Tourism was suddenly recognised by bankers and politicians as an 'industry' and one with immense potential for countries such as Britain replete with attractive scenery and historic sites. As one visionary speculated as early as 1923: 'it is even possible that the part ultimately reserved for the British Isles in the scheme of the international division of labour will be that of a playground and park and museum to exercise the youth and soothe the declining years of the strenuous industrial leaders congregated on either side of the Pacific Ocean'.

Not all were content with this emerging new scheme of things. In Italy, where Mussolini really had eased the travel agent's life by making the trains run on time, upper-class British visitors were horrified to find themselves rubbing shoulders with compatriots the very sight of whom made them shudder: 'the most awful people with legs like flies who come into lunch in bathing costumes'. The American novelist Scott Fitzgerald was just as disgusted with his countrymen abroad who displayed 'the humane values of Pekinese, bivalves, cretins, goats'.

For the beneficiaries, rich and not so rich, of the new

AWAY FROM IT ALL
The development of skiing as a fashionable sport in the early part of the century transformed remote mountain communities into prosperous resorts.

tourism, there were many new choices, including all kinds of specialist packages. At the beginning of the century, it had already been possible for travel-trade analysts to identify 'the Cairo crowd, the Riviera crowd, the Swiss winter sport crowd, and the more go-ahead set who are off to the States, to India or to the Colonies'. Bermuda and Cuba were being colonised as winter playgrounds; it was possible to book special holidays for golfers, skiers, daredevils who wanted a balloon ascent over Mont Blanc and rowing fanatics who just had to be at the World Sculling Championships, which were held on the Zambezi in 1910. By the 1920s one could go trail riding in the Canadian Rockies or travel to Timbuktu in a Citroën. The discovery of Tutankhamun's tomb in 1922 sparked a renewed rush to Egypt. Idealists organised

trips to Bolshevik Russia to inspect the workers' paradise, archaeologists to Lascaux near Toulouse to see newly discovered prehistoric cave paintings.

The 'great outdoors' exercised a growing appeal, and would continue to do so for the rest of the century. The first youth hostels had appeared in Germany before the First World War, catering for students and young people taking walking or cycling holidays in places such as the Black Forest. The youth hostel movement spread rapidly in the interwar years which saw the craze for weekend 'rambling' at its height. The International Youth Hostel Federation was founded in 1932 – by the 1970s it had some 20 million members in 50 countries.

National parks represented another growth area. One of the earliest had been

WANDERLUST The growth of youth hostels in the 1920s and 30s helped to spread the German cult of hiking and made 'rucksack' (literally 'back sack') an English word.

Yellowstone National Park in the United States, sprawling over almost 3500 sq miles (9000 km^2) of Wyoming, Montana and Idaho, and offering an abundance of rare plant and animal life. As early as 1872 it had been established as a major ecosystem to be protected from disturbance. By the 1890s the national park concept had spread to Canada, South Africa, Australia and New Zealand. Europe

then started creating its own national parks, starting with Sweden in 1909. The interwar period brought Argentina, Chile and Japan into the national park movement. Britain delayed until 1949, though this was partly because its privately funded National Trust had been taking over precious natural sites since its formation in 1895. Tourism was big business in the parks. By 1986, America's 300 National Parks, historic sites, protected shores, rivers and trails were attracting more than 364 million visitors a year.

The interwar decades also introduced a new attraction to the seaside holiday. Where earlier generations had shrouded themselves against the sun, fearing the harmful effects of too much exposure to its rays, the opposite

NATURAL WONDERS In 1872 the USA began the creation of National Parks to preserve areas of wilderness – but not, as this Redwood in Yellowstone shows, from all forms of commercial intrusion.

now came to be the rule. Sunbathing was becoming all the rage, and remained so until the depletion of the ozone layer towards the end of the century renewed fears of excessive exposure. Devotees of the new fad clustered in the mushroom-growth cities of Florida – 'the Riviera of America'.

Cheap and cheerful

The Depression of the 1930s meant a bleak time for the travel business. The number of Britons taking winter sports holidays fell by almost 90 per cent. The very rich, however, cushioned from the inconvenience of poverty, continued to take luxury cruises. The demand for air travel also continued to grow. By 1939 it was possible to go 'Round the World in Thirty Days'.

But the real growth came at the bottom end of the market, with the opening of the first major commercial 'holiday camp' at Skegness on the east coast of England in 1936. This was the brainchild of the former

LUXURY TRAVEL ON THE QUEENS OF THE ATLANTIC

travelling showman Billy Butlin. He was following a path first trodden by high-minded socialists and teetotallers before the First World War, when campers had slept in tents or huts made from old tramcars.

Billy Butlin accommodated his campers in neat rows of purpose-built chalets and gave them three sit-down meals a day and free entertainment for the price of a workman's weekly wage. By 1938 his experiment had proved so successful that Cook's and the London Midland Scottish Railway had sunk £250 000 into creating a rival establishment at Prestatyn on the North Wales coast. By 1939 Britain had more than 100 holiday camps in operation, capable of accommodating half a million people each season. In Nazi Germany, the *Kraft durch Freude* (Strength through Joy) organisation sponsored similar camps.

As in the 1920s, the ending of war in 1945 inaugurated a boom in travel. But this time the boom just went on booming. In 1950 a million Britons went abroad and 200 000 North Americans visited Britain. The mass of people in war-shattered continental Europe had yet to catch the travel bug, but that too would shortly change. In 1950, Gerard Blitz from Antwerp went a step farther than Billy

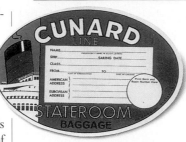

FLYING FASHIONS

Germany's first airline, Deutsche Luft-Reederei, began its service in 1919 with open cockpit biplanes – obliging passengers to don flying suits, helmets, goggles and fur-lined boots and gauntlets.

Butlin, replacing Butlin's 'cheap'n'cheerful' formula with one combining romance and simple elegance. Using US Army surplus tents for accommodation, Blitz advertised an informal holiday camp on the Spanish island of Majorca. A staggering 2600 people, most of them French, responded to his invitation. Club Méditerranée was born.

Blitz knew what he was offering: 'Today's luxury is not comfort, but open space. Adventure is dead and solitude is dying in today's crowded resorts. But if you can no longer go on holiday alone without finding yourself in a crowd, it ought to be possible to go off in a crowd in order to find yourself alone. The individual . . . needs a very flexible holiday community where at any moment he can join in, or escape . . .' Within 20 years of its birth 350 000 'Club Med' clients were

The Cunard line built its reputation as a transatlantic carrier around the motto 'Speed, Comfort, Safety'. Senior officers were strictly instructed to avoid 'racing, rivalry or risk-taking'. Having never lost a life at sea, the company prospered as a passenger carrier until faced with cut-price competition. Its response was to move up-market and focus on providing travellers with unashamed luxury aboard two of the most famous ships in the world – the *Queen Mary* (launched in 1934) and the *Queen Elizabeth* (1938). In 1938 the *Queen Mary* made the fastest Atlantic crossing to date in 3 days, 21 hours, 48 minutes and then held the Blue Riband – the award given to passenger ships holding the record for fastest crossing – until 1952, when the title passed to the SS *United States*.

During the Second World War both Queens served as troopships, each carrying up to 15 000 servicemen, ten times their normal complement of passengers. Their destinations included the Middle East and Australia and they had to rely on their speed to keep them safe from attack. Both were modified to fit their unaccustomed role. On the *Queen Elizabeth* the dance salon became a hospital ward and the Turkish bath became an X-ray room.

The heyday of the Queens came in the decade after 1945, when liners rather than planes were still the most popular way of crossing the Atlantic and the two great ships ran a back-to-back weekly service between Southampton and New York. Along with thousands of postwar refugees and migrants travelling tourist or cabin class, regular voyagers aboard the Queens included well-known celebrities such as Bob Hope, Noël Coward, Marlene Dietrich, Fred Astaire, Gary Cooper, Cary Grant, Bing Crosby, Bette Davis and Liberace.

At the peak of their popularity the Cunard fleet of 12 ships carried between them more than a third of all transatlantic passengers. Airline competition then forced a reassessment and the Queens were

reallocated to cruising. Too big to berth in many ports, they became major loss makers. *Queen Mary* was sold (1967) to become a tourist attraction, combining hotel facilities with a maritime museum, in Long Beach, California. *Queen Elizabeth* was refitted to become a floating university but caught fire and sank in Hong Kong harbour (1972), to be broken up later for scrap. The Queens' successor, the *QE2*, launched in 1969, is now the only liner to offer a transatlantic service, although even that is not a regular one.

A WORLD APART The cruise liner represented the ultimate in luxury but has been forced by airline competition to redefine its market appeal.

being accommodated in pseudo-Polynesian villages located in Tunisia, Morocco, Israel, Spain, Italy, Yugoslavia – and Tahiti itself.

Germany's version of Club Med was Club Robinson, which established centres as far away as Brazil and Sri Lanka. The Germans were, indeed, to become the keenest of all foreign holidaymakers. In 1954 only 15 per cent of the holidays Germans took were spent abroad; by 1990 they were the world record-holders. More Germans than Americans had spent their holidays abroad each year since 1976, even though the USA had a population four times as large. Germans accounted for more than 40 per cent of all visitors to Italy and 70 per cent of visitors to Austria.

The French, meanwhile, took to *le camping*. In 1950 a million French people went on camping holidays. By 1990, 5 million did so, mostly at sites renowned for their comfort and efficiency. Having part of the Alps in their country, some 4 million were able to take holidays skiing – a less class-biased sport in France than in Britain. The French also

owned more second homes than any other nation in Europe. Many families of relatively modest means were thus able to imitate the wealthy middle classes of the previous century by deserting sweaty cities each summer to relish the fresh air of the countryside.

While European holiday patterns began to change from the 1950s – partly through the impact of short-haul flights – in North America and Australasia mass motoring was enabling nations of suburbanites to renew contact with real or imagined rural roots. Queensland's spectacular Gold Coast and Great Barrier Reef began to attract interstate visitors. Americans were drawn to the majesty of the Grand Canyon and the Rockies.

By 1965, 114 million people worldwide were travelling abroad. Spain now relied on tourism for 40 per cent of its export earnings. The UN designated 1967 as International Tourist Year and endorsed a resolution recognising it as 'a basic and most desirable human activity, deserving the praise and encouragement of all peoples and all governments'. The

SUNSPOTS Mass-migrations from northerly climes towards sun-soaked beaches are now a well-established tradition – although fears of skin cancer have modified the trend.

British broadcaster Malcolm Muggeridge opined that 'tourism today is a more dynamic force than revolution . . . Thomas Cook and the American Express . . . unite the human race'. By 1972 tourism was the world's single biggest international business. Fifteen years later it was not only the biggest but the fastest-growing. In 1988, 355 million tourists travelled abroad and twice as much was spent on tourism as on the international arms trade.

Adventure and honeypots

The very fact, in 1900, that millions of ordinary families could get a break at the seaside ensured that many of the wealthy and adventurous wanted to go somewhere else – to avoid what Cook's trade magazine referred to as 'those who find happiness in spending their holiday in Ramsgate eating shrimps'.

The Englishman Richard Gordon Smith, both wealthy and adventurous, had the additional incentive of escaping an unhappy marriage. For 20 years he steamed the oceans of the world on liners, visiting everywhere from Quebec to Kobe, accompanied by the impedimenta of the intrepid professional traveller – shotguns, snowshoes, a camera, a gramophone and huge supplies of Stilton cheeses. He shot mountain goats in the Pyrenees and collected wildlife specimens in Korea for the British Museum.

THEME DREAM With new technologies, the travelling Victorian fairground has evolved into a fixed-site fantasy world providing all-in entertainment.

By the last decades of the century, adventure on this scale was no longer the privilege of the wealthy few, though much of the new adventure was packaged. By the 1950s it was possible to go in a group to Nepal, in a safari Cape-to-Cairo, or round Cape Horn in a

square-rigger. The first package tour to Mount Everest was organised in 1970, although the tourists confined themselves to the lower slopes. Cheap international air travel, meanwhile, was bringing everywhere from the Andes of South America to the islands of Indonesia within the reach of increasing numbers of youthful backpackers.

Nowadays, some are still content to go on safari in Kenya or scuba-diving off an island in the Indian Ocean – and then return to a five-star Western-style hotel each evening. But there are others who are lured by the prospect of crossing Greenland on dog-sledges or of meeting 'Stone Age' peoples in New Guinea or Amazonia. Doggedly seeking spectacle or solitude or the exotic, these leading-edge tourists of the late 20th century have ensured that almost nowhere, except perhaps Antarctica, can now be regarded as remote. Fragile ecosystems are, ironically, now threatened by the too frequent passage of even those who recognise and treasure their fragility.

Whole cities have become what the travel trade calls 'honeypots', attracting swarms of free-spending visitors. In Venice one person in four is directly employed in catering to their demands. The noise and bustle they generate at the height of the season make the city ever less worthy of its proud title – *La Serenissima* ('the most serene'). Florence,

VIRTUAL REALITY? A Las Vegas hotel offers its guests a flirtation with Egypt – without all the time-consuming bother of having to travel there.

Versailles, Windsor and Stratford-on-Avon are similarly in thrall to the sightseer. Benidorm, an insignificant Spanish fishing village in the 1950s, had a permanent population of 25 000 some 30 years later – except in summer, when it welcomed a million seekers after sun, sea, sand and sangria. The islands of Corfu, Majorca, Tenerife and dozens of others in the Mediterranean, Atlantic and Caribbean have followed the same path to tourism-dependency.

Some centres have become honeypots by design. These include the Disneylands in California and Florida and outside Tokyo and Paris, which aim primarily at families with young children. Others are coastal enclaves, such as Acapulco in Mexico and Konya in

MODERN TRADE In past centuries, Venice prospered by controlling East-West commerce. Now it lives by peddling culture, romance and nostalgia.

Turkey, which have been allocated massive state funding for roads, sewage systems, hospitals, recreational facilities and the other bits of infrastructure required to keep affluent visitors amused, contented, healthy and safe.

Some capital cities have become honeypots almost by default as the numbers of vacationing tourists have been swelled by business travellers or students filling in spare hours by visiting the sights. London by the 1990s had 6 million tramping round the British Museum annually and 2.5 million each around the Tower of London and Westminster Abbey. London and Paris are big enough to take on yearly invasions of even 20 million people without being overwhelmed by them. But smaller sites risk overloading themselves to the point of self-destruction, as the veteran travel writer Jan Morris observed: 'I went to the coast of Maine and found its old seaports swamped one and all by Collectible Shoppes, Sea'n'Surf restaurants and Davy Jones Boutiques. I went to the Caribbean island of St Maarten, and found its old Dutch waterfront garishly dominated by duty-free shops for cruise passengers, I went to the Côte d'Azur and ran away again.'

GOING OUT, STAYING IN

FROM MUSIC HALL TO CINEMA TO TV – OUR NOTION OF AN EVENING OUT (OR IN) HAS BEEN TRANSFORMED DURING THE 20TH CENTURY

The moving image more than anything else has transformed entertainment in the 20th century. A night on the town in 1900 meant just that. Only large cities offered commercial entertainment on a regular basis – and the bigger the city, the bigger the choice. Berlin, which doubled its population between 1900 and 1914, had no fewer than 33 theatres and four opera houses. Elsewhere, Montmartre in Paris, New York's Broadway, London's Strand and Leicester Square, all were synonymous with pleasure. But these places were so famous largely because they were so few.

Already, however, a new force was starting to make itself felt: the 'bioscope' or cinema. The first public demonstration of 'moving pictures' had taken place in Paris in 1895 before an audience of 34, who were only mildly impressed by the novelty. By 1907, however, the United States alone had 3000 'nickelodeons' – charging a nickel, 5 cents, with accompaniment from harmonium-like organs called melodeons. By 1910 the USA had 10 000. The silent screen gave way to the 'talkies' after 1928; then, after the Second World War, came the all-invading television. Ready-made entertainment, provided by nationally or internationally acclaimed stars, was no longer the prerogative of the great cities. The cinema had brought it to the street corner or town square; television brought it into the living room.

Homemade fun

At the start of the century, most Americans and Canadians still lived in small towns or on farms. They could gather only at the general store, in a church hall or on each other's porches, to while away idle hours with gossip and homemade music, unless their isolation was interrupted by a travelling 'tent show', circus or 'showboat' presenting popular melodramas. The *fiestas, festas, fêtes* and feasts of

FUN OF THE FAIR Jumbo leads the circus parade into an American town. Tobogganing without snow offers fun at Munich's *Oktoberfest.*

the Church year were occasions for jollification in Europe, with parades, firework displays and much feasting and drinking. In Germany such celebrations were especially strong in the Rhineland and Bavaria. Munich's celebrated *Oktoberfest*, spread over 16 days, was dominated by serious consumption – of 40 roast oxen, 500 000 chickens and nearly 8 million pints (4.5 million litres) of beer. Traditionalists supported Germany's 14 500 choral societies, which claimed 1.5 million members.

In Britain the music hall was in its heyday, though it could hardly compete with the pub. London had the most halls, more than 60 – but even that meant only one music hall for over 100 000 people. Nationally there was one pub for every 300 people. In France, where alcohol was even more central to working-class leisure, there were three times as many outlets per head as in Britain. A trip to the music hall – or in American cities the vaudeville, in Paris the *café-concert*, in Berlin the *Kabarett* – meant getting dressed up and paying for a tram ride to the city

PARISIAN PLEASURE Paris was renowned for its saucy cabarets, of which the most famous was the Moulin Rouge (Red Mill), founded in 1888 and still thriving in the 1930s (below).

centre. For this reason, the best customers were young, employed men revelling in the few years before early marriage relieved them of their spare cash. At the end of a working day that often began at 6 am most married working men were content to stroll to their corner 'local' for a few sedative drinks. Pubs and bars offered not only alcohol but cheery company, music and laughter, cards and dominoes, and a brightness and warmth that contrasted with the dingy, cramped and chilly homes they would totter back to.

Observers were concerned by the phenomenon of solitary drinking, to be observed in the lowest dives in many European working-class districts. The condition was memorably portrayed by the French painters Degas and

HAVE A SWIG A woman sits in an English pub, with a pram beside her, offering her child a sip of beer. Consumption of alcohol by juveniles was banned in Britain in 1908.

Toulouse-Lautrec. Historians have explained the solitary drinker as a reaction to the decline in traditional festivals in big industrial cities, the loss of craft skills which had once been a source of self-respect, and the increasing monotony of work governed by machinery – coupled with increased leisure and income, which meant time to fill or to kill.

The top end of the entertainment market, meanwhile, was dominated by the huge spending power of the 'idle rich'. Winston Churchill's mother could spend £200 on an evening gown – almost two years' income for

an average British working-class family. Around the turn of the century, some 250 000 adult male Britons of property were reckoned to be 'without trade or profession'; France had twice that number of *rentiers*. Such people could seek their pleasures, not weekly, but nightly, dining at Maxim's in Paris, Delmonico's in New York or the Savoy Grill Room in London, before applauding the performances of a new breed of international superstar represented by Sarah Bernhardt, Ellen Terry or Nellie Melba. Other hits included the Hungarian-born Franz Lehár's operetta *The Merry Widow* and the Russian Sergei Diaghilev's Ballets Russes.

The silver screen

Even before 1914, people started flocking to the cinema. Unlike the music hall, it was untainted by smut or strong drink. Even respectable women could go to see 'moving pictures'. Captions carrying dialogue or

STARS AND SUPERSTARS
Classical actresses like Sarah Bernhardt (left) and Ellen Terry (top) were idolised on both sides of the Atlantic. German cabaret artists such as Betty Berane (above) and Wilhelm Bendow (right) often used musical aids, props, costume and gesture to overcome barriers of language when working abroad.

CINEMA IDOLS Films brought a new crop of stars: (clockwise from left) the Keystone Kops, Jean Harlow, Rudolf Valentino and Vilma Bankey, and Germany's Emil Jannings.

narrative links required a minimum literacy in the audience. The unlettered brought their offspring as translators. Robert Roberts, who grew up in the slums of the northern English industrial city Salford, recalled that 'when picture gave place to print on the screen a muddled Greek chorus of children's voices rose from the benches, piping above the piano music only to falter when confronted with an unfamiliar long word'.

France was the biggest pre-1914 producer of motion pictures, its industry dominated by the former magician George Méliès. His quirky, fantastical films such as *A Trip to the Moon* (1902) and *Conquest of the Pole* (1912) entertained growing worldwide audiences. From the expanding US industry came epic dramas such as D.W. Griffiths' *The Birth of a Nation* (1915) and the crazy antics of Mack Sennett's Keystone Kops.

The interwar years brought the cinema's golden age. Already in the early 1920s the silent screen had generated a cluster of superstars, from the comics Charlie Chaplin and Buster Keaton to the romantic husband-and-wife team of Mary Pickford and Douglas Fairbanks Snr, the vampish Pola Negri to the supreme sex symbol Rudolf Valentino. The German horror film *The Cabinet of Dr Caligari* (1919) sent shivers down audiences' spines with its tale of the mad, murderous head of an insane asylum. Sergei Eisenstein's *Battleship Potemkin* (1925) stirred them with its celebration of the Bolshevik revolution of

1917. In *The Italian Straw Hat* (1927) the Frenchman René Clair poked fun in a lighter vein at the values of the bourgeoisie.

Gradually, the cinema overhauled other forms of entertainment. In the USA, nickelodeons gave way to 'picture palaces' seating not a few hundred but 2000 or more. New

York's biggest, the Roxy, could take 5889. The typical cinema-goer was young, female, urban and working class. Many went two or even three times a week. Australia, which still had a population smaller than London's, led the world in cinema attendances, clocking up 126 million in 1929.

By now Hollywood, whose sunny climate and ample labour market made it an ideal movie-making location, dominated the commercial film business, and the coming of sound in 1928 confirmed its supremacy. The 'talkies' would carry American culture into the far corners of the English-speaking world and beyond. As the New York *Morning Post* declared: 'If the United States abolished its diplomatic and consular services, kept its ships in harbour and its tourists at home, and retired from the world's markets, its citizens, its problems, its towns and countryside, its roads, motor cars, counting houses and saloons would still be familiar to the uttermost corners of the world . . . The film is to America what the flag was once to Britain. By its means Uncle Sam may hope some day, if he is not checked in time, to Americanise the world.'

Escapism was always one of the cinema's chief appeals. A 1925 advertisement for

Paramount showed that the studios understood this clearly: 'All the adventure, all the romance, all the excitement you lack in your daily life are in – Pictures.' Romances were the most popular type, followed by lavish musicals. Hollywood obliged; nine out of ten films featured romance as the main plot or a major subplot. Men favoured Westerns and gangster movies, both essentially American genres. A stream of classics emerged, from musical blockbusters such as Busby Berkeley's *Gold Diggers* films to the raunchy humour of Mae West in *I'm No Angel* (1933), from the sultry decadence of the German import Marlene Dietrich in *Blue Angel* (1930) to the

STUDIED CRAZE Professionals demonstrate the re-bob-bob in a 1947 London ballroom. Invented by South African music publishers, the new dance was intended to start a fad which would boost their sales.

wistful mystery of her Swedish-born rival Greta Garbo in *Queen Christina* (1933), from the cool elegance of Fred Astaire and Ginger Rogers in *Flying Down to Rio* (1933) to the Boy's Own frolics of Ronald Colman in *The Prisoner of Zenda* (1937).

SIMPLY SHOCKING! New, more daring dance crazes have followed one another, including (left to right) the tango, black bottom and jive.

Movie-makers elsewhere coped with the competition as best they could. In films such as Jean Renoir's *Grand Illusion* (1937), French directors offered more intellectual subject matter, treating cinema as an art. The Germans followed the same path until their film-makers were diverted to propaganda work by the Nazi regime. The British excelled in films that drew on local nuances of language and manner, or historical traditions, as in comedies and costume dramas. They also produced some notable thrillers such as the early Alfred Hitchcock classic, *The Thirty-nine Steps* (1935).

Dance mad

The most typical patrons of the cinema – young, urban working girls – were also the most enthusiastic supporters of another craze, the dance hall. Here again, the Americans mostly set the pace. Even before the First World War, jazz and syncopated rhythms had started to cross the Atlantic to Europe, and America had established itself as the source of vibrant new dances such as the cakewalk, grizzly bear and turkey trot.

In 1913 the comedian Harry Fox devised the foxtrot for a Broadway review, the Ziegfeld Follies – based on the Parisian Folies-Bergère. At the same time, the sensuous tango, originating in the slums of Buenos Aires, was sweeping all before it. The 1920s

A SCHOOL OF LIFE AT THE MOVIES

For Polish-born Kate Simon, growing up in New York's Bronx between the wars, the cinema was an education:

'The brightest, most informative school was the movies. We learned how tennis was played and golf, what a swimming pool was and what to wear if you ever got to drive a car. We learned how tables were set, "How do you do? Pleased to meet you", how primped and starched little girls should be, how neat and straight boys should be, even when they were temporarily ragamuffins. We learned to look up soulfully and make our lips tremble to warn our mothers of a flood of tears, and though they didn't fall for it (they laughed), we kept practising. We learned how regal mothers were and how stately fathers, and of course we learned about Love, a very foreign country like maybe China or Connecticut. It was smooth and slinky, it shone and rustled. It was petals with Lillian Gish, gay flags with Mario Davies, tiger stripes with Rudolf Valentino, dog's eyes with Charlie Ray.'

brought many more new steps as short-skirted 'flappers' and their male partners danced the nights away. In 1926 the British magazine *Modern Woman* advised its readers that the 76-year-old Lord Aberconway had just celebrated his golden wedding anniversary by dancing the foxtrot, 'though he does not quite manage the Charleston'. In hotels and restaurants professional dancing couples instructed clients in the latest steps. In the USA there were gruelling marathons where the object was to keep on dancing until all other couples had collapsed. On the eve of the Second World War, the athletic jitterbug

SHOW OFF! The dynamism and daring of rock and roll in the 1950s was accentuated by the flamboyant clothes of the time.

first hit European dance floors from the USA, a taste of dance crazes to come, including swing, the jive and the twist.

Sporting lives

Throughout the century sport has reflected differences between nations. By 1900 Americans had evolved their own form of football, a sport so lethal that several college presidents banned it from their campuses. In

1906 President Theodore Roosevelt intervened, demanding rule changes to cut down the annual crop of deaths and injuries. Only baseball, another sport unique to the United States, could rival football in popularity.

In Canada, American-style football was played by the wealthy but lacrosse was still the most popular game in 1900; ice hockey would overhaul it among Canadian sportsmen by the 1920s. The Tour de France, established in 1903, rapidly became a French national institution and also boosted cycling as the most favoured sport in neighbouring Belgium and Italy. Germany and the Scandinavian nations were pre-eminent in gymnastics.

Britain, having given the world soccer, cricket, rugby and snooker, and devised the internationally accepted standards for boxing, horse racing and athletics, considered itself the world's sporting nation par excellence. In sport, as in society, the nation was divided along class lines. Although watching cricket transcended social barriers, rowing, squash, hockey, a handful of arcane games such as fives and real tennis, equestrian sports such as polo and most forms of hunting, were largely the prerogative of the public-school elite, as were sports involving travel or major expense, such as yachting and mountaineering. Tennis, croquet and golf had their following largely among the middle class. Soccer was the proletarian game. Rugby was divided between two codes – the amateur, 15 man Union

CASH OR CACHET? Professional sportsmen like this baseball player (left) came to earn big money, but these English girls (below) probably thought of tennis as a social asset.

game, played in the south of England by 'gentlemen' and in Wales by working men, and the professional, 13 man League game, which was almost entirely confined to the industrial regions of Yorkshire and Lancashire.

Female participation in sport throughout the advanced world was severely limited by

> ### DIVIDING LINE
> In prewar England the distinction between professional and amateur cricketers was marked by the way their names appeared on the score card. The initials of 'gentlemen' were printed before their surname; for 'players' the order was reversed. An unwritten law decreed that county sides and the England team could be captained only by amateurs.

prevailing notions about femininity, modesty and health. Archery was regarded as eminently suitable. Readers of the British *Badminton Magazine* were warned, however, that 'unlimited indulgence in violent outdoor pursuits, cricket, bicycling, beagling, otter-hunting, paper-chasing and – most odious of all games for women – hockey, cannot but have an unwomanly effect on a young girl's mind, no less on her appearance. Let young girls ride, skate, dance and play lawn tennis . . . but let them leave field sports to those for whom they are intended – men.'

Hi-tech sport

From the 1920s onwards advances in technology created new sports and had a profound impact on existing ones. In Britain, greyhound racing relied on electricity to power the hare, light the stadium and operate

TEEING UP Cartoonists in the interwar years poked fun at women playing traditionally male sports such as golf.

the totalisator which calculated betting odds. By 1966, with a 12 million annual attendance, it had become Britain's second most popular spectator sport after soccer. Motor racing emerged from its infancy to be joined by rally driving, speedway, dirt-track racing (which began in Australia) and go-cart racing (which began in the USA).

Radio, and later television, created mass audiences among sports fans too far away or too poor to be there in person at Wimbledon for tennis, the World Series for baseball or the Melbourne Cup for horse racing. Sports

that lent themselves to detailed commentary, such as cricket, or close-up visual coverage, such as golf, snooker or darts, came to rely increasingly on their association with broadcasting and the business interests that controlled it. At the same time, commercial opportunities for successful professional sports stars eroded the cult of the amateur – a trend that many deplored.

Politics, too, entered sport. 'Sport for All' was a slogan that governments of very different political complexions felt they could endorse and support. Nazi Germany's *Kraft durch Freude* (Strength through Joy) programme of state-sponsored sporting activities and outdoor holidays for workers and youth groups was widely noted abroad. France's left-wing Popular Front government of 1936-9 established an Office of Sport and Leisure Time and subsidised a network of *auberges de jeunesse* (youth hostels).

In 1936 a British government white paper noted that 'other nations have stolen a march on Britain in this primary matter of pursuing

LEADER OF THE PACK The final phase of the 1991 Tour de France. Cycling has won a passionate following in mainland Europe.

health'. The Conservative government accordingly allocated £2 million for a three-year programme to 'make British citizens

BIG MATCH Soccer has been England's most successful sporting export. Here Pelé scores for Brazil in the 1970 World Cup Final.

COMPETING FOR GLOBAL GLORY: THE OLYMPIC GAMES

The Olympic games have regularly brought together more people from more countries than any other event – with the exception perhaps of the annual pilgrimages of Muslims to Mecca. In spite of this record, the Olympics have also included some notable disasters. The Paris Olympics of 1900 lasted for five months and were so disorganised that many competitors did not even know what they were taking part in. Sprints were run downhill. Discus and hammer-throwers in the Bois de Boulogne kept hitting the trees. The Parisian waiter who won the marathon was suspected of taking short cuts through back alleys.

RECORD-BREAKERS In four Olympics American Ray Ewry (above) won ten golds for standing jumps. The Olympic spirit survived Hitler's attempt to turn the 1936 Berlin games (right, below) into a Nazi showcase.

The St Louis Games (1904) were financially out of reach for most Europeans. Of the 625 competitors, 533 were American and 41 Canadian. The London Games (1908) were better run. They took place in a brand-new 70 000-seater stadium at White City, the largest in the world. For the first time countries were limited to 12 competitors for each event and winners were given gold medals. The Stockholm Games (1912) were the first to combine efficiency with hospitality. The Swedes made useful technical innovations, such as electric devices to make timings as accurate as possible.

War scuppered the 1916 games planned for Berlin and the defeated nations were pointedly not invited to Antwerp in 1920. In the interwar years events such as standing jumps, tug of war and rugby were dropped from the Olympic schedule and new ones admitted – weightlifting, yachting, ice hockey, speed skating, canoeing and basketball. Winter Games were staged from 1924 and the number of events for women increased. Taking an Olympic oath (1920), flying the Olympic flag (1928) and lighting an Olympic flame (1936) were added to the opening rituals.

During the postwar decades the games were held outside Europe or North America for the first time. The number of competing nations increased. In Rome (1960), 83 nations competed and a member of the Emperor of Ethiopia's bodyguard, Abebe Bikila, became the first black African to win a gold – in the marathon, barefoot. He repeated this triumph in Tokyo (1964). At Barcelona (1992), 169 nations took part. Cuba, which had not participated since 1980, won 31 medals, coming fifth in the overall table. By then many purists were complaining that the modern Olympics' lofty vision had been clouded by professionalism, advertising, sponsorship and the demands of television. The games had become a mega-business – risky but potentially rewarding. Montreal in 1976 had budgeted for costs of $310 million and ended up facing a bill for $1.4 billion. By contrast, Los Angeles in 1980, thanks to the backing of sponsors like General Motors and Xerox, showed a $200 million surplus. By the 1996 Atlanta games, commercialism had reached the point where, as disgusted commentators pointed out, the logos of the sponsors were often more prominent than the five-ring logo of the games themselves.

more robust' by encouraging local government authorities to establish communal fitness facilities. But it took another generation for the idea to take off. In 1968 the UK had just ten sports centres providing gymnasiums, swimming pools and indoor racing tracks for local communities; by 1976 there were 400.

By the 1980s football was Germany's top sport, with 4.3 million members enrolled in clubs of one sort or another. Gymnastics, with 3.1 million active participants, was still a national passion, while the new popularity of tennis – boasting 1.2 million regular players – reflected the international triumphs of the German players Boris Becker, Steffi Graf and Michael Stich.

Many of the most popular activities in the advanced world were now non-competitive, health-orientated and even narcissistic. These included jogging, aerobics, fitness training and body building. Others required a level of income unimaginable to ordinary families even a generation before. In the France of 1960 there were just 20 000 people sailing dinghies at weekends; by 1990 there were more than 30 times that number.

A quiet night in

As homes became more comfortable, more spacious, warmer and better lit, they became more popular as a place for entertainment and a focus for leisure. Before 1914, family get-togethers, especially at birthdays and weddings, on saint's days or at Christmas, were often enlivened by singing round a piano or playing forfeits or charades. Fortunetelling was much favoured at all-female gatherings. A 1910 issue of the British magazine *The World and His Wife* featured 15 'impromptu laughter-making games' for winter parties. These included threading needles at speed, flipping a cork off the neck of a bottle while walking past it and picking up dried peas with two pencils.

Some families kept up the Victorian custom of reading aloud from a novel in the evenings. There was also an abundance of

GONE FISHING In contrast to the thrill of competitive sport, fishing – one of the most popular of all sports – allows fans to enjoy the tranquillity of a quiet day in the open air.

WORK OVER? WORK OUT The staff of a British Columbia paper mill work out. In an increasingly sedentary age, getting fit and staying fit are growing obsessions.

periodicals, many of them illustrated, for individual perusal. The adventures of Sherlock Holmes in the British *Strand Magazine* were at the height of their popularity at the start of the century. Best-selling authors for adults included Jack London, Anatole France, Colette, Thomas Mann, H.G. Wells, Arnold Bennett, Joseph Conrad and John Galsworthy. Children adored Rudyard Kipling's *Puck of Pook's Hill* (1906), Lucy Maud Montgomery's *Anne of Green Gables* (1908), set on Canada's

Prince Edward Island, and Kenneth Grahame's *Wind in the Willows* (1908). The fantasies of Jules Verne and the swashbuckling adventures of Alexandre Dumas' *Three Musketeers* – originally written for adults – held their own as international children's favourites, as did the Swiss Johanna Spyri's *Heidi*.

The less bookish played with train sets or constructional toys if they were boys, Kewpie or

Raggedy Ann dolls if they were girls. Collecting picture postcards, most of them printed in Germany, and mounting them in elaborate albums was another popular pastime. The busy-handed occupied themselves by making rag-rugs or using their skills of embroidery, fretwork or rafiawork to create knick-knacks for use as gifts or decorations in the home. Whist and bridge were socially acceptable amongst the middle and upper classes, although some strict churchgoers still regarded all card games as tantamount to reading 'the devil's books'. Older men often indulged in harmless outbursts of petty malice by trouncing each other at cribbage, dominoes or draughts (checkers). In Britain, above all, pottering in the garden or on a vegetable patch was an unfailing delight. Apartment-dwelling continentals perfected the rival arts of growing plants in window boxes and sheltered courtyards, and on balconies and rooftops.

Between the wars radios and cheap gramophones reinforced the attraction of the home at the expense of the pub. This was especially true among the unemployed and couples with children, who had little cash to spare for going out. For the better-off it was an era of crazes. Mah-jong, a Chinese gambling game, was regarded as chic

in the 1920s. Crossword puzzles became an obsession throughout the English-speaking world. The board game Monopoly swept all before it in the mid 1930s.

Radio was the most universal source of home entertainment and dance-band music the most popular form of programming. By 1930 Denmark had the highest level of radio ownership, followed by the USA, Sweden and Britain. Australia lagged a little behind but ahead of Germany, Canada, France and New Zealand. In Britain the BBC developed a strong public-service ethos under the authoritarian leadership of its first Director-General John Reith. Its mission was to inform, educate and entertain – in that order. A BBC symphony orchestra was established to keep up a constant output of classical music. Major royal ceremonies and great sporting occasions were covered as 'outside broadcasts' in the interests of national solidarity. Talks by eminent public figures were

GUESS WHO? The oldest and simplest games are often the best and never lose their popularity. Squeak, Piggy, Squeak requires the blindfold child to identify his 'victim' by sound alone.

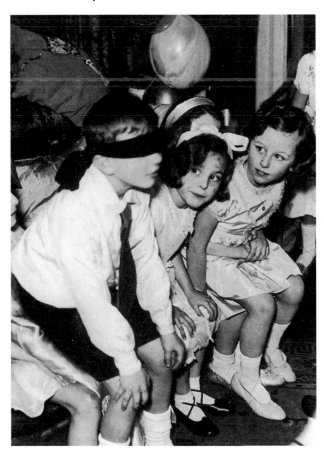

THE OLD DAYS Televisions in the 1950s were cumbersome affairs. Before the arrival of satellite and cable, programmes had to appeal to wide audiences.

scheduled but care was taken to avoid divisive issues and political extremes. Reith believed in giving people what was good for them, not whatever they wanted.

In the USA advertisers pressed radio stations to reverse this commitment. A distinctive new form of radio serial, based on

BIG BUDGETS As TV won mass audiences and improved its technology more money was spent on series such as *Dallas* (right) or *The Forsyte Saga* (below) or outside broadcasts of sporting events and public occasions.

the saga of an imaginary family, emerged under the patronage of various companies plugging household products, most typically washing powder – the 'soap opera'.

The Box in the corner

After the wireless came television. TV services began experimentally in the mid 1930s but did not start in earnest until after the Second World War a decade later. Televisions then sold faster than any other consumer durable in history. By 1954 half the households in America had one and so did a quarter of all homes in Britain and Canada.

TV output soon became the despair of cultural critics and even some of those engaged in the industry. As early as 1961 America's TV watchdog, Newton N. Ino of the Federal Communications Commission, denounced American broadcasting as: 'A

GLOBAL FOOTPRINT

In 1986 there were 4937 people for every TV set in Cameroon – and 0.9 in Bermuda, where there were, therefore, slightly more sets than people. In the United States there were 1.7 people for every set. Austria, at 2.5, had the highest level of ownership in Europe, closely followed by Denmark (2.6), West and East Germany and Finland (2.7). The UK (3) was slightly ahead of France (3.1); Poland (4.0) was on a par with Japan. Pakistan (55) was well ahead of neighbouring India (155) and war-torn Afghanistan (860). Only a few areas still remained beyond the reach of terrestrial television altogether – either because they were too poor (Botswana, the Central African Republic), too small (The Gambia) or too remote (Fiji and the Falkland Islands).

FANTASY FUN The cast of
Monty Python's Flying Circus satirise
television presenter Alan Whicker's taste
for exotic locations.

vast wasteland – a procession of game shows, violence, audience participation shows, formula comedies about totally unbelievable families . . . blood and thunder . . . mayhem, violence, sadism, murder . . . and, endlessly, commercials . . . screaming, cajoling, and offending.'

The earliest TV programmes assumed that viewers had a limited attention span and imitated the old vaudeville format of unconnected 'turns' or 'spots'. Other genres soon emerged – the celebrity chat show, the big money quiz show (such as *Wheel of Fortune*) and the formula drama (*Ironside*, *Colombo*, *Cannon* and countless others), in which the central character, a detective, lawyer, doctor or teacher, encounters a different guest star in each weekly episode. Sports coverage attracted a large male audience.

In the USA, the Public Broadcasting System was established in 1969 to raise programming standards, largely by importing productions from 'the least worst TV in the world' – that is, Britain's – and won a limited but loyal following for such diverse offerings as the classic *Forsyte Saga*, based on John Galsworthy's Edwardian novels, and the surreal *Monty Python's Flying Circus*. The establishment of international audiences for quality drama and natural history series encouraged co-production across national frontiers. The sumptuously produced *Brideshead Revisited*, a dramatisation of the novel by the English writer Evelyn Waugh, was made by a British commercial company Granada, drawing on finance from an American PBS station, a German national network and the Exxon oil corporation.

The British-made two-hour mysteries solved by ale-swilling, classical music buff Inspector Morse found a loyal audience in Australia, as did Granada's long-running soap

Coronation Street. Britain returned the compliment by making *Neighbours* a youth cult. Language barriers were readily crossed with the use of dubbing and subtitles – though as with films in the interwar years the traffic was mostly one-way, from the English-speaking world to the rest. *Dallas*, the everyday story of Texan oil tycoons, became a national obsession in the socialist Islamic republic of Algeria – everybody there apparently understood family rivalries and the abuse of wealth and power. *Yes, Minister*, which revelled in revealing the manipulative machinations of British bureaucracy, was well received in China as an accurate exposé

of how the People's Republic actually worked. And a number of Mexican and Brazilian soaps found a ready market in post-Soviet Russia.

Pop and rock

As TV was entrenching itself in the world's living rooms, popular music was turning into 'pop'. In the 1940s the big bands still held sway, producing music by adults for adults. In the 1950s solo artists like Frank Sinatra,

OL' BLUE EYES TV has enabled cabaret and concert artists like Frank Sinatra to reach simultaneous audiences of tens of millions.

Ella Fitzgerald, Perry Como and Nat King Cole began to command the adult market, while younger talents, such as Pat Boone, Elvis Presley and, in France, Johnny Halliday appealed to a booming teenage market demanding 'rock'n'roll'. Jazz and country-and-western added mainstream appeal to their established cult followings. New genres developed, such as bluegrass and rhythm and blues. The huge growth of the music business was reflected in the sales of individual 'hits'. In 1946 and 1947 around 20 records reached the million mark in the United States; a decade later the figure was over 100. Individual commercial radio stations flourished by serving specific musical markets; by 1953 there were 270

YEAH! YEAH! YEAH! By the 1960s groups such as the Beatles (below), embodiments of the newly emerging 'youth culture', inspired an almost religious fervour in their fans (left).

BEATLEMANIA! THE 'FAB FOUR' HIT NEW YORK

In February 1964 Tom Wolfe chronicled the arrival of the 'Fab Four' for the *New York Herald Tribune*:

'By six-thirty a.m. half the kids . . . were already up with their transistors plugged in their skulls . . . You could turn anywhere on the dial . . . and get the bulletins: "It's B-day! . . . The Beatles left London 30 minutes ago! . . ." By one p.m. about 4000 kids had finished school and come skipping and screaming into the international terminal at Kennedy Airport. It took 110 police to herd them. At one-twenty p.m. The Beatles' jet arrived . . . To get a better look, some of the kids came plunging down the observation deck, and some of them already had their combs out, raking their hair down over their foreheads as they ran . . . some of the girls tried to throw themselves over a retaining wall. The Beatles left the airport in four Cadillac limousines . . . Five kids in a powder blue Ford overtook the caravan on the expressway, and as they passed each Beatle, one guy hung out the back window and waved a blanket . . .

'At the Plaza Hotel there were police everywhere . . . The Plaza was petrified . . . Every entrance to the hotel was guarded. The screams started as soon as the first limousine came into view . . . The kids were still hanging around the Plaza hours after they went inside . . .

A policeman came up and one of them yelled, "He touched a Beatle! I saw him!". The girls jumped on the cop's arms and back . . . There were goony smiles all over their faces.'

American stations focusing their output on the black community alone.

By the 1960s music in the hands of groups and singers such as the Beatles, Rolling Stones, Bob Dylan and Joan Baez had become the pivotal feature of a youth sub-culture which expressed itself in dance crazes, 'way out' fashions and experiments with drug-taking. The Vietnam War and the massive expansion in the proportion of young people at college across the developed world made music more socially engaged, critical of existing society and confrontational towards authority in all its forms. The nihilistic, self-loathing Punk movement of the mid 1970s marked the most extreme expression of this trend.

Down at the flicks

As television came to monopolise family entertainment and pop music became central to youth culture, the cinema seemed to be facing terminal decline. The 1950s had their share of stars, notably Marilyn Monroe and James Dean, whose cult status in both cases was confirmed by early tragic deaths – aged 24 in a car accident for Dean, aged 36 of an overdose of sleeping pills for Monroe. Even so, by 1956 the major Hollywood studios were producing less than half as many feature films each year as they had in 1946. A decade later only one film in ten was making a profit. Britain's 1947 peak weekly cinema attendance figure of 30 million slumped to 6 million by the mid 1960s. Grudgingly, some studios survived by churning out formula weekly Westerns for the despised small screen. (Initially, Warner Brothers had refused to allow the word 'television' even to be mentioned in their films.)

In 1963 *Cleopatra*, made for 20th Century Fox at a cost of $40 million and starring Elizabeth Taylor and Richard Burton, nearly bankrupted the studio and flopped at the box

MOVIE MAGIC *Cleopatra* with Elizabeth Taylor was a box-office flop but inspired stamp designers in Mali. More successful financially were *The Godfather* (right) and *The Graduate* (below).

office. After that Hollywood began to abandon the strategy of competing with television by producing stupendous spectacles or special effects, such as Cinemascope, which could not be reproduced on the small screen. The fact that good movies did well if they were good movies was painfully rediscovered. *The Sound of Music*, made in 1965 for $8 million, grossed $78 million in North America alone.

The real turnaround came in 1967 when *The Graduate*, starring Dustin Hoffman, and *Bonnie and Clyde*, with Warren Beatty and Faye Dunaway, drew young people back into the cinemas. Audience figures turned up again for the first time in 20 years. In 1968 Hollywood finally abandoned the hallowed Production Code which for decades had established standards of taste, decency and

social acceptability. Films became more violent, more sexually explicit – and often more original in content and treatment.

The next year *Easy Rider*, made for a mere $400 000, grossed $25 million. In the same year *Midnight Cowboy*, directed by an Englishman, John Schlesinger, became the first 1960s movie to win the Best Film Oscar without being based on a musical or an existing book. In 1971 *The French Connection* became the first crime story to win the Best Film accolade. It was followed in 1972 by *The Godfather* and in 1973 by *The Sting*. During the following decades a number of directors showed that it was perfectly possible to combine quality with profits in widely acclaimed box-office hits such as Alan J. Pakula's *Sophie's Choice* (1982) and Steven Spielberg's *Schindler's List* (1993).

1900s buzzwords: nickelodeon, suffragette, chauffeur, hamburger

1900

The World Exhibition and the second Olympiad are held in Paris. The first escalator for public use is demonstrated at the exhibition. The Paris **Métro** is opened and motorised ambulances are introduced, also in France.

PALACE OF GLASS The Horticultural Pavilion at the Paris exhibition.

Hamburgers are first sold in New Haven, Connecticut.

The first **Zeppelin** airship – designed by the retired German army officer, Ferdinand, Graf von Zeppelin – makes its maiden flight from a floating hangar on Lake Constance.

Harvey Samuel Firestone founds the **Firestone** Tire and Rubber Company in Akron, Ohio.

1901

In the USA **Oldsmobile** becomes the first motor manufacturer to turn out more than ten cars a week.

The first **Nobel** prizes are awarded, under terms laid down in the will of the Swedish inventor of dynamite, Alfred Nobel. The first winner of the prize for physics is the German Wilhelm Röntgen, discoverer of the X-ray.

The first electric **hearing aid** is patented in the USA. In Britain, the first practical **vacuum cleaner** is invented by Hubert Cecil Booth, a bridge engineer.

The first **body-building** contest is held in the Royal Albert Hall, London.

1902

The **Pepsi-Cola** and **Texaco** companies are founded.

Beatrix Potter's *The Tale of Peter Rabbit* is published in Britain. A **wax disc** of the Italian tenor Enrico Caruso singing 'Vesti la giubba' from the opera *I Pagliacci* sells over a million copies.

Berlin's **U-bahn** (Underground) opens.

The **Teddy Bear**, named for US President Theodore 'Teddy' Roosevelt is invented in the USA.

1903

The Boston Red Sox win the first **World Series** baseball tournament. The first **Western** movie, *Kit Carson*, opens in the USA – it has a running time of 21 minutes.

The Wright Brothers achieve **powered flight** at Kitty Hawk, North Carolina. In Detroit, farmer's son Henry Ford founds the **Ford** Motor Company.

The first **Tour de France** cycle race takes place.

1904

Some 150 000 people use the first section of the New York **subway** on its opening day.

The Fédération Internationale de Football Association (**FIFA**) is set up in Paris.

The **tea bag** and the **caterpillar** tractor are pioneered in the USA. The domestic **Thermos** flask is marketed in Germany. The Parisian jeweller Louis Cartier invents the **wristwatch**.

Premiere of **J.M. Barrie**'s *Peter Pan*.

1905

The Pittsburgh-based firm H.J. Heinz markets **baked beans** in Britain.

The first **nickelodeon** opens in Pittsburgh. New York sees the first gallery dedicated to **photography**.

The electrification of London **Underground** is completed. In France, **oxyacetylene** welding, intelligence tests and factory production of aircraft are pioneered.

1906

England beats France 35-8 in the first international **rugby** match.

The first **Mozart Festival** is held in Salzburg. The first **animated cartoon** is released in the USA.

1907

The Australian Arbitration Court establishes the concept of the **basic wage**.

The Shell Oil Trust is founded, and the **Boy Scouts** movement established.

Persil washing powder is produced in Germany. **Meccano** construction sets are marketed in Britain.

1908

Filming of *The Count of Monte Cristo*, one of the earliest story-telling movies, is completed in **Hollywood**. The next year a former tavern on Sunset Boulevard is converted into Hollywood's first film studio.

The Ford Motor Company begins production of the **Model T**. Buick and Oldsmobile merge to create **General Motors**.

Disposable **paper cups** are introduced by a New York company.

Advertisements in the US press offer householders the chance to buy an upright vacuum cleaner for $70 after ten days' free trial. The man behind this scheme is a former harness-maker from Ohio, W.H. **Hoover**.

The first international meeting of **psychiatrists** is held at Salzburg.

1909

The General Electric Company produces the first electric **toaster**.

Frenchman Louis **Blériot** flies the English Channel.

1910s buzzwords: ace, chow, civvies, dud, red tape, rookie, shell shock, vamp

1910

The **tango** craze sweeps the USA and Europe. The 5000 seat Gaumont Palace, the world's largest cinema, opens in Paris. Also in France, fluorescent **neon** lights are introduced.

Father's Day is first celebrated in Spokane, Washington state.

Iodine proves useful as a disinfectant and antiseptic.

1911

The first **Indianapolis '500'** motor race is held.

The **Olivetti** company is founded in Italy.

The US introduces **white lines** to mark the middle of roads. The US Army adopts the **Colt .45** automatic pistol.

1912

American Albert Berry makes the first **parachute jump** from a plane – the aircraft is flying at a height of 1500 ft (460 m). A London-Paris **airmail** postal service is introduced.

Morse code **SOS** is adopted as international distress signal.

Manhattan delicatessen-owner Richard **Hellmann** sells his ready-made Blue Ribbon Mayonnaise in wooden containers.

Coco **Chanel** opens her first salon in the resort of Deauville, France.

1913

Grand Central Station in New York is opened – it is the world's largest railway station. The **Panama Canal** is completed linking the Atlantic and Pacific oceans.

NO 5 Coco Chanel, *marquise* of the perfume bottles (*flaconnerie*). Eugene Sandow (background), American apostle of body building.

The first **crossword** puzzle is published in the *New York World*.

The first home electric **refrigerator** is marketed in the USA.

The Ford Motor Company's moving **assembly line** reduces production time per vehicle from $12\frac{1}{2}$ hours to $1\frac{1}{2}$ hours.

1914

The **First World War** breaks out in Europe.

Edgar Rice Burroughs' *Tarzan of the Apes* is published. It is the first **Tarzan** book.

1915

The first **tanks** are developed in Britain. The German, Hugo **Junkers**, develops the first all-metal aircraft.

Heatproof **Pyrex** glass is developed in the USA.

FIRST THROUGH The SS *Ancon* was the first ship through the Panama Canal.

1916

Britain introduces **British Summer Time** – clocks are put forward one hour in summer as a measure to 'save' daylight and fuel.

The first **self-service** store is opened in Memphis, Tennessee.

The first **birth-control** clinic is opened in the USA by Margaret Sanger.

Jeanette Rankin becomes the first **woman member** of US Congress.

American automobile manufacturers introduce **windshield** wipers and the Dodge Company produces the first all-steel automobile bodywork.

The Canadian, Peter Nissen, designs the **Nissen hut** to house troops.

Lightweight, non-corrosive **asbestos** cement pipes are developed in Italy.

The German company Telefunken begins the mass production of **radio valves**.

1917

The **Trans-Australian** railroad is completed; the last 300 miles (480 km) being the longest straight stretch in the world.

German soap shortages stimulate the production of the pioneer **detergent** Nekal. The US Navy adopts windproof flying jackets with **'zip'** fastenings.

In the USA, the annual **Pulitzer** prizes are established for outstanding achievements in journalism and letters. The awards were endowed by the late Hungarian-born journalist and newspaper editor Joseph Pulitzer.

1918

New Mexico store-owner Conrad Hilton buys the Mobley Hotel in Cisco, Texas. Before long he acquires hotels in Waco, Dallas and Fort Worth – the start of the **Hilton** chain.

Outbreak of the worldwide **influenza** epidemic which kills more people than the First World War.

1919

The **jazz** craze spreads from the USA to Europe.

British flyers John Alcock and Arthur Brown complete the first **transatlantic** flight (Newfoundland-Ireland) in 16 hours 27 minutes.

AT & T introduces the first **dial telephones** in the USA.

The **Bauhaus** group is established in Germany to promote modern design.

1920s buzzwords: blind date, bootlegger, flapper, goofy, hooch

1920

The first international **feminist** conference opens in Geneva.

Transcontinental **airmail** services begin between New York and San Francisco.

The USA adopts **Prohibition**; the sale of intoxicating liquors remains illegal until 1933.

Marconi establishes the first public **radio station** in the USA. In Britain, HMV devises the first gramophone **disc autochanger**.

America's Jantzen Company markets the first elasticised **one-piece bathing suit**.

1921

The first **Autobahn** is completed in Germany.

The **BCG** tuberculosis vaccine is pioneered in France.

Coco Chanel markets **Chanel No 5** perfume in France. The first bathing beauty contest is organised for the title **Miss America**.

1922

The **BBC** is founded.

The **Reader's Digest** is founded in the USA.

American **cocktails** become fashionable in Europe. The **dance marathon** craze seizes the USA. The first improvised **water-skis** are used at Lake Pepin, Minnesota.

The Canadian scientists Frederick Banting and Charles Best successfully treat diabetes with **insulin**.

London's Piccadilly Line introduces the first underground train with **automatic doors**.

1923

Time magazine is first published in the USA. The BBC introduces daily **weather forecasts**.

The **Charleston** dance craze sweeps the USA. The American celebration of **Mother's Day** is adopted in Europe.

The first **speedway** motorcycle races are organised in NSW, Australia. Littlewoods **football pools** are founded in Britain. In London, **Wembley** Stadium opens as part of an Imperial exhibition.

The American LaPlante-Choate Company introduces the **bulldozer**.

1924

The **MGM** motion-picture company and **IBM** corporation are founded.

The German **Leica** company pioneers mass production of a precision miniature camera.

The first **Zeppelin** transatlantic flight takes place, from Friedrichshafen on Lake Constance to New York.

The first **Surrealist** exhibition is held in Paris.

MODERN LINES The surrealist Salvador Dalí with his wife Gala. A tubular chair (background), designed in 1926.

British hairdresser Antoine introduces the **blue rinse** for grey hair.

1925

The Exposition des Arts Décoratifs in Paris popularises the **Art Deco** style.

The *New Yorker* magazine begins publication. The world's first **motel** opens at Monterey, California.

1926

ICI is founded in Britain. **Lufthansa** is founded in Germany.

Lone Scottish inventor John Logie Baird demonstrates **television**.

1927

Charles A. Lindbergh makes the first **solo transatlantic flight** (New York-Paris) in 33 hours 39 mins.

Pan American Airways is founded. A London-New York **transatlantic telephone** service is inaugurated.

Shingled haircuts become fashionable.

1928

Australia introduces the **flying doctor** service.

Walt Disney produces his first **Mickey Mouse** cartoon, *Steamboat Willie*. Mickey Mouse and later Donald Duck and the dogs Pluto and Goofy entertain growing audiences during the Great Depression.

Scottish researcher Alexander Fleming discovers **penicillin** by accident but fails to exploit its potential.

1929

The **Wall Street Crash** and central European banking crises trigger worldwide depression.

The Anglo-Dutch **Unilever** Corporation is founded, manufacturing margarine, soaps and other fat-based products.

SYDNEY'S PRIDE The Harbour Bridge and, later in the century, the Opera House became Sydney's world-famous landmarks.

The French-born Raymond Loewy founds the bureau that will pioneer **streamlined** industrial design in the USA. Some of his famous designs include a refrigerator for Sears, Roebuck, automobiles for Studebaker, railway locomotives and passenger carriages and Greyhound buses.

The first Academy Awards are distributed. They are nicknamed the **Oscars**, apparently because an official quipped that the statuettes looked like his uncle Oscar.

The cartoon characters **Tintin** and **Popeye** make their first appearance.

The **iron lung** life-support machine is developed in the USA for polio victims.

The British Dunlop Company develops **foam rubber**.

1930s buzzwords: dole, fireside chat, jitterbug, New Deal, swing

1930

Uruguay beats Argentina 4-2 to win the first-ever soccer **World Cup**.

PVC and **Scotch Tape** are invented in the USA.

1931

J. Schick markets the **electric razor** in the USA and **Alka Seltzer** makes its appearance there, too.

The **Empire State Building** is opened as the world's tallest structure.

Britain's King George V makes the first **royal radio broadcast** 'to the children of the Empire'.

1932

The BBC launches its first **regular television service**. It broadcasts four programmes a week.

The **Sydney Harbour Bridge** is opened in Australia.

1933

The **Boeing** 247 airliner, capable of cruising at 189 mph (304 km/h), enters regular service.

Monopoly, the world's best-selling board game, is invented in the USA.

1934

ICI produces clear plastic **Perspex**.

Cat's-eyes road reflectors are invented in Britain.

1935

George **Gallup** pioneers reliable opinion polling in the USA.

Catastrophic **dust storms** devastate American farmlands, forcing mass migrations.

Penguin Books launch the 'paperback' revolution in Britain.

1936

The first **Butlin's** holiday camp is opened at Skegness, Lincolnshire, on England's east coast.

FLYING HIGH The cover for *Picture Post*'s first issue, October 1, 1938.

Ferdinand Porsche unveils the prototype Volkswagen **'Beetle'**; millions of German workers subscribe to savings schemes to buy one, but few will be built until after the Second World War.

Roll-on roll-off (Ro-Ro) ferries are introduced on cross-Channel routes between England and France.

The first **vitamin pills** are marketed in the USA.

1937

The **Golden Gate** bridge is opened to traffic in San Francisco.

British engineer Frank Whittle builds the first **jet** engine.

The first **magnetic tape recorder** is marketed in Germany.

Nescafé, the first commercially successful **instant coffee**, is made by the Swiss Nestlé Company.

Disney issues *Snow White and the Seven Dwarfs* – the first all-colour **cartoon** feature film with sound.

1938

New Zealand introduces a **state medical service**.

The first issue of the **photo-illustrated** weekly news magazine *Picture Post* appears in Britain.

Hungarian Laszlo Biro patents the **ballpoint** pen, using quick-drying printer's ink. America's Du Pont corporation manufactures **nylon** to

make toothbrushes; nylon stockings are first sold in 1939.

1939

Pan American Airways begins regular **transatlantic flights**.

The **Citroën 2CV** (*Deux Chevaux*) is initially launched in France but is shelved after the outbreak of war.

The **Second World War** breaks out.

1940s buzzwords: blitz, ersatz, gobbledygook, kamikaze, Mae West, PoW, walkie-talkie

1940

The **'Jeep'** (General Purpose) four-wheel-drive vehicle is adopted by US forces.

The US pioneers **freeze-drying** for food preservation.

1941

The **aerosol** can is developed for spraying insecticides. Massey-Harris manufacture the first **combine harvesters**.

In Britain the RAF's first **jet-powered aircraft**, the Gloster E28/39, has a successful test flight.

WHITE CHRISTMAS Irving Berlin's Christmas musical, starring Bing Crosby, became a firm favourite.

1942

The Oxford Committee for Famine Relief (**OXFAM**) is founded by Oxford classics professor Gilbert Murray to relieve famine in Greece which kills 350 000.

Napalm is invented in the USA.

Bing Crosby records Irving Berlin's **'White Christmas'**.

1943

The first **kidney dialysis** machine is improvised in the Netherlands.

The **aqualung** is invented in France.

IKEA, the Swedish furniture retailer, is founded.

1944

DDT insecticide is used for the first time on a large scale – to halt a typhus epidemic in Naples.

1945

The USA introduces **fluoridation** of water to combat tooth decay.

1946

The **jukebox** craze spreads from the USA to Europe. The two-piece **bikini** swimsuit is designed in France.

1947

Christian Dior's lavish **New Look** revolutionises Parisian haute couture.

Edinburgh launches its **International Festival** of Music and Drama.

US presidential adviser Bernard Baruch coins the term **'Cold War'**.

The **polaroid** camera is demonstrated for the first time. The first **microwave** cooker is marketed in the USA.

The Goodyear company pioneers the **tubeless tyre**. The **Vespa** motor scooter is launched in Italy.

1948

Scientists at the USA's Bell Laboratories invent the **transistor** to replace the thermionic valve. The **Morris Minor** saloon car is manufactured in Britain.

PENNY IN THE SLOT Postwar US exports to Europe included the jukebox.

The **Velcro** fastener is invented by the Swiss engineer George deMestral.

1949

The maiden flight takes place of the De Havilland Comet, the world's first **jet airliner**.

Scrabble, the word game, is launched in the USA.

1950s buzzwords: beatnik, fallout shelter, station wagon

1950

Diners' Club pioneers the first **credit card**.

The first **kidney transplant** operation is performed in the USA.

1951

Deutsche Grammophon markets the first 33 rpm **long-play record**. Chrysler pioneers **power-steering**.

Colour TV becomes available in the USA.

1952

The airline TWA pioneers **'tourist class'** flights.

The world's first **sex-change** operation is performed in Denmark.

The first pocket-sized **transistor radio** is marketed by Sony in Japan.

1953

An Anglican clergyman, the Rev Chad Varah, founds the **Samaritans** organisation in London to counsel potential suicides.

The *Kinsey Report* declares that a quarter of American wives are **unfaithful** to their husbands.

1954

Frozen food sales in the USA surpass $1 billion a year.

Medical student Roger Bannister becomes the first man to run a **four-minute mile**.

Photochemical **smog** identified in Los Angeles.

Rock'n'roll sweeps the USA with The Crew Cuts' 'Sh-Boom', Bill Haley and the Comets' 'Rock Around the Clock' and Elvis Presley's 'That's All Right Mama'.

1955

Disneyland opens in California.

Commercial TV begins in Britain. Also in Britain, the **hovercraft** is developed, and frozen **fish fingers** are marketed.

1956

Ampex of California launch the first commercially viable **video recorder**. Long-life stainless-steel **razor blades** are marketed in Britain.

1957

France, Germany, Italy, Belgium, the Netherlands and Luxembourg sign the Treaty of Rome to form the European Economic Community (**EEC**).

The first **stereo** discs are marketed in the USA. Also in the USA, the **Frisbee** disc-throwing craze sweeps college campuses.

The **Citroën DS19** is launched.

1958

The lightweight, cheap **aluminium can** is developed in the USA. **Lycra** artificial elastic is marketed in the USA. **Nonstick** frying pans are marketed in France.

The **Honda 50** is launched in Japan – it will become the world's biggest-selling motorcycle.

1959

The **Mini**, designed by Alec Issigonis, is first manufactured in Britain. The first commercial **Xerox** copier is introduced.

FALLOUT Cold War jitters brought devices such as the family fallout shelter. Background: the Vespa motor scooter, synonymous with youth and romance.

IAN FLEMING'S **DR. NO**

THE FIRST JAMES BOND FILM!

KING OF COOL   Sean Connery, the original film James Bond.

Sony market a transistorised **portable television**. The Barbie doll is launched in the USA.

The four-hour film epic *Ben Hur* wins **11 Oscars** – an all-time record.

1960s buzzwords: commune, flower power, gear, LSD, tie-dye, trendy

1960

After being cleared of **obscenity** charges, Penguin Books sell 200 000 copies of D.H. Lawrence's *Lady Chatterley's Lover* on the first day of publication.

Britain's Hawker **'jump jet'**, the first vertical takeoff plane, is test flown successfully.

Surgeons in Birmingham, Britain, develop the first **heart pacemaker**. The oral contraceptive pill is marketed in the USA.

1961

Three million copies of the **New English Bible** version of the New Testament are sold in its first year of publication.

The 'freedom riders' campaign ends **segregation** on US interstate buses.

Chubby Checker inspires the **twist** dance craze.

Miniskirts are shown as haute couture at the Dior and Courreges fashion houses.

Texas Instruments patents the **silicon chip**.

1962

Amnesty International is founded in London to campaign for political prisoners.

The first **James Bond** film, *Dr. No*, comes out.

Lasers are first used for eye surgery. General Motors installs the first **industrial robots**. Canadian thinker Marshall McLuhan predicts that electronic communications will make the world a **global village**.

1963

The first giant **hypermarket** is opened in France by Carrefour. Kodak launch the **Instamatic** camera using cartridge film.

1964

The 130 mph (210 km/h) Shinkansen – **Bullet Train** – service is launched to link Tokyo and Kyoto.

Ships designed to carry standardised containers revolutionise international trade. IBM introduce the first **word processor**.

Beatlemania sweeps the USA. The world's first **discotheque** – Whiskey-a-Go-Go – opens in Los Angeles.

British youth styles are dominated by designer Mary Quant and hairdresser Vidal Sassoon. Terence Conran opens **Habitat** home-ware store in London.

High-yielding rice strains developed in the Philippines initiate a **'green revolution'** in developing countries.

1965

BP discovers **natural gas** in the North Sea.

The Early Bird **communications satellite** enables the exchange of TV programmes between Europe and North America.

Soft **contact lenses** are invented.

1966

TV sci-fi serial ***Star Trek*** begins.

1967

South African surgeon Christiaan Barnard performs the first **heart transplant** operation.

France pioneers construction of a **tidal barrage** to produce electricity.

1968

Student riots in Paris.

1969

Hundreds of millions of people worldwide watch US astronauts **land on the Moon**.

Massive **anti-Vietnam** War demonstrations erupt across the USA. Some 400 000 attend the Woodstock Rock Festival in New York State.

Monty Python's Flying Circus is shown on British TV for the first time.

The Anglo-French supersonic airliner **Concorde** makes its maiden flight.

1970s buzzwords: encounter group, jogging, singles bar, streaking, transcendental meditation

1970

Expo '70 in Osaka is Asia's first world fair.

The **Gay Liberation Front** holds its first demonstration in Britain.

The Boeing 747 **'jumbo jet'** enters transatlantic service.

IBM develop the **floppy disk** for storing computer data.

1971

The US Intel Company introduces the microprocessor. Texas Instruments

BEAM ME UP   *Star Trek*, one of many 1960s institutions that would outlast the decade. Disposable mini dresses (background) were less successful.

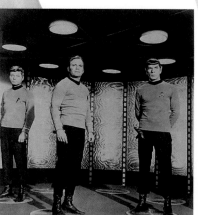

---

markets the first **pocket calculator** – weighing some 2^{1}/$_2$ lb (1.1 kg).

The Magi-Mix **food processor** is exhibited in Paris.

1972

Total sales of the Volkswagen **Beetle** overtake those of the Model T Ford.

The **feminist** magazines *MS* and *Spare Rib* appear in the USA and Britain.

1973

An Arab-led oil-price hike provokes a global **energy crisis**.

Britain, Denmark and Ireland join the **EEC**.

The **Sydney Opera House** is opened.

Supermarkets introduce **computer-coded labels**.

1974

Richard **Nixon** becomes the first US President to resign.

British fashion designer Laura Ashley opens her first US shop. **McDonald's** opens its first British hamburger restaurant in south-east London.

The **IRA** launches a bombing campaign in mainland Britain.

1975

Liquid crystal displays are used for calculators and digital watches.

In the **International Women's Year** Japanese Junko Tobei becomes the first woman to reach the top of Mount Everest.

1976

Punk style and music emerge in Britain.

The USA celebrates its **Bicentennial**.

1977

Saturday Night Fever inspires a worldwide **disco-dancing** craze.

The Apple II **personal computer** is launched. The first cheap autofocus camera is marketed.

THE VICTIMS A vast quilt was one memorial to those killed by the new plague of AIDS.

1978

Louise Brown, the first **test-tube baby**, is born in Manchester, Britain.

Compact discs (CDs) are first demonstrated.

1979

Canada becomes the first country to operate a **satellite TV** broadcasting service. The **mobile cellular phone** is launched.

The Sony **Walkman** personal stereo is launched in Japan.

The game **Trivial Pursuit** is invented in Canada.

1980s buzzwords: cellulite, interface, nerd, quality time, safe sex, sound bite, yuppie

1980

The laser-scanning process for **bar codes** is perfected by IBM in the USA and NEC in Japan.

SINGING FOR THE STARVING Bob Geldof's Live Aid concert built on the success of the Band Aid record.

Rollerblades are invented in USA as a summer training tool for ice-hockey players.

1981

AIDS is first officially recognised in the USA.

The **Rubik's Cube** puzzle (invented in 1974) becomes a global craze.

Some 700 million people worldwide watch the marriage of Britain's Prince **Charles** and Lady **Diana** Spencer.

1982

Rap music becomes the rage in the USA and Britain. The first **CD players** are marketed in Japan.
Michael Jackson's *Thriller* LP is released. It goes on to sell an all-time record of 47 million copies.

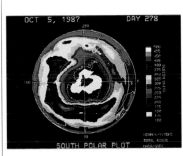

HOLE IN THE SKY Satellite images brought proof of ozone depletion.

1983

Widespread **anti-nuclear** demonstrations take place in Britain, West Germany, Italy and the Netherlands.

1984

Apple's user-friendly **Macintosh computer** is launched.

The **Band Aid** record raises money to relieve famine in Ethiopia.

1985

The World Health Organisation declares **AIDS** an epidemic.

The 17-year-old German, **Boris Becker**, becomes Wimbledon's youngest-ever men's singles lawn tennis champion.

The **Home Shopping Network** TV sales channel is launched in the United States.

LAST GUARD East German guards line the Berlin Wall, whose fall shortly afterwards marked the end of an era.

1986

The first **heart, lung and liver transplant** is performed in Cambridge, Britain.

Scientists express concern over the **greenhouse effect** and the thinning of the ozone layer.

1987

A freak **hurricane** destroys 15 million trees in southern England.

A worldwide **stock exchange crash** creates turmoil on Black Monday, October 19.

Solar-powered cars race across Australia from north to south.

1988

Australia marks the **bicentennial** of European settlement. The Reserve Bank of Australia issues a laminated **counterfeit-proof** banknote.

1989

France celebrates the **bicentennial** of the Revolution of 1789.

The **Berlin Wall** is demolished.

Nintendo produces the handheld video **Game Boy**.

1990s buzzwords: BSE, double whammy, ethnic cleansing, road rage

1990

West and East Germany are **reunited**.

The **Teenage Mutant Ninja Turtles** craze is at its height.

1991

Operation **Desert Storm** liberates Kuwait from the attentions of Iraq's Saddam Hussein.

The last **apartheid** laws are abolished in South Africa.

Sales of **CDs** outstrip those of tapes and records.

1992

The **Euro Disney** amusement park opens near Paris. **Madonna**'s photo-album *Sex* sells 100 000 copies in 12 hours.

1993

A British insurance company values a **wife's work** at £349 a week.

Rolls Royce opens its first showroom in Russia.

1994

The **Channel Tunnel** is opened. London-Paris and London-Brussels Eurostar train services begin.

Nelson **Mandela** is sworn in as the first black president of South Africa.

1995

The USA is mesmerised by the murder trial and acquittal of former football-player **O.J. Simpson**. A civil court later finds him liable for the deaths of his ex-wife and her friend, and awards huge damages against him.

1996

European farming is traumatised by the **BSE** beef crisis.

Bands such as Oasis and Blur pioneer **Britpop.**

1997

At 43, **Tony Blair** becomes the youngest British prime minister for nearly 200 years.

Unprecedented public mourning sweeps Britain after **Diana,** Princess of Wales, is killed in a car accident in Paris. A record audience, estimated at up to 2 billion, watch the funeral which is televised worldwide.

INDEX

ACKNOWLEDGMENTS

Abbreviations:
T=top; M= middle; B= bottom;
L= left; R= right.

3 Ullstein Bilderdienst, L; Corbis-Bettman, LM; Popperfoto, RM; Hulton Getty, R. 6 Corbis-Bettmann, BL; Dennis Gilbert, Arcaid, BR. 7 Illustrated London News, L; Popperfoto, R. 8 Popperfoto, TM; Corbis-Bettmann, BL. 9 Popperfoto, TL; Vintage Magazine Company, BR. 10 Illustrated London News, TR; N.D. Comtec, M; Mary Evans Picture Library, BL. 11 Chris Bland/Arcaid; Michael Nichols/Magnum, L; Hulton Getty, ML; Giraudon/Bridgeman Art Library, MR; Mary Evans Picture Library, R. 12 Camera Press, BL, TR. 13 AKG Photo, TR; Corbis-Bettmann, B. 14 Giraudon/Bridgeman Art Library, L; Mary Evans Picture Library, TR; Corbis-Bettman, MR, BR. 15 Corbis-Bettmann, TL; Popperfoto, MR. 16 AKG Photo, TR; Corbis-Bettmann, L. 17 Hulton Getty, TR. 18 Mary Evans Picture Library, TM, BL; Popperfoto, LM. 19 Corbis-Bettmann, TR, TM; Simon Kenny/Belle/Arcaid, MM; Constantine Manos/Magnum, BL. 20 Corbis-Bettmann, T, ML. 21 Popperfoto, TL; Hulton Getty, MR, B. 22 Hulton Getty, TL; Orde Eliason/Link,TR; John Parkin/Link, BL. 22-23 Alex Bartel/Arcaid. 23 Richard Bryant/Arcaid, TR; David Hurn/Magnum, BR. 24 Hulton Getty, TR; Popperfoto, BL. 24-25 Burt Glinn/Magnum. 26 Corbis-Bettmann, BL; Mary Evans Picture Library, MR. 27 Topham Picturepoint, TL; Ullstein Bilderdienst, BR; Mary Evans Picture Library, MR, ML. 28 Popperfoto, TL; Corbis-Bettmann, M. 29 Popperfoto, TL; Sygma, BR. 30 Roger-Viollet, TL; Hulton Getty, BR; Alfred Dunhill Archive, BL. 31 Illustration by Graham White, reference courtesy of Corbis-Bettmann and Hulton Getty, TL; Michael Nichols/Magnum, BR. 32 Fred Mayer/Magnum, TR; J.R. Eyerman, Time Inc./Katz Pictures, BL. 33 Clarence Saunders/ Library of Congress; Ullstein Bilderdienst, L; Advertising Archives, ML; Anthony Blake Photo Library, MR; Roger-Viollet, R. 34 Topham Picturepoint, B. 35 Mary Evans Picture Library, TL; Corbis-Bettmann, MR. 36 Mary Evans Picture Library, TM, BM; Ullstein Bilderdienst, L. 37 Mary Evans Picture Library, M; Corbis-Bettmann/UPI, BL. 38 Hulton Getty, TR; Mary Evans Picture Library, M; Image Library of New South Wales, BL. 39 Topham Picturepoint. 40 Camera Press, L, BR. 41 Jean-Loup Charmet, MR; The Granger Collection, BR. 42 Corbis-Bettmann/UPI, ML; Cadbury Ltd, BR. 43 Collection of the New York Historical Society, TL; Roger-Viollet, R. 44 Corbis-Bettmann/UPI, TL; Topham Picturepoint, TM; Mary

Evans Picture Library, M; Hulton Getty, BR. 45 The Granger Collection, TL; Topham Picturepoint, B. 46 Topham Picturepoint. 47 Ullstein Bilderdienst, TR; Peter Paz/Image Bank, BR. 48 Jon Love/Image Bank, TL; Lou Jones/Image Bank, BL. 49 Topham Picturepoint, TL; Philip J. Griffiths/Magnum, R. 50 Topham Picturepoint. 51 Corbis-Bettmann. 52 Ullstein Bilderdienst, TR; Popperfoto, L. 53 Advertising Archives, TR; Popperfoto, B. 54 Corbis-Bettmann/UPI, L; Mary Evans Picture Library, TM; Robert Harding Picture Library, BR. 55 Popperfoto, TL; American Vogue 1926/Condé Nast Publications, New York, BR. 56 Topham Picturepoint, TL; SuperStock, TR; Corbis-Bettmann, BL. 57 SuperStock, BL; Paul Bremen Collection, USA/Bridgeman Art Library, BM; Vintage Magazine Co., TR; Topham Picturepoint, RM. 58 Robert Opie Collection, TL; Popperfoto, BL; Hulton Getty, TM; Topham Picturepoint, MR. 59 Advertising Archives, TR,B. 60 Topham Picturepoint, TL; Pictorial Press, R, BM. 61 Pictorial Press, L, M, BR. 62 Advertising Archives, LM; Corbis-Bettmann/UPI, R. 62-63 Illustration by Kevin Jones Associates, B. 63 Camera Press, TM; Gary Parker/Photofusion, R. 64 Hulton Getty. 65 Mary Evans Picture Library, TL, ML, BR. 66 G. Spencer Pryse/Public Records Office, TM; Fred Taylor/Public Records Office, M; Robert Opie Collection, TR, B. 67 The Granger Collection. 68 Ullstein Bilderdienst, L; Popperfoto, TR. 69 Robert Opie Collection, TL; Corbis-Bettmann, R; Mary Evans Picture Library, TM, BM. 70 Corbis-Bettmann/UPI, ML. 70-71 Corbis-Bettmann/UPI. 71 Roger Viollet. 72 Corbis-Bettmann, TL, ML, BR. 73 Illustration by Kevin Jones Associates. 74 Hulton Getty, TL; Popperfoto, B. 75 Hulton Getty, BL; Pictorial Press, TL, TR. 76 Anthony Blake Photo Library, TR, B. 77 Anthony Blake Photo Library, TM; Camera Press, TL, TR, BL, BR. 78 Kermani-Liaison/FSP/Gamma, TL; Chris Steele Perkins/Magnum, ML. 79 Popperfoto; Robert Opie Collection, L; Andreas Springer/Ullstein Bilderdienst, ML; Mary Evans Picture Library, MR; Ullstein Bilderdienst, R. 80 Pictorial Press, TR; AKG Photo, BL. 81 Hulton Getty, ML; Popperfoto, B. 82 L'Illustration/Sygma. 83 Eve Arnold/Magnum, TL; Hulton Getty, M, BR. 84 Keystone/Sygma, B; Robert Opie Collection, M; Ullstein Bilderdienst, MR. 85 Ullstein Bilderdienst, TL, B. 86 Eve Arnold/Magnum, TL; Marie Stopes International, BM. 86-87 Ullstein Bilderdienst. 87 Hulton Getty, TL,

BR. 88 Rotolo-Liaison/FSP/ Gamma, TR; Noël Quidu/FSP/ Gamma, ML; Hulton Getty, BR. 89 Burt Glinn/Magnum, TL; P. Zachman/Magnum, R. 90 Mary Evans Picture Library, BL, MR. 91 Corbis-Bettmann, TL; Hulton Getty, B. 92 Ullstein Bilderdienst, TL; Hulton Getty, B. 93 Hulton Getty, TL; Mary Evans Picture Library, BR; Süddeutscher Verlag, BL. 94 Corbis-Bettmann. 95 Popperfoto, TR; Ullstein Bilderdienst, BL. 96 Corbis-Bettmann, TR, BL. 97 Corbis-Bettmann, TR, B; Hulton Getty, MR. 98 Camera Press, TR; Corbis-Bettmann, BL. 99 Mirror Syndication International, TL, TM, BL; Corbis-Bettmann, TR; Science Photo Library, M. 100 Corbis-Bettmann, L; John Walmsley Photo Library, TM; Hulton Getty, TR. 101 Corbis-Bettmann, ML, B. 102 Mary Evans Picture Library, L; Robert Opie Collection, TM; John Frost Historical Newspaper Service/ illustration by Kevin Jones Associates, MR. 103 Eve Arnold/Magnum, BL; Mary Evans Picture Library, M. 104 Sygma. 105 Corbis-Bettmann, TL, BR. 106 Keystone/ Sygma, BL; Ullstein Bilderdienst, TR. 107 J.P. Laffont/Sygma, R; Frederic Stevens/Rex Features, BL. 108 Frank Spooner Pictures, BL, TR. 109 Frank Spooner Pictures, TL; Abbas/Magnum, BL; Eve Arnold/ Magnum, TR. 110 Christoph Henning/Ullstein Bilderdienst, TR; Rex Features, BL; Jon Walter/Katz, M. 111 D. Goldberg/Sygma, TL; Andreas Springer/Ullstein Bilderdienst, MR; Denis Doran/Network, BR. 112 Ullstein Bilderdienst, BL, T. 113 Donald McLeish/Robert Harding Picture Library, T; Lapi/Roger-Viollet, B. 114 Ullstein Bilderdienst, TL, B; Jean-Loup Charmet, M. 115 Süddeutscher Verlag, T; Hulton Getty, BL; Topham Picturepoint, MR. 116 Popperfoto, T; Corbis-Bettmann, BL; Mary Evans Picture Library, M. 117 Mary Evans Picture Library. 118 Corbis-Bettmann, TR, MR, B. 119 John Walmsley Photo Library, T; Corbis-Bettmann, B. 120 Dr M. Mundle, TL, ML; Hulton Getty, BL. 121 Raymond Depardon/Magnum, T; Marc Riboud/Magnum, MR; Ulrike Preuss/Format, BL. 122 Paul Lowe/Magnum, TL; Novosti (London), ML; Steve Strike/Image Library of New South Wales, BL; John Walmsley Photo Library, BR. 123 SuperStock; Popperfoto, L; Sygma, ML; Robert Opie Collection, R. 124 Popperfoto, MR; Frank Spooner, B. 125 Jean-Loup Charmet, TR; Robert Opie Collection, ML; Hulton Getty, BL; Popperfoto, BR. 126 Ullstein Bilderdienst, TR, M, BL. 127 Hulton Getty, TL; Robert Opie Collection, TR, TM, MR, MM; Popperfoto, BR. 128 Hulton Getty, TL; Robert Opie Collection, TM, B.

129 Jean-Loup Charmet, TR; Keystone/Sygma, M; Popperfoto, BL; Hulton Getty, BR. 130 Hulton Getty, TL, BR; Robert Opie Collection, BM. 131 Hulton Getty, TR, BL; Robert Opie Collection, TL. 132 Robert Opie Collection, TM, M; Camera Press, BR. 133 Burt Glinn/Magnum, T; Malak/Camera Press, BR. 134 Hiroji Kubota/Magnum, R; Craig Davis/Sygma, BL. 135 Richard Smith/Sygma, TR; Peter Brooker/Rex Features, BL. 136 Hulton Getty, ML; Ullstein Bilderdienst, B. 137 Popperfoto, TR; J.A Grun, Private Collection/Bridgeman Art Library, M; Sygma, B. 138 Hulton Getty, L; Popperfoto, TM; Ullstein Bilderdienst, M, BR. 139 Hulton Getty, TM, MR; Robert Opie Collection, TM; Ullstein Bilderdienst, BR. 140 Hulton Getty, TR; Popperfoto, BR; Ullstein Bilderdienst, BL, BM. 141 Pictorial Press. 142 Ullstein Bilderdienst, L; Hulton Getty, B. 143 Sygma, TL; A. Gyori/Sygma, TR; Colorsport, B. 144 Popperfoto, TL; Robert Opie Collection, M. 144-5 Martin Parr/Magnum. 145 Hulton Getty, TL, BR. 146 Ullstein Bilderdienst, TL; Sygma, M; Popperfoto, BL, BR. 147 Hulton Getty, TL; Dennis Stock/Magnum, BR. 148 David Hurn/Magnum, L; Keystone/Sygma, M. 149 Sygma, TL, TM; Pictorial Press, TR. 150 Hulton Getty, TL, M; Jean-Loup Charmet, BR. 151 Victoria & Albert Museum/Bridgeman Art Library; Popperfoto, ML; Corbis-Bettmann, MR. 152 Image Library of New South Wales, ML; Hulton Getty, M; Corbis-Bettmann, BR. 153 Popperfoto, M, BR; Pictorial Press, TM. 154 Hulton Getty, M; The Ronald Grant Archive, TL; Pictorial Press, BM. 155 Corbis-Bettmann, TL, TR, BL; Hulton Getty, M.

Front cover: SuperStock, T; Allsport, B; Pictorial Press, L; Robert Opie Collection, ML; Roger Viollet, MR; Mary Evans Picture Library, R.

Back cover: SuperStock, T; Allsport, B; Alex Bartel/Arcaid, TL; Mary Evans Picture Library, TR; Hulton Getty, BL, BR.

Endpapers (front and back): All from John Frost Historical Newspaper Service except left-hand page, LM, RM from The Vintage Magazine Picture Library.

The editors are grateful to the following individuals and publishers for their kind permission to quote passages from the publications listed below:

Chatto & Windus, from Gift From the Sea, by Anne Morrow Lindbergh, 1955. Collins and Brown, from Motor Mania: Stories from a Motoring Century by Richard Sutton, 1996. The Daily Telegraph, June 4, 1979. Express Newspapers, from the Daily Express, February 18, 1993. Victor Gollancz, from A Wild Herb Soup by Emilie Carles, trs. by Avriel H. Goldberg. HarperCollins Publishers Ltd., from Nineteen Sixty Eight: A Personal Report by Hans Koning, 1988. New York Herald Tribune, Tom Wolfe, © 1964 by The New York Times Co. Martin Secker & Warburg Ltd., from Collected Essays by George Orwell, ©The estate of the late Sonia Brownell Orwell & Secker & Warburg Ltd. Richard Scott Simon Ltd., from Bronx Primitive by Kate Simon, © Kate Simon 1982, 1986, 1989. Souvenir Press Ltd., from Beyond All Pity by Caroline Maria De Jesus, trs. by David St Clair.